D0099392

The Human Tradition in America

CHARLES W. CALHOUN
Series Editor
Department of History, East Carolina University

The nineteenth-century English author Thomas Carlyle once remarked that "the history of the world is but the biography of great men." This approach to the study of the human past had existed for centuries before Carlyle wrote, and it continued to hold sway among many scholars well into the twentieth century. In more recent times, however, historians have recognized and examined the impact of large, seemingly impersonal forces in the evolution of human history—social and economic developments such as industrialization and urbanization as well as political movements such as nationalism, militarism, and socialism. Yet even as modern scholars seek to explain these wider currents, they have come more and more to realize that such phenomena represent the composite result of countless actions and decisions by untold numbers of individual actors. On another occasion, Carlyle said that "history is the essence of innumerable biographies." In this conception of the past, Carlyle came closer to modern notions that see the lives of all kinds of people, high and low, powerful and weak, known and unknown, as part of the mosaic of human history, each contributing in a large or small way to the unfolding of the human tradition.

This latter idea forms the foundation for this series of books on the human tradition in America. Each volume is devoted to a particular period or topic in American history and each consists of minibiographies of persons whose lives shed light on that period or topic. Well-known figures are not altogether absent, but more often the chapters explore a variety of individuals who may be less conspicuous but whose stories, nonetheless, offer us a window on some aspect of the nation's past.

By bringing the study of history down to the level of the individual, these sketches reveal not only the diversity of the American people and the complexity of their interaction but also some of the commonalities of sentiment and experience that Americans have shared in the evolution of their culture. Our hope is that these explorations of the lives of "real people" will give readers a deeper understanding of the human tradition in America.

Volumes in the Human Tradition in America series:

Ian K. Steele and Nancy L. Rhoden, eds., *The Human Tradition in Colonial America* (1999). Cloth ISBN 0-8420-2697-5 Paper ISBN 0-8420-2700-9

Nancy L. Rhoden and Ian K. Steele, eds., *The Human Tradition in the American Revolution* (2000). Cloth ISBN 0-8420-2747-5 Paper ISBN 0-8420-2748-3

Ballard C. Campbell, ed., *The Human Tradition in the Gilded Age and Progressive Era* (2000). Cloth ISBN 0-8420-2734-3 Paper ISBN 0-8420-2735-1

Steven E. Woodworth, ed., *The Human Tradition in the Civil War and Reconstruction* (2000). Cloth ISBN 0-8420-2726-2 Paper ISBN 0-8420-2727-0

David L. Anderson, ed., *The Human Tradition in the Vietnam Era* (2000). Cloth ISBN 0-8420-2762-9 Paper ISBN 0-8420-2763-7

Kriste Lindenmeyer, ed., *Ordinary Women, Extraordinary Lives: Women in American History* (2000). Cloth ISBN 0-8420-2752-1 Paper ISBN 0-8420-2754-8

Michael A. Morrison, ed., *The Human Tradition in Antebellum America* (2000). Cloth ISBN 0-8420-2834-X Paper ISBN 0-8420-2835-8

Malcolm Muir Jr., ed., *The Human Tradition in the World War II Era* (2001). Cloth ISBN 0-8420-2785-8 Paper ISBN 0-8420-2786-6

Ty Cashion and Jesús F. de la Teja, eds., *The Human Tradition in Texas* (2001). Cloth ISBN 0-8420-2905-2 Paper ISBN 0-8420-2906-0

Benson Tong and Regan A. Lutz, eds., *The Human Tradition in the American West* (2002). Cloth ISBN 0-8420-2860-9 Paper ISBN 0-8420-2861-7

Charles W. Calhoun, ed., *The Human Tradition in America from the Colonial Era through Reconstruction* (2002). Cloth ISBN 0-8420-5030-2 Paper ISBN 0-8420-5031-0

Donald W. Whisenhunt, ed., *The Human Tradition in America between the Wars, 1920–1945* (2002). Cloth ISBN 0-8420-5011-6 Paper ISBN 0-8420-5012-4

Roger Biles, ed., *The Human Tradition in Urban America* (2002). Cloth ISBN 0-8420-2992-3 Paper ISBN 0-8420-2993-1

Clark Davis and David Igler, eds., *The Human Tradition in California* (2002). Cloth ISBN 0-8420-5026-4 Paper ISBN 0-8420-5027-2

THE HUMAN TRADITION IN
CALIFORNIA

THE HUMAN TRADITION IN
CALIFORNIA

No. 14
Human Tradition in America

Edited by
Clark Davis
and
David Igler

SR BOOKS

Lanham • Boulder • New York • Toronto • Oxford

Published by SR Books
An imprint of Rowman & Littlefield Publishers, Inc.
A wholly owned subsidiary of The Rowman & Littlefield Publishing Group, Inc.
4501 Forbes Boulevard, Suite 200
Lanham, MD 20706

PO Box 317
Oxford
OX2 9RU, UK

First SR Books edition 2004
Copyright © 2002 by Scholarly Resources Inc.

Library of Congress Cataloging-in-Publication Data

The human tradition in California / edited by Clark Davis
and David Igler.
     p. cm. — (The human tradition in America ; no. 14)
     Includes bibliographical references and index.
     ISBN 978-0-8420-5027-2 — ISBN 0-8420-5027-2 (pbk. :
alk. paper)
     1. California—Biography. 2. California—History—Anecdotes.
I. Davis, Clark, 1966– II. Igler, David, 1964– III. Series.

CT225 .H86 2002
979.4—dc21   2002021676

To
Cheryl Koos
and
Cynthia Willard

About the Editors

CLARK DAVIS received his Ph.D. from the University of Southern California and is associate professor of history at California State University, Fullerton. He is the author of *Company Men: White-Collar Life and Corporate Cultures in Los Angeles, 1892–1941* (1999), and codirector of the Huntington Library Los Angeles History Research Seminar.

DAVID IGLER received his Ph.D. from the University of California, Berkeley, and is assistant professor of history at the University of Utah. He is the author of *Industrial Cowboys: Miller & Lux and the Transformation of the Far West, 1850–1920* (2001) as well as numerous articles on California, western, and environmental history.

Contents

Introduction

Clark Davis and David Igler

California enters the twenty-first century occupying a unique place among American states. Not only does its population surpass 34 million people, more than any other state, but its inhabitants comprise one of the world's most ethnically and racially diverse populations. There is currently no racial or ethnic majority group among California's population, while the state also contains the largest immigrant communities from many nations in the world, including Korea, Vietnam, Mexico, and Armenia. Economically, California's rich natural resources, powerful technology sector, and vital position at the intersection of Pacific trade make it the country's largest state economy as well as the fifth largest economy among nations worldwide. California is also the point of origin for much of the world's popular and mass cultures. Since the 1920s, Hollywood has been the home of the American film industry and a center of network television production.

Californians' versions of the American dream—celluloid images of prosperity, redemption, and the human desire for reinvention—every day cross state, national, and international boundaries. How accurately such images reflect California's reality remains debatable and opinions on this matter vary from Beverly Hills to Watts, from Barstow to Eureka; for amid the state's periods of growth and prosperity, Californians have found plenty of reasons for pessimism. In recent years, natural disasters in the form of earthquakes, fires, and floods, episodes of major civil unrest, and economic and energy crises have repeatedly underscored the fragility of the California dream.

At first glance, California today is a world far removed from that of 200 years ago. In 1802 three decades of Spanish colonization had produced a system of Franciscan missions along the coast from San Diego to Sonoma. The Spanish population numbered in the mere hundreds, while European diseases and social dislocation had already wrought havoc on the once vibrant and populous Indian communities. For Spain,

California served as a colonial outpost to ward off Russian and British threats against its faltering New World empire. For native peoples, California remained a richly endowed—and tragically altered—homeland.

Remarkable differences obviously separate colonial California from the state today, yet a closer look reveals many common characteristics across these 200 years. The native population in 1802, for instance, easily matched today's diverse social milieu in terms of linguistic variations, cultural beliefs, and kinship networks. International commerce forms another link between the past and the present: in the early 1800s, California received French, British, U.S., Russian, and Spanish trading vessels carrying cargo and crews from all points around the world. Indeed, colonial California soon developed into an active trading center for the Pacific Basin and, similar to today, that international commerce brought laborers, ideas, and economic competitors from ports near and far. Even the American dream had its counterpart two centuries ago. Franciscan missionaries sought redemption and Indian conversions, while Spanish and mestizo soldiers hoped for land and opportunity on a new frontier. The fact that those colonial ambitions culminated in a demographic nightmare for native populations underscores another continuity—the persistent interplay between utopian and dystopian forces in Californians' lives.

Distinct continuities as well as significant changes therefore run throughout California history. Not surprisingly, its story has attracted considerable interest. The California public remains keenly intrigued by their history, as suggested by the numerous civic historic pageants, commemorations, and celebrations that dot the state's cultural calendar. All of its fourth-grade students spend the year studying California history, a subject also required for all credentialed teachers. And from Antonio María Osio's 1851 *History of Alta California* to contemporary historian and state librarian Kevin Starr's ongoing multivolume study, California's past has also been the focus of considerable scholarship. In recent decades, historians of U.S. politics, urban affairs, and environmental issues have increasingly turned to California as a site of national and international importance. Scholars from around the world now examine California not only as an archetype of the modern experience but also as a model for other regions to emulate or avoid.

California's rich and complex history—as well as its often puzzling juxtaposition of past and present—challenges us with many questions. How should we interpret the replication of eighteenth-century Mission architecture in a twenty-first-century Bakersfield strip mall? To what extent did the heated immigration debates of the 1990s echo similar debates in the late 1870s? In what ways do Silicon Valley immigrant engineers resemble the middle-class immigrant gold-seekers of 1849? These questions, involving Californians' efforts to create a romanticized historic legacy, the continuing process of immigration, and the opportunities offered by a booming economy, present just a few examples of historical themes that Californians revisit on a regular basis.

The Human Tradition in California investigates this history through the lives of ordinary individuals—and those not so ordinary—at key moments in time. California certainly has its share of renowned figures: Father Junípero Serra, Leland Stanford, Aimee Semple McPherson, Upton Sinclair, Earl Warren, Ronald Reagan, and Mickey and Minnie Mouse. While these individuals have undeniably shaped California's past, the lives of such historical celebrities can obscure the experiences of ordinary people, especially the majority of the population who are neither white, nor male, nor privileged by wealth and status. *The Human Tradition in California* instead offers a more inclusive composite of the region's social experience. If some figures in the following pages are well known, such as César Chávez and John Steinbeck, the majority will be unfamiliar to most readers. Their lives, however, intersected with crucial historical events, and in many cases their actions profoundly swayed the state's social, political, cultural, and economic development.

In the pages that follow, sixteen historians explore the major themes and issues of California history through the lives of individual persons who sometimes shaped and sometimes responded to the dynamic forces that have created modern California. The essays are ordered chronologically and span several major eras. The first chapter in the state's story began several thousand years ago when Asian peoples settled in California, having migrated across the Bering Strait and down through what is now Canada and the Pacific Northwest. By 1500 as many as 300,000 native peoples lived in the region that became Alta California. The Spanish colonization of Alta California in the eighteenth century began a new era in the state's history as Spanish, mestizo, and mulatto people established a system of missions, pueblos, and presidios—dislocating native populations in the process. In 1821, California fell under Mexican rule, and, amid the transition in power, its people wrestled with the new government's program of mission secularization. The steady immigration of Americans in this period further added to the social and political complexities of Mexican-era California as different groups vied for regional power and control. In 1848 the United States acquired

California from Mexico through the Treaty of Guadalupe Hidalgo that ended the Mexican-American War. From the outset, the American period of California history has been characterized by massive population growth, urbanization, and the diverse challenges posed by an economically, racially, and culturally mixed population.

Five critical issues have influenced the fabric of California society and underlie the lives of Californians explored in the following essays. Perhaps no issue has more consistently influenced the nature of its society than the national and transnational flow of immigration into the state. Its massive population today rests on the arrival of wave after wave of immigrants from virtually every part of the nation and globe. From the earliest Californians, descendants of those who migrated across the Bering Strait from Asia thousands of years ago, to the international cast of Forty-niners, to the latest groups of Asian and Latin American arrivals, steady streams of immigration have defined California's social, economic, and political history. California residents have often welcomed new arrivals, while at other times immigrant groups faced hostility and even forced deportation. For instance, cartoons in the popular late nineteenth-century San Francisco newspaper *The Wasp* repeatedly portrayed Chinese immigrants as an alien and dangerous force in the Golden State. In the 1930s, Dorothea Lange's photographs of Dust Bowl migrants revealed the plight of the latest poverty-stricken arrivals and leveled an implicit critique of their treatment by established Californians. In the 1990s, news coverage of immigration focused on the militarized wall of the California-Mexico border and the "illegals" who crossed it. These three periods witnessed particularly strong public debates over immigration, but every generation of Californians has struggled through its own conflicts over newly arrived groups.

In California as elsewhere, debates over immigration pose basic questions about *community* itself: who is inside and who is outside the community, who is welcome and who is not? Many essays in this volume examine this dilemma and offer personal examples of the struggles between immigrants and California's established population. Erika Lee's essay on Wong Kim Ark and the 1882 Chinese Exclusion Act revisits the state's first major conflict over immigration and restriction. Charles Wollenberg's study of John Steinbeck reveals how one young writer attempted to influence the public debate over Dust Bowl refugees. Gretchen Lemke-Santangelo's sketch of four African American migrant women suggests the many ways that immigration from the American South transformed California during World War II. These and other essays explore the opportunities and restraints that confronted each immigrant group, and in the process they shed light on the complex negotiations between newcomers and self-defined California "natives."

Immigration leads directly to a second prominent theme: the state's unmistakable social and cultural diversity. As with the issue of immigration, some Californians have celebrated their state's social diversity while others have feared and resisted the social and political consequences of racial and ethnic heterogeneity. Most all Californians, however, recognize the complex mix of peoples and cultures as one of the state's distinguishing characteristics. This attribute has a long lineage. Steve Karr's essay on the Luiseño Indian Pablo Tac shows the pre-mission indigenous communities as highly diverse in terms of language, culture areas, and community structures. Many aspects of life changed when Indians and Spaniards "discovered" one another, and yet the basic fact of native diversity persisted despite Spanish attempts to simplify Indians' identities. Doug Cutter and Iris Engstrand explore the social tensions and cultural complexities in Spanish California from the perspective of Father Mariano Payeras. Franciscan friars succeeded in building a far-flung system of missions in large part by their coercion of Indian groups, and Father Payeras understood the many ramifications of this enterprise. The secularization of the mission system in the 1820s pushed Californians to reconsider and renegotiate lines of power, status, and authority. Miroslava Chávez-García's essay on the murder trial of Guadalupe Trujillo, who killed her Indian servant Ysabel, explores the social dynamics between Mexicans and Indians in Mexican Los Angeles. Throughout her murder trial, Trujillo struggled to defend her *gente de razón* identity despite the mixed ethnic background she shared with most other Mexican Californians. Brian Roberts's treatment of the gold rush reveals the remarkably diverse and contentious society created in the years immediately following the discovery of gold. Finally, Elisabeth Orr takes the story of social heterogeneity into the modern era in exploring how white residents of postwar Orange County suburbs attempted to build a stable and homogeneous community amid the state's rapid development. Orr shows how behind California's vast diversity existed considerable racial, class, and cultural segregation. These five essays bear testament to the complex social fabric that has consistently characterized the state.

A third central theme is the vital role of industry in the state's legendary prosperity. California's economic prowess has always rested on the propensity of its rich natural resources, favorable climate, and diverse labor pool to attract massive capital investment. Large-scale industry arrived in a fast and furious way with the gold rush, as individual miners quickly lost place to hydraulic and hard-rock mining companies. Agriculture, too, rapidly grew into an industry of concentrated landownings, costly farm technology, irrigation, and marketing innovations. The twentieth century witnessed California's transformation into a global industrial power, led by Hollywood and the film business, the defense industries of World War II, and, most recently, Silicon Valley's high-tech sectors. Quite simply, few places on Earth have matched California's path of industrial development—a path manufactured by countless individuals. The development of the state's massive water delivery system is one of the most pivotal and legendary stories in California history. Jessica Teisch's essay on State Engineer William Hammond Hall illuminates how the social and political battles involved in securing water for the major urban centers transformed him from idealistic water engineer to opportunistic urban planner. Lary May's study of filmmaker Cecil B. DeMille recounts how and why southern California became a locus for American film production by the 1920s, a fortuitous occurrence for the state as the entertainment industry would bolster its economy through the rest of the century. Teisch and May both capture the human side of California's diverse economic development, and this theme reappears in many other essays throughout this volume.

Much of California's prosperity has rested on an abundance of both skilled and unskilled labor. From the many Indians who were coerced into mission labor during the Spanish era through the Asian and Latino immigrant sweatshops today, cheap and easily exploitable labor has been pivotal to California's business and industry. In more recent years, few groups have endured a harsher pattern of economic exploitation than immigrant Mexican farmworkers. Frank Bardacke's essay recounts how Mexican and Mexican American workers fought to improve these conditions under the powerful leadership of César Chávez and the United Farm Workers (UFW). But Chávez, Bardacke argues, chose a particular strategy for his union members that contained significant pitfalls. Glenna Matthews brings us to the present day with her essay on workers in the Silicon Valley. Though best known for its legions of skilled programmers and astronomical property values, the Silicon Valley's economic success is also due to the poorly paid labor of recent immigrants from Mexico and Asia.

The issues of immigration, diversity, business, and labor have reverberated throughout the state's political arena during the nineteenth and twentieth centuries. For better or worse, California's political arena has also decidedly influenced the nation's political environment during periods of reform, reaction, and radicalism. Judith Raftery's essay on Caroline Severance explores the pivotal role played by Californians in the early twentieth-century Progressive movement. Raftery shows how Severance, like many women Progressives, assumed leadership positions at the state level and ultimately influenced the nation's reformist environment. During World War II, California once again promoted significant change in the nation's public arena—this time spearheading the drive for forced internment of Japanese immigrants (issei) and Japanese American citizens (nisei). Alice Yang Murray's recounting of Edison Uno's experience reveals the level of discrimination faced by Japanese internees during this tragic period of racial politics. In the 1960s, California's political pendulum swung widely between both left and right, leaving a tenuous liberal center holding the key to the state's political future. Daryl Maeda explores the boundaries of California's political culture in the 1960s and 1970s through the life of Senator S. I. Hayakawa, who, while championing and symbolizing opportunities for people of color, became an outspoken critic of student protestors and racial political movements. These essays spotlight only three important moments in twentieth-century state politics, and yet together they suggest California's power to shape the nation's political culture.

These five themes only begin to capture the human experience in California history, and we could easily draw on many other themes to organize the state's past. For instance, the power of religious communities has had a strong impact on California society, from the era of Franciscan friars to Protestant Evangelicalism in the 1920s and 1930s, to today's broad spectrum of devotional groups throughout the state. Environmental politics and activism represent another powerful and persistent theme. Sierra Club founder and California transplant John Muir created a lasting legacy from which late twentieth-century environmental groups have decidedly benefited. Agriculture, too, provides a crucial theme in the state's past and present, given that industry's economic, social, and ecological impact. The important point here is that California history possesses a wealth of thematic continuities and individuals who personify those themes. The essays contained in the following pages represent just an introduction—and we hope a useful one—to the human tradition in California.

1

Pablo Tac
Native Peoples in Precontact California

Steven M. Karr

The missions, Forty-niners, and major modern cities that often domi-nate narratives of California history all speak to only a small and very recent part of the region's past. While written documents about California's his-torical record date from the European navigators in the 1500s, California had been populated for thousands of years before that time. Demographers now believe 300,000 native peoples lived in California at the time of the Spanish conquest, comprising one of the largest concentrations of Native Americans on the continent.

California's precontact population included diverse geographic cultural groups spread throughout the area. While their languages, cultures, and bases for survival varied greatly, there was much interaction between these groups. Extensive trading networks not only existed regionally but also spread to other parts of North America.

Plenty of archaeological and anthropological evidence exists on the diversity of established Native American communities in California, but his-torians have found few written sources through which to learn about precontact life. One of the most intriguing windows into the precontact past is the accounts and records of Pablo Tac, a Luiseño born at Mission San Luis Rey in the early 1820s. Though acculturated by Spanish padres and educated in California, Mexico, and Rome, Tac's life provides one of the richest insights into native California communities and the mission system that dominated this era. In this essay, Los Angeles Museum of Natural His-tory researcher Steven M. Karr probes Pablo Tac's experiences in order to describe native life prior to the Spanish period.

> When the missionary arrived in our country with a small troop, our captain and also the others were astonished, seeing them from afar, but they did not run away or seize arms to kill them, but having sat down, they watched them. But when they drew near, then the captain got up (for he was seated with the others) and met them. They halted, and the mis-sionary then began to speak, the captain saying per-haps in his language "*hichsom iva haluon, pulùchajam cham quinai.*" "What is it that you seek here? Get out of our country!"[1]
>
> PABLO TAC, LUISEÑO INDIAN

Like all indigenous groups throughout North America, the native peoples of California possessed no written language. Only after the arrival of the Spaniards to this coastal land did any native person learn to read or write. Pablo Tac's account of his life and of the experiences of his Luiseño ancestors is therefore unique. Published in 1835, Tac's writing represents the first indigenous recording of life in California. Through this source as well as the written records kept by Franciscan missionaries in California and Catholic priests in Rome, we can understand a great deal about Tac's brief but eventful life.[2] Perhaps equally important, Tac's writing reveals what life may have been like for the Luiseños and their neighbors prior to first contact with European explorers.

Tac was one of six children born to Pedro Alcántara and his wife, Ladislaya Molmolix, both Luiseño Indians, at Mission San Luis Rey de Francia, most likely in the first weeks of 1822.[3] Similar to most Indians living near Mission San Luis Rey, Tac was baptized by the Franciscan fathers. His name first appeared in the mission's *padrón* (a register of all Indians known to be living within its sphere of influence) on January 15, presumably shortly after his birth. Though the mission's baptismal records have long since been lost, the original *padrón*, today housed in the Santa Barbara Mission Archives in California, lists Pablo Tac's baptism as number 3,896. Since they had founded the Mission San Luis Rey in 1798, the fathers had therefore baptized nearly 4,000 native Californians by the time of Tac's own baptism.

Educated at the mission, Tac demonstrated a particular aptitude for learning and catechism. Because of their intelligence, Tac and one other Indian boy, Agapito Amamix, left Mission San Luis Rey and California in 1832, never to return. Under the guardianship of San Luis Rey's former administrator, Fray Antonio Peyri, they were taken first to the Franciscan Mission College of San Fernando in Mexico City. They remained there until February 1834, when Fray Peyri took both boys to Rome, Italy, where they registered at the city's Urban College on September 24, 1834. In Rome, both Tac and Amamix began their formal training in Latin grammar and additional religious instruction. Father Antonio Peyri testified to Amamix and Tac's exceptional character as well as their scholarly performance in Rome: "I brought with me two Indian youths, Pablo and Agapito, whom you knew already in California. I had the good fortune of being able to place them in Rome, at the College of Propaganda, where they are very contented and which I doubt not will leave bright men, for they are very talented, and they are very much appreciated by the entire College, for being from such distant countries, true Indians, and of good comportment. Would that they continue!"[4]

Only three years later, however, Agapito Amamix fell ill, and he died on September 26, 1837. Despite contracting smallpox in late 1840, Tac completed studies in grammar, rhetoric, and the humanities, and subsequently took his vow to continue preparation for the priesthood and missionary work, presumably in his native country. A year after initially contracting smallpox, Tac became ill again and he died on December 13, 1841. Prior to his death, however, Tac wrote a unique narrative about his Luiseño people. Barely twenty years old and so far removed from his home in California, Tac's strong recollections of his people and their culture are powerful reminders of not only how native peoples lived but also how they viewed themselves and their world.

While Pablo Tac's life may stand in contrast to the lives of most precontact native Californians, he was well acquainted with his people's culture and lifeways prior to Spanish settlement. Tac's account, "Conversión de los San Luiseños de la Alta California" (Conversion of the San Luiseños of Alta California), discusses in detail some aspects of the Luiseños' traditional precontact lives, providing a compelling window into the past. Among its many topics, Tac's account lends considerable insight to our understanding of ceremonial dances, weaponry and warfare, and a type of recreational ball game played against the neighboring Juaneño Indians. He also sheds light on various traditional Indian "districts" or villages, including Pala and Temécula, both of which remain to this day home to significant numbers of Luiseño and Cupeño Indians.[5]

Among the more important topics Pablo Tac mentions is the number of native peoples he claims lived in and around the area of Mission San Luis Rey. When the Franciscan fathers first arrived in his people's country, Tac wrote in his account, "there were five thousand souls (who were all the Indians there were)."[6] He gives more detail later in his narrative: "In Quechla not long ago there were 5,000 souls, with all their neighboring lands. Through a sickness that came to California 2,000 souls died, and 3,000 were left."[7]

Though Tac touches only briefly on the Indian population in his native land, his estimates raise difficult questions that to this day remain controversial for many historians and anthropologists.[8] If Tac's estimates are indeed correct, then between 1798 (when Mission San Luis Rey was founded) and 1832, when he left California, nearly half the entire Luiseño population died of disease, certainly of European origin. What then are we to assume was the population for the rest of California prior to contact with Europeans? How many native Californians died as a result of European contact? Moreover, how did these people live both individually and in groups before the arrival of any European? Based on a wide range of evidence—including accounts like Tac's, archaeological data from old Indian village sites, early mission baptismal records kept by Franciscan priests, and oral histories shared by Indian peoples—we have a fairly clear view into the lives of California's first people.[9]

Demographic distribution varied throughout this vast area, with the highest concentration levels often determined by the regional environment. There is general consensus among historians and anthropologists today that at the beginning of Spanish settlement in 1769, California's indigenous population may have been as high as 310,000.[10] Certain parts of California were able to sustain greater numbers of people primarily because they provided a wider range of food sources, both plant and animal life. The most abundant and diverse regions were generally coastal zones, particularly those along the northwestern and southern California coast. These areas also harbored greater numbers of indigenous peoples because of their easy access to the interior where additional food sources, equally as diverse as those along the coast, could be found. Other favorable environmental zones included lands around inland lakes and along large rivers. Good examples of these two zones are the Sacramento River Delta and large portions of the San Joaquin Valley. Not only did these areas provide a wide variety of marine life and other aquatic foods year-round, but they also supplied seasonal foods in the way of migrating birds moving on a north-south axis along the Pacific Flyway. As abundant as food sources may have been for coastal groups and those living near lakes and large rivers, subsistence for others was far more tenuous. These mountain and desert groups relied heavily on acorns from California's numerous oak species as well as piñon nuts, roots, and various plant and grass seeds. Like coastal, riverine, and lake groups, mountain and desert peoples supplemented their diets with wild game, most typically rabbits and other small rodents along with larger game such as antelope and deer.[11]

Coastal groups carried out most of their fishing from the shore, while northwestern and some southern California coastal peoples undertook deep-sea fishing from boats. Northwest peoples made their canoes from hollowed-out redwood logs, while some southern California groups, particularly the Chumash, made their small sea craft by lashing together wood planks and sealing the open seams with asphaltum. With these boats, sea mammals could be hunted, most often with harpoons and clubs. Small and large game were generally hunted with a bow and arrow, while some groups in southern California commonly hunted with a curved throwing stick. Snares, traps, and nets were frequently used for capturing game as well.[12]

Both gender and age generally determined the division of labor among all culture groups throughout California. To this fact Tac stated: "When the sun rises and the stars and the moon go down, [the man] takes his bows and arrows and leaves the house with vigorous and quick steps. (This is if he is going to hunt.) . . . his old woman staying at home makes the meals. . . . The son, if he is a man, works with the men. His daughter stays with the women."[13] As Tac clearly states, men were responsible for hunting and fishing while women, small children, and the elderly processed most plant resources. Still, work activities for men and women did at times overlap, particularly among those groups who relied heavily on the seasonal acorn crop. Because it was the primary food staple for so many groups, entire villages might assist in gathering the year's crop from oak groves often located some distance from the main living area. Men conducted many rituals, trading ventures, and warfare. Older men supervised a wide range of ceremonial activities, passing much of their sacred knowledge to designated boys. Older men also produced many of the tools and hunting implements, such as arrows and basket traps, in addition to various ceremonial items.[14]

As Tac noted, women's roles tended to be more secularly oriented. In addition to collecting and preparing food, younger women also made the majority of utilitarian items used among their respective groups, including baskets, cooking vessels, and clothing. Older women, in addition to instructing girls and young women about child rearing, were responsible for educating females in a multitude of gender-specific roles and duties.[15]

These social customs could be applied to many culture groups throughout California. Still, there were other customs that remained quite different for various Indian groups. Of course, it was the Indians themselves and not the Europeans who were most keenly aware of these differences, as Tac details in his discussion of Indian dances:

> Each Indian people have their own dances, different from other dances. In Europe they dance for joy, for a feast, for any fortunate news. But the Indians of California dance not only for a feast, but also before starting a war, for

grief, because they have lost the victory, and in memory of grandparents, aunts, uncles, parents already dead. . . . The Dance of the Yumas is almost always sad, and thus the song; the same of the Diegeños. But we Luiseños have three principal kinds [of dances] for men alone, because the women have others and they can never dance with the men.[16]

The Geographical Spread of Native Californians

For purposes of research and identification, anthropologists and historians generally divide the state into six primary culture areas, all of which, to varying degrees, possess unique regional lifeways. These areas are the Colorado River, Southern, Great Basin, Central, Northeast, and Northwest. The Colorado River groups, in a strict Euro-American perspective, were California's only agriculturists. Using the same type of flood-plain irrigation employed by many southwestern culture groups, the Mohave, the Yuma, and the Halchidhoma planted maize, beans, squash, and watermelons along the low dry banks of the Colorado River. With the seasonal rising of the river in the late spring or early summer, their crops could then be irrigated in this extremely arid desert region. All three groups possessed sizable populations, numbering between 2,000 and 2,500 per tribe.[17]

Like the Colorado River region, California's Great Basin region represents a desert adaptation. Among several other groups, the Paiute, Shoshone, and Chemehuevi are perhaps best known for their ability to adapt to such an inhospitable environment. Numbering between 2,000 and 3,000 per tribe, the Great Basin cultures, unlike most other groups, did not rely on acorns or varied marine life as food staples. Where bodies of water did exist, most carried a high salinity content, though a few did support some fish and waterfowl life. And again, unlike groups in much of the rest of California, Great Basin groups were neither sedentary nor semisedentary peoples. They were instead nomadic, traveling throughout much of the vast desert region in small groups and carrying with them only what was needed to process and collect grass seeds, mesquite beans, and piñon nuts. Also in their possession might be rabbit-skin blankets and bedding for winter months, along with bows and arrows to hunt mountain sheep and deer. Living much as they had for centuries, these groups experienced little if any Euro-American contact prior to the Mexican-American War.[18]

Occupying both coastal and inland areas were numerous Hokan and Uto-Aztekan language families in the Southern California culture

area. Among the larger groups were the Kumeyaay or Diegeño, the
Cahuilla, the Luiseño, the Gabrielino, and the Chumash. The Chumash
were among the most sea-oriented groups in California. Traveling in
their plank canoes throughout the Santa Barbara Channel region, they
not only colonized the offshore archipelago comprised of San Miguel,
Santa Rosa, Santa Cruz, and the Anacapa Islands, but also lived as far
inland as the western edge of the San Joaquin Valley. From island quar-
ries the Chumash harvested steatite, or soapstone, which they traded
with interior groups or from which they fashioned cooking vessels and
delicate carvings, often of sea mammals. Interior groups were also known
for their rock paintings, many found in the Cuyama Valley and the
Carrizo Plains. Known for their exceptional polychrome abstract de-
signs, Chumash paintings rank as some of the finest prehistoric rock art
in the United States.[19]

In present-day San Diego, Riverside, and Imperial Counties, Cahuilla, Kumeyaay, and perhaps Cupeño Indians made fine pottery in the
form of small-mouthed water jars, cooking pots, pipes, and ollas, used
primarily for seed and grain storage. Tac's group, the Luiseño, employed
a sophisticated crop management technique with the use of fire. Semi-
annual seasonal burns often ensured greater yields of much-needed grass
seeds, greens, basket grasses, and other useful plants. With such tech-
niques, California native peoples (like all human cultures) did in fact
work to alter certain elements of the environment in which they lived.
Because of the wide variety and abundance of food sources, both floral
and faunal, Southern California's coastal zones contained the majority
of its indigenous peoples.[20]

Central California subcultures collectively represented the largest
population throughout the state. Numbering upward of as many as
185,000 people in total, these groups also inhabited the largest geographical area, which included the San Joaquin and Sacramento Valleys
and the coastal range from roughly San Luis Obispo to the San Francisco Bay's southerly reaches. Among the numerous tribes throughout
this vast territory were interior groups such as the Yokuts, Maidu,
Wintun, and Yana; the coastal range groups including the Salinan,
Esselen, Costanoan, or Ohlone; and the Pomo of the northwest coast.
Because of the abundance of food, Central California groups were able
to sustain large, permanent villages that numbered as many as 1,000 people.
In part because of the lifestyle provided by a townlike atmosphere, craft
specialists developed, devoting their time to the production of a single

item, whether an arrow point or a basket. In turn some of their surplus items were traded for other necessities, thus creating a sophisticated trade economy throughout California and beyond.[21]

Northwest California cultures included the Hupa, Yurok, Tolowa, and Shasta. Ecologically unique to California, the northwestern subculture was in many respects more closely related to the rain-forest environment of the Pacific Northwest and its cultures. Living primarily along riverbanks and the coastline at stream outlets and lagoons, northwestern peoples moved easily along coastal shores and deep rivers in their dugout canoes. For their canoes and for other needs, the main building and craft material for these peoples was the coast redwood.[22] The main tribes of Northeast California were the Achomawi, Modoc, and Atsugewi. Numbering approximately 9,600 in total population, these groups harvested acorns and fished for salmon wherever possible, mostly in the western half of the area. Common to these groups were sweat baths taken in domed, hide-covered structures heated with water poured over rocks from an outside fire.[23]

Major trade routes throughout California brought numerous groups in contact with others, not only within the area itself but also with culture groups from the Southwest, the Great Basin area, and the Pacific Northwest. Many of these routes, although well traveled, were nothing more than foot trails leading from one region to another, some from north to south, others from east to west. Eventually these trails would be traversed by early European explorers, white soldiers, and settlers, and some even became the major thoroughfares of today.[24]

Trade relations in aboriginal California were both reciprocal and one-way, the most common being a one-for-one exchange of items. Although it is widely held that there were no professional traders among precontact peoples, there is little question that some groups participated in trade more frequently than others, primarily because of their control over scarce or desirable resources such as steatite, salt, or obsidian. It is also believed that some large villages strategically located near tribal boundaries may have developed into important trade centers.[25] Trading generally took place between tribes on either friendly or ceremonial visits. Clearly, amicable relations between groups encouraged intertribal trade, especially when the groups lay in ecologically distinct areas, each possessing or producing items the other desired. Often, if open conflict occurred, trade relations might be disrupted for years.

Based upon archaeological evidence, it appears that shell beads are the oldest documented trade items. Ethnographic evidence supplied by native peoples in the postcontact era suggests the most frequently traded items were marine shell beads, salt, and baskets, in that order, followed by hides and pelts, bows, acorns, fish, and obsidian. More interesting than these items themselves are the specific articles traded between various groups. The Diegeño of southern California commonly traded acorns with the Yuma of Arizona and in return received gourd seeds. The southern Yokuts of the Central Valley supplied obsidian to the Chumash, who provided them with shells and shell beads. And the northwestern Shasta peoples often traded bows and baskets to the Klamath of Oregon for otter skins.[26]

The Arrival of the Spaniards

Long before Pablo Tac wrote his narrative, the Luiseño community had been radically changed by European contact. First visited by Spanish explorers sailing up the California coast as early as 1542 with the Juan Rodríguez Cabrillo expedition, the native peoples did not experience sustained contact until 1769, with the founding of Alta California's first Franciscan mission, San Diego de Alcala. Though there were encounters between Europeans and Indians along California's coast during the intervening 200 years, drastic changes to Indian cultural orientations did not occur until permanent Spanish settlements and institutions were established among the various Indian groups. As Pac wrote: "It is known from history that the first of the missionaries who came to California were the Jesuit Fathers. . . . The Dominicans came to Baja California, and the Franciscans came to Alta California."[27]

The Spaniards viewed Indians as cultural primitives, immoral and ignorant. They believed it their duty to lift Indian peoples from their heathen state to one that was God-fearing, virtuous, and enlightened. With this in mind, from 1769 to 1823 the Spaniards established a string of missions along California's coastal range spanning from Mission San Diego in the south to Sonoma Mission in the north. Tac, like thousands of other California Indians, was himself a product of these missionary efforts. And through his education, carefully administered by the Franciscans, Tac was well aware of the Catholic Church's influence throughout California: "These Fathers came to Alta, and one of them came to our country. . . . The god who was adored at that time was the sun and the fire. Thus we lived among the woods until merciful God freed us of these miseries through Father Antonio Peyri, a Catalan, who arrived in our country in the afternoon with seven Spanish soldiers."[28]

Ethnocentric

Still, strategic considerations also guided Spanish colonization. Together with the mission, the presidio worked to safeguard Spain's political, economic, military, and religious interests along the most northerly reaches of the Spanish American frontier. In theory, surplus agricultural produce from the missions, administered in Alta California by Franciscans, would help defray the costs of colonization by reducing the amount of money spent on presidios, or military garrisons. Eventually the missions' populations would grow to become pueblos, or towns, inhabited by a loyal, taxpaying Catholic citizenry, thus expanding Spanish hegemony throughout the region. Essential to this economic system, however, was the Franciscans' control over Indian labor.[29]

Many Indians were initially amenable to the mission lifestyle. Different foods, strange animals, and new technologies surely piqued their curiosity. Few understood, however, that once they agreed to be baptized by the Franciscans and taken into the mission fold, their tenure would be permanent. These Indian neophytes, as converts were called, were then expected to abide by a rigid system of rules and demands meted out indiscriminately by both priest and soldier. Moreover, Indians were forced to labor in the mission fields, tend to the flocks, and carry out domestic chores at the mission, entirely uncompensated, with little if any regard for their wants or desires. An Indian who refused to work was often flogged by soldiers or *alcaldes*, a type of Indian overseer chosen by the priests. For other offenses, Indians might be put in the stocks, hobbled, placed in solitary confinement, or in some cases even executed. A strict Catholic moral code dictated that unmarried men and women were locked in separate dormitories at night and were unable to leave until morning. Church attendance among neophytes was compulsory, as was the Indians' total rejection of their traditional religion and spiritual beliefs.[30]

Despite these harsh, often cruel realities, Indian peoples by no means merely accepted their fate. Native resistance, both disguised and overt, was present from the very beginnings of Spanish settlement in California. This we can understand more clearly by remembering Tac's narrative of his peoples' first encounter with the Spaniards: "It was of great mercy that the Indians did not kill the Spanish when they arrived, and very admirable, because they have never wanted another people to live with them."[31] The most common form of open resistance among Indians was simply to flee the mission and its environs. Doubting the intellectual capacity of their Indian wards, Spanish priests were unable to see that resistance could take many forms.[32] Such resistance could be as simple and seemingly benign as practicing any traditional custom, either religious or secular, deemed inappropriate or sinful by the priests, or it could take on far more serious implications. Women practiced abortion and infanticide, for instance, which was sometimes an awful reminder of their agonizing hardships suffered at the hands of some European men and at other times an act of defiance at the prospect of subjecting a child to an intolerable existence.[33]

Violent resistance in the way of open rebellion was not uncommon among native peoples. The two largest incidents took place some fifty years apart, the first at Mission San Diego in 1775 and the second in 1824 at Missions Santa Ynez, La Purísima, and Santa Barbara. These two revolts, although occurring half a century apart, indicate that Spanish domination did little to suppress native feelings of injustice and outrage. At Mission Santa Barbara, some 800 Kumeyaay from nine villages organized to completely destroy the mission structure and kill three Spaniards, including a friar. In 1824 at Mission Santa Ynez, in response to their own ill treatment and the flogging of a visiting neophyte, Indians burned many of the mission buildings. Emboldened by events at Santa Ynez, some 2,000 Indians attacked and captured Mission La Purísima later the same day. Word of the attacks reached neophytes at Mission Santa Barbara and soon they, too, took up arms against the Spaniards. Within two months of these episodes, signs of rebellion among Indians as far south as Missions San Fernando and San Gabriel greatly alarmed Spanish officials. Though it took the Spaniards almost three months to quell the native rebellion, many Indians were able to flee the missions for the safety of the California interior.[34]

Despite the efforts to resist Spanish domination, Indian peoples were sometimes utterly helpless at fighting Spain's influences. The most glaring reason for this was certainly the rapid decline of the Indian population in California due to the introduction of European diseases. Often congregating in large groups and living in conditions to which they were entirely unaccustomed, Indians were exposed to numerous viruses to which they had no immunity. Tuberculosis, measles, smallpox, and cholera had devastated mission communities throughout the Spanish colonial era. The first notice of significant deaths by disease recorded in Upper California was mentioned by Fray Francisco Palóu in the vicinity of Mission Santa Clara in 1777, when he noted that "there had come upon the people a great epidemic."[35] In 1802, at Missions San Luis Obispo, Soledad, and San Carlos, pneumonia and diptheria seem to have been the main culprits when, at the peak of the epidemic, five or six Indians died each day at Soledad. By the time the outbreak had died down, perhaps as many as 200 to 300 Indians had died at both missions. The most serious measles outbreak during the mission era occurred in 1806, killing as many as 1,600 Indians throughout the entire system and at Mission San Francisco alone wiping out the entire population under ten years of age. Like so many other California Indians, Tac was also a victim of smallpox, which led to his early death. In a somewhat ironic twist, however, unlike his Indian brethren, Tac contracted the disease in Europe rather than in his native land.[36]

More insidious and certainly the most detrimental affliction to Indian peoples was the occurrence of venereal diseases, mostly syphilis. Introduced in California within the first decade of Spanish settlement, syphilis and other venereal diseases contributed not only to Indian deaths, most commonly of women, but also to female sterilization which, among other causes, greatly reduced birthrates among mission Indians.[37] Clearly there were numerous causes, many unknown, for the deaths of so many California Indians during this period. We know, however, that between 1769 and 1834, as many as half (or 150,000 people) succumbed to deadly diseases. And yet this startling number pays little attention to the numbers of native people and cultures that did survive these traumatic times.

Looking back at Pablo Tac's brief account of the Luiseño people, it appears, despite his own religious convictions, that he was well aware of his people's fate at the hands of Spanish missionaries, noting among other examples their significant population decline. Yet unlike his ancestors who asked, "What is it that you seek here?" when they first met the Spaniards, Tac had the advantage of retrospection—he knew what it was the Spaniards sought. They came to California and other parts of the New World in search of wealth and converts, and the Indians, Tac among them, provided ample opportunity for both. Equally important, Tac witnessed and recorded the incredible devastation suffered by the Luiseño Indians as a result of Spain's colonization efforts.

Notes

1. Minna and Gordon Hewes, eds. and trans., "Indian Life and Customs at Mission San Luis Rey: A Record of California Indian Life Written by Pablo Tac, an Indian Neophyte (Rome, 1835)," *Americas* 9 (1952): 94.

2. Importantly, Tac made the distinction that before the arrival of the Spaniards his people called themselves *Quechnajuichorn*, inhabitants of *Quechla*. Luiseño was the name given by the Spanish missionaries to the Native American groups who lived in

proximity to or came to live at a particular mission: the Luiseño at San Luis Rey, the Juaneño (*Acâgchemem*) at San Juan Capistrano, and the Diegeño (*Quichamcauichom*) at San Diego de Alcala.

3. See Tac, "Indian Life and Customs at Mission San Luis Rey," 87–91.

4. Zephyrin Engelhardt, *San Luis Rey Mission* (San Francisco, 1921), 84–85.

5. Tac, "Indian Life and Customs at Mission San Luis Rey," 93, 98, 100–106.

6. Ibid., 94.

7. Ibid., 98.

8. In his publication, *Numbers from Nowhere: The American Indian Contact Population Debate* (Norman, 1998), David Henige raises questions over the widely varying estimates of precontact North American indigenous populations and a tendency in recent decades toward increasingly high numbers. Henige is particularly critical of the Berkeley school's Sherburne F. Cook, whose precontact population estimates for California remain the standard for most scholars today.

9. Michael Moratto, *California Archaeology* (New York, 1984); Zephyrin Engelhardt, *Missions and Missionaries of California*, 4 vols. (San Francisco, 1912); Delfina Cuero, *The Autobiography of Delfina Cuero: A Diegeño Indian* (Banning, CA, 1970).

10. The most current discussion of California precontact Indian demographics can be found in M. Kat Anderson et al., "A World of Balance and Plenty: Land, Plants, Animals, and Humans in a Pre-European California," and William S. Simmons, "Indian Peoples of California," both in Ramón Gutiérrez and Richard Orsi, eds., *Contested Eden: California before the Gold Rush* (Berkeley, 1998), 18, 48.

11. Lowell J. Bean, "Indians of California: Diverse and Complex Peoples," *California History* 71, no. 3 (1992): 308–9; Martin Baumhoff, "Environmental Background," in Robert F. Heizer, ed., *Handbook of North American Indians*, 17 vols. (Washington, DC, 1978), 8:16–17; Robert F. Heizer and Albert B. Elsasser, *The Natural World of the California Indians* (Berkeley, 1980), 82–85.

12. Bean, "Indians of California," 308–9; Heizer and Elsasser, *The Natural World of the California Indians*, 804–29.

13. Tac, "Indian Life and Customs at Mission San Luis Rey," 100–101.

14. Bean, "Indians of California," 309–10.

15. Ibid., 310.

16. Tac, "Indian Life and Customs at Mission San Luis Rey," 101–2.

17. Heizer and Elsasser, *The Natural World of the California Indians*, 52–56.

18. Ibid., 45–46.

19. Campbell Grant, "Chumash: Introduction," and "Interior Chumash," both in Heizer, ed., *Handbook of North American Indians*, 8:505–8, 530–34; Alfred L. Kroeber, *Handbook of the Indians of California*, Bureau of American Ethnology Bulletin 78 (Washington, DC, 1925), 550–52; Heizer and Elsasser, *The Natural World of the California Indians*, 47.

20. Heizer and Elsasser, *The Natural World of the California Indians*, 47–52; Lowell John Bean and Florence C. Shipek, "Luiseño," in Heizer, ed., *Handbook of North American Indians*, 8:552; Cook, "Historical Demography," in *Handbook of North American Indians*, 8:91.

21. Heizer and Elsasser, *The Natural World of the California Indians*, 37–42.

22. Ibid., 30–34.

23. Ibid., 36.

24. James T. Davis, *Trade Routes and Economic Exchange among the Indians of California* (Berkeley, 1961).

25. Robert F. Heizer, "Trade and Trails," in Heizer, ed., *Handbook of North American Indians*, 8:690.

26. Davis, *Trade Routes and Economic Exchange among the Indians of California*, 20, 37, 39; Heizer, "Trade and Trails," 690–91.

27. Tac, "Indian Life and Customs at Mission San Luis Rey," 93.

28. Ibid., 94.

29. David J. Weber, *The Spanish Frontier in North America* (New Haven, 1992), 236–65.

30. Edward D. Castillo, "The Impact of Euro-American Exploitation and Settlement," in Heizer, ed., *Handbook of North American Indians*, 8:100–101.

31. Tac, "Indian Life and Customs at Mission San Luis Rey," 94.

32. James A. Sandos, "Between the Crucifix and Lance: Indian-White Relations in California, 1769–1848," in Gutiérrez and Orsi, eds., *Contested Eden*, 203–9.

33. Heizer and Elsasser, *The Natural World of the California Indians*, 228.

34. Castillo, "The Impact of Euro-American Exploration and Settlement," 102–4.

35. Cook, *The Conflict between the California Indians and White Civilization* (Berkeley, 1976), 18.

36. Ibid., 18–19.

37. Ibid., 23–29.

Suggested Readings

Cook, Sherburne F. *The Conflict between the California Indians and White Civilization.* Berkeley: University of California Press, 1976.

Cuero, Delfina. *The Autobiography of Delfina Cuero, a Diegeqo Indian.* Banning, CA: Malki Museum Press, 1970.

Davis, James T. *Trade Routes and Economic Exchange among the Indians of California.* Berkeley: University of California Press, 1961

Gutiérrez, Ramón, and Richard Orsi, eds. *Contested Eden: California before the Gold Rush.* Berkeley: University of California Press, 1998.

Heizer, Robert F., and Albert B. Elsasser. *The Natural World of the California Indians.* Berkeley: University of California Press, 1980.

Heizer, Robert F., and M. A. Whipple. *The California Indians: A Source Book.* Berkeley: University of California Press, 1971.

Hurtado, Albert L. *Indian Survival on the California Frontier.* New Haven: Yale University Press, 1988.

Margolin, Malcolm. *The Ohlone Way: Indian Life in the San Francisco-Monterey Bay Area.* Berkeley: Heyday Books, 1978.

Phillips, George Harwood. *Indians and Intruders in Central California, 1769–1849.* Norman: University of Oklahoma Press, 1993.

Rawls, James. *Indians of California: The Changing Image.* Norman: University of Oklahoma Press, 1984.

2

Father President Mariano Payeras
A View of the California Missions

Douglas Cutter and Iris Engstrand

In the decades following Christopher Columbus's legendary 1492 voyage, the Spanish government launched repeated expeditions to North America with the desire to colonize the rich region and Christianize its peoples. The Spanish conquest of North America initially focused on what is now Mexico, and by the late 1600s, "New Spain" extended far north into what is now the southwestern United States.

Spain's conquest of California began in 1769 when the Franciscan missionary Junípero Serra and Spanish military leader Gaspár de Portola set north from Baja California to claim the northern region for Spain and to establish a series of missions. Between 1769 and 1823 the Spaniards founded twenty-two missions spanning from San Diego to Sonoma, as well as several military presidios and pueblos, including Los Angeles and San José. Spanish control of southern California would last from 1769 through 1821, during which time mission settlements spawned a new infrastructure of towns, farms, and trade routes throughout the region. While the mission system cleared the way for future European immigration to California, it resulted in the decimation of the Native American population. Spaniards not only introduced European diseases to the Indians, but many native peoples died from both economic dislocation and oppressive labor conditions created by the mission system.

In this essay, University of San Diego historians Iris Engstrand and Doug Cutter explore how one Franciscan missionary, Father Mariano Payeras, struggled with his mission duties amid alarming evidence of staggering Indian mortality rates. Engstrand and Cutter suggest that Franciscan fathers were neither villains nor saints, but committed missionaries carrying out their work against the backdrop of challenges from both Native American communities as well as Spanish authorities and other Catholic orders.

As the morning sunlight streamed into his cell-like room, Father Mariano Payeras groggily opened his eyes to gaze at his water clock, which had risen to the level of eight o'clock. "That worthless clock," he mumbled to himself. "You would think that after two decades of service to His Majesty and now to the Emperor Agustín Iturbide, the College of San Fernando could have sent me a decent alarm clock!" Payeras had

15

begged in his correspondence for an alarm clock for over twenty years—"one that was especially loud"—because he was notorious for oversleeping. For whatever reason, the college never saw fit to grant this request. Although the supply ships were not always reliable, the procurer for the college managed to send regular shipments of chocolate, the missions' subscriptions to periodicals, lots of poison for bears and wolves, and even a piano to accompany an Indian choir—but no clock. As a result, Payeras and his fellow prelate at the Mission La Purísima Concepción had set up a water clock, which kept decent time but did not help Mariano's oversleeping.[1]

Mission La Purísima Concepción. *Courtesy of the Bancroft Library, University of California, Berkeley*

Now in his mid-fifties, Payeras worried more about awakening because it seemed to indicate his poor general health. Even bloodlettings "no longer reduced his sluggishness."[2] As one of two fathers stationed at the mission in the early 1820s, Payeras had always been the one who pulled more than his own weight, but circumstances had now changed. As he opened his door to let in some fresh air, he could see Father Antonio Rodríguez out in the wheat fields giving orders to the male Indian neophytes, while the females were busy tending to the morning laundry closer to the main building. "Father Rodríguez is a marvel," Payeras wrote, "even though he wants to retire, he can get a couple of hours of work out of the neophytes before breakfast." In this respect Father Rodríguez was like almost all of the other missionaries in Alta California. Even though he felt devoted to his mission and to the Indian charges, he still hoped to retire to the College of San Fernando in Mexico.[3]

Father Payeras also wanted to retire from the mission field. He had complained a few years earlier that he and his fellow Franciscans "had grown gray and lost their teeth in the service of God and His Majesty [King Fernando VII]," but now at age fifty-three, his time was running short. Not only had he had trouble waking up in the previous years but one of his legs had become infected during a horseback ride through the province—preventing further travel—and now he had a bleeding tumor on his head that required continual bandaging.[4] This morning, as Father Payeras looked over his mission, he knew there would be no retirement to Mexico for him. He would soon die in California.

Few historical arenas can claim such an abundance of historical materials as the California missions. Yet because Spanish officials kept these records, the Franciscan padres often appear as benevolent creators of a new civilization, while Indian perspectives remain largely unrecognized.[5] Since the aboriginal population had no written language, centuries of cultural change, disease, persecution, and censure have limited what anthropologists and historians can reconstruct of the Native American past.[6] Recent historiography, however, has changed the accepted picture of California life during the Spanish and Mexican periods, and despite certain shortcomings, this new literature has allowed a more balanced picture of mission life to emerge.

When the Spaniards arrived in 1769, they found the natives generally divided into semiautonomous bands of fifty to seventy-five households whose economy depended upon hunting and gathering. Often an entire Indian village (*rancheria*) would move within a given geographic area to take advantage of seasonal natural resources. In conformance with general Spanish policy, missionaries induced California Indians to settle in small, permanent villages called *reducciones*, where they could be taught the rudiments of a "civilized" and Christian life. Those Indians already settled in established coastal communities received religious instruction in their native *rancherías* and were allowed to retain their existing social structure, which was normally based upon a patriarchal kinship system. The mission system was unquestionably paternalistic, and native leaders who had formerly administered economic and social affairs often assumed similar roles when brought within the Spanish mission organization.

Under the Spanish "Laws of the Indies" compiled in 1680, control of Indians by the missionaries was to be temporary—ideally to last only ten years. Religious duties would be turned over to a parish priest and mission lands distributed among converted Indians. In many cases, however, the missionaries insisted that independence was not practical, especially within ten years, and conflicts between secular and religious authorities became a major source of tension in later years. Spanish law also provided that the royal treasury bear the expense of the missionary's initial equipment and transportation, pay him a small annual salary, share the cost of mission buildings, and furnish a small military guard. As soon as the fathers could enlist Indian support, however, the missions were supposed to become self-sustaining economic units through farming, stock raising, and some manufacturing.

Even though California settlement began in 1683 on the southern gulf coast of Baja California, the mission system within California's present borders emerged during the latter years of the Franciscan effort in New Spain.[7] The founding of Mission San Diego de Alcalá in July 1769 under Father Junípero Serra, president of the California missions from 1768 until his death in 1784, established the final effort in Spain's northward expansion. Serra's actions have been well documented and reported, as have those of his successor, Father Fermín Francisco de Lasuén. Unfortunately, much less has been written about the presidency of Father Mariano Payeras from 1815 to 1823.[8] Payeras's career provides new insights into the thoughts and doubts of Spanish missionaries during this pivotal period of California history.[9] Mariano Payeras has been overlooked by historians because his tenure as president and prelate contained neither the drama of mission founding enjoyed by Serra and Lasuén nor the finality of mission secularization witnessed by the last father president, Narciso Durán. Even so, Payeras's presidency and prefecture from 1815 until 1823 deserves greater attention because it occurred during a critical juncture in early California history. The year 1821 marked the independence of Mexico from Spain and the beginning of a strong government and civilian effort to secularize the missions, thereby removing them from Church control.

Source material for mission history has been available to scholars since the time Hubert Howe Bancroft compiled his massive, 39-volume *Works*, but interpretations of mission history have been, quite naturally, widely divergent.[10] These interpretations have characterized the Franciscans as everything from saints to promoters of genocide.[11] The missionaries' actions often seem paradoxical. For example, Franciscan fathers locked unmarried Indian women in sleeping rooms at night to protect their chastity and make them desirable spouses, but such crowded living conditions made them more susceptible to infectious diseases such as measles and smallpox. These diseases killed countless natives in the mission confines. Venereal disease also spread quickly due to unregulated sexual intercourse between Spanish settlers and Indians. In terms of work, the unpaid Indian laborers tilled the fields, constructed buildings, tended cattle, wove cloth, and performed the other tasks necessary to keep the missions running. Some Indians adapted to these circumstances while others sought freedom and ran away. Missionary treatment of Indians differed greatly depending on many factors, and historical interpretations of the missionaries' actions have swung like a pendulum from evil to sublime and back again.[12]

A major problem in the historiography of mission development is the historian's inability to look objectively at both mission and Indian history. For a balanced mission and Indian history to be written, historians must begin from the position that Indians were victims of forced cultural change. The focus should therefore shift from whether missionization was right or wrong, and instead view it as a matter of fact. In an effort to avoid taking sides on the morality of the mission system, we present Father Mariano Payeras as a person doing a job for which he was trained and which he believed was a beneficial force in human salvation: the conversion of nonbelieving persons to the Christian faith. He was also given the challenge of maintaining a mission system in an economically profitable manner despite the frequent neglect of Spanish officials. Payeras struggled as much with Spanish government officials and fellow missionaries as with Native Americans. In fact, no substantive Indian uprising took place during his administration. It is therefore as important to understand the daily activities of Father Payeras and his relationship to the Spanish government as to criticize or defend the mission system itself.

Mariano Payeras was born in 1769, the same year that the expedition from Baja California led by Gaspar de Portolá and Father Junípero Serra laid the foundations for the occupation of Alta California. Born Pedro Antonio in Inca, Mallorca (Spain), Mariano was the first son of Antonio Payeras and Gerónima Borras.[13] He was baptized the day after he was born at the parish church of Santa María la Mayor and confirmed on November 28, 1770, in the same parish church.[14] As a young boy, Pedro Antonio was enrolled in school at the Convento San Francisco de Inca, where, as was typical for young Mallorcans, he came under the influence of his Franciscan teachers. At age fourteen he joined the Franciscan Order at Palma and was given the name of Mariano.[15]

It was not unprecedented that Payeras joined the order at such an early age. Many youthful Spaniards joined military or religious orders during this era, and an early acceptance in the order generally indicated exceptional ability.[16] In addition, there were only two real opportunities for sons of peasant families such as Payeras: an ecclesiastical life or that of a farmer. Parents often encouraged their sons to become priests in a country where the austere lives of the poor were filled with religious rules and traditions.[17] Young Mariano embarked for New Spain as a missionary in 1793. At this time he was described in his passport records as being of medium stature, of swarthy complexion, with chestnut-colored eyes, dark hair, and a light beard.[18]

The College of San Fernando in Mexico City, the first destination of newly arrived missionaries, was founded by royal decree on October 15, 1733, one of seven colleges in New Spain. These colleges were not only centers of learning but also sites for missionary recruitment and orientation.[19] San Fernando served as an intermediary between civil and mission authorities throughout New Spain, and the college supervised the placement of missionaries throughout New Spain. Additionally, each college served as a base for missionaries to which they could retire when their tours of duty were over or they were physically or mentally incapacitated.[20]

After two years of training at San Fernando College, Payeras was evaluated by his superiors as "a person of approved conduct and entirely satisfactory to the college membership."[21] Eagerly following the footsteps of his role model, Junípero Serra, Payeras volunteered to participate in the expansion of the Alta California missions conducted by Father Fermín Francisco de Lasuén, the second father president who succeeded Junípero Serra in 1784. To this end Payeras left the college on March 1, 1796, and traveled to San Blas to board a supply ship headed for California.[22] Up until this point there was no indication that Payeras was anything other than an ordinary missionary, much less that he would become president of the California missions.

In June 1796 young Mariano Payeras and his fellow travelers arrived in San Francisco aboard the *Aránzazu* and were met by Father President Lasuén, who had made the trip north from Mission Santa Cruz where he had been visiting. Lasuén wanted to give the new missionaries their assignments as soon as possible. Although Lasuén seemed generally displeased with the capabilities of the new recruits, he took a shine to Payeras, who arrived bearing an insignia of the heraldic symbol of Santiago as a gift for Lasuén and was the only missionary who had been granted the authority to hear confession.[23]

From the beginning of their working relationship, Lasuén trusted Payeras implicitly and obviously recognized him as a man of ability. Having reached his sixties, Lasuén was feeling his age and no longer had the physical stamina to move easily from mission to mission. The two men worked well together, and within six months of his assignment Payeras's authority extended over Missions San Carlos (including the Monterey presidio), San Juan Bautista, San Antonio, and La Soledad.[24] The training Payeras received during his two years with Father Lasuén would serve him well during his own presidency from 1815 to 1823.[25]

Stationed at a number of different missions before receiving a permanent abode at Mission La Purísima Concepción, Payeras became well acquainted with various missionaries and their methods of instruction. He personally visited each of the twenty-one missions and gained considerable knowledge of the California countryside through these travels. Known to his companions as Father Mariano, he made it his business to personally interview each of the priests and discuss the operation of their missions. In December 1820, under official orders, Payeras wrote short biographies and performance evaluations of each of the father-ministers. This document has been extremely useful to historians and shows the objectivity with which Payeras viewed his colleagues.[26]

Among the more common claims in Native American and Franciscan history is the brutalization and domination of California Indians by intolerant mission fathers, who presumably used native labor for their own profit. Interaction between Indians and Franciscans was far more complex, even to the extent that Native Americans used the missions for their own economic advantage or to retaliate against traditional enemies. The correspondence of Father Mariano Payeras during his presidency and prelacy in California helps to diffuse the binary conception of missionaries and Indians as oppressors and oppressed. Payeras's letters reveal his attempt to understand two opposing cultures striving to negotiate the limits of their control. Rather than as subjugators, this interpretation presents missionaries as quite ordinary men given to the whims of everyday life and genuinely concerned with their Indian neophytes, if not always tolerant of their disobedience. Franciscan missionaries considered their role to be that of fathers looking after their children.

The mission fathers were well aware of their limited power in Alta California, especially with regard to Native Americans. Indians often influenced mission agendas through passive and aggressive resistance, forcing the missionaries to succumb at least in part to Indian demands. The coastal Chumash, for instance, resisted acculturation through the continued practice of abortions, horse raiding, and an unwillingness to learn Spanish. Franciscan fathers were forced to translate Catholic doctrine into native languages, even though this practice contradicted the rules of their order. On the other hand, Native Americans' willingness to farm, build mission structures, and even militarily protect Spanish settlements is befuddling to historians looking for a coherent sense of Indian objectives. In the end, Native Americans' responses to the missions and to the larger Spanish presence are beyond simple classification.

Father Payeras's attitudes toward the California Indians, particularly the Chumash among whom he spent most of his missionary career, were fairly consistent throughout his tenure. Anthropologists have consistently depicted the Chumash as having the most materially advanced culture among the California Indians.[27] They also proved the most receptive to missionization. Therefore, when Payeras was elected president of the California missions, he remained with the Chumash at Mission La Purísima Concepción instead of moving to Carmel, the traditional political center. La Purísima was in the process of being rebuilt after the old mission had been destroyed by an earthquake in 1812, and Payeras viewed the Chumash as probably the most effective labor force in the province. Chumash labor was instrumental in rebuilding the mission, and their agricultural output rivaled that of missions with larger neophyte populations.

However adaptable the Chumash were to mission life, vestiges of their native religion nevertheless remained in clear view of the Franciscans, who were in many ways powerless to change native beliefs. The secret ceremonial life of the Chumash surfaced occasionally and reminded Father Payeras how little success the Franciscan indoctrination enjoyed. Payeras spent a great deal of time tracking down *cimarrones* (escaped neophytes) in the San Joaquin Valley, otherwise known as the Gran Tular because of the reed-covered marshes that dominated the local terrain. To bring back particularly well-trained neophytes, the Spaniards planned battle strategies that employed both leather-jacket soldiers (*soldados de cuera*) and Indian *gentiles* (non-mission Indians) as auxiliaries. However, the majority of Indians who left the missions to gather acorns or other foodstuffs at harvest time returned voluntarily. Other Indian groups, such as those attached to Mission San Luis Rey, lived far from the mission but nonetheless remained under its tutelage.

An early illustration of Payeras's attitude toward his Indian charges is contained in a 1798 letter he composed as a young mission trainee at Mission San Carlos. Payeras expressed his doubt about the potential for success among these California natives, because "rational men" should naturally favor learning methods of agriculture in order to avoid the uncertainty of hunting and gathering. He wrote to Governor Diego de Borica:

> In order to fulfill the great task that has been entrusted to us of teaching these neophytes to be both rational men as well as to be good Christians, we have focused all our attention on gathering in some [Indians] from the direction of Calendarruc[28] and others from Mutsun.[29] Motivated solely by the natural inclination of living among the beasts, they have spent all their lives in the woods. We pleaded with them often to present themselves, inviting them by offering them pardon. We have threatened them with recourse to government intervention if they do not appear; but all of our efforts have accomplished nothing. Our efforts can achieve nothing more; and therefore we beseech Your Lordship to take the measures that may seem best to you so that the aforementioned may be brought in. May God Our Lord protect Your Lordship many years![30]

Like so many other Spanish missionaries, Payeras clearly found it difficult to understand the Indians' rejection of mission life.

In the next decade, however, increasing numbers of Chumash appeared to accept the missionaries' offerings. During the years 1803–04 over 1,600 Chumash entered the three missions erected in their domain: Santa Inés, Santa Bárbara, and La Purísima. This figure represents nearly 25 percent of all neophytes registered during the mission era.[31] Payeras corroborates these statistics by stating, "In this area the unconverted have vanished . . . the few *gentiles* who appear . . . live 25 to 30 leagues away, perhaps because of such a great distance it would not be advantageous to baptize them."[32]

Payeras frequently painted a positive picture of Indian life at La Purísima, but he also agonized over the loss of native life. He was painfully aware of the statistical evidence of neophyte mortality because, by 1808, Payeras had become the senior padre at La Purísima, responsible for the reports concerning production and population statistics for the mission, a duty he fulfilled for the rest of his life. After becoming president in 1815, he received reports from all of the missions regarding Indian mortality. Faced with the evidence of thousands of Indian deaths, Payeras was concerned that other religious orders, as well as Spanish officials, would discover the truth about neophytes entrusted to Franciscan care.[33]

After twenty-three years as a missionary in California, Payeras felt it was his duty to inform the College of San Fernando of his view of Indian mortality and to question the methods of the California missions.

On February 2, 1820, he wrote to the ruling body at the College, informing the Father Guardian and the Discretorio of his misgivings. After a short preamble on the basic purpose of the Alta California endeavor, he wrote: "Where we expected a beautiful and flourishing church and some beautiful towns which should be the joy of the sovereign majesties of Heaven and Earth, we find ourselves with missions or rather with a people miserable and sick, with rapid depopulation of *rancherías* which with profound horror fills the cemeteries."[34]

The father-prelate continued, reporting that while the *gentiles* were healthy and procreated easily in spite of the fact that they lived "almost like beasts," as soon as they entered the missions "they become extremely feeble, lose weight, get sick, and die." Mission fathers assumed that the change of environment contributed to the decline in health and that the Indians would soon adjust. Children born in the mission, they reasoned, should be as healthy and robust as their non-mission counterparts, but population records did not prove this to be the case. In his letter to the college, Payeras explained: "However, the sad experience of 51 years has showed us all too well that we have erred in our calculation. Having already seen two generations in the missions, we sadly observe that the mission native dies equally, and perhaps more so than the Indian in the sierra, that they are consumed indiscriminately and are rapidly vanishing."[35]

The historian of today can find much to criticize with regard to the high Indian death rate in the missions. It should be kept in mind, however, that death resulted mainly from disease, the spread of which the padres did not understand, rather than from malnutrition, overwork, or oppressive measures. The padres were at a loss to explain the high death rate among the natives. Moreover, devastating plagues hit other places and other peoples during these times for similarly misunderstood reasons.

Surprisingly, Payeras seems to have been one of the few people in authority to recognize (or one of the few willing to write about it) that mission populations were frequently bolstered by bringing in natives from other areas. Even though he was fond of traveling and working among non-mission Indians, Payeras was unwilling to seek out *gentiles* to bring back to La Purísima. Other missions, he noted in the letter to the College of San Fernando, disguised the "reduction" in mission population in their annual reports:

> [By] baptizing *gentiles*, and by mixing one group with another, we still come
> out ahead in the total. But this decline cannot be hidden in the places where

the conquest has ended. Here is an example of the mission of my actual residence, La Purísima, last year, 1819: out of 228 couples, the greater portion at the age of procreation, only 26 children were baptized from among them while 66 of its neophytes died of the 800 to 900 which it had. This means that in one year alone it had a decrease of 40 individuals. About the same thing happens, more or less, in the greater part of the missions so that this subject is for many of the Father Ministers the touchstone of their greatest despair and affliction.[36]

Although the missions were at the height of their productivity under the prelacy of Payeras, changes beyond the control of the padres were taking place that would ultimately bring about the end of the missions. Ideas about the status of man, engendered by the Enlightenment, brought the function of the missions into question; the issue of whether the Indians should continue in a state of tutelage was central to antimission ideas.[37] Missionization had long been unpopular in New Spain, but José de Gálvez in 1773 had exempted Alta California from the rules regarding secularization.[38] The echoes of complete independence from Spain now cast an additional shadow upon the missions. As representatives of the Bourbon monarchy, the Franciscans and their neophytes were viewed with suspicion. It seemed that in postcolonial Latin America there would be no place for the missions. Nevertheless, the California mission fathers continued to labor in the "Lord's vineyard" as if their way of life would never end.

Father Payeras was a typical Franciscan caught up in these changes. Fortunately, as the highest authority over the California missions, his opinions are frequently reflected in his continual correspondence between La Purísima and the College of San Fernando. Although he had no less apostolic zeal than the indefatigable Serra or the cerebral Lasuén, the circumstances brought on by Mexican independence in 1821 made Payeras's service in California from 1797 until 1823 distinct from that of his predecessors. During this so-called Golden Age of the missions, both Alta and Baja California changed from ecclesiastical havens controlled by the Franciscans to territories controlled by Mexico's secular government. Nevertheless, Father Payeras, as the main representative of the gray-robed Franciscans, possessed the ability to weather these changes because of his decades-long training, business ability, and intimate knowledge of California. Even Hubert Howe Bancroft, often a critic of the mission system, wrote: "There was no friar of better or more balanced ability in the province. He was a personally popular man on account of his affable manners, kindness of heart, and unselfish devotion to the welfare of all. . . . His death just at this time [1823], in the prime of life, must be considered as a great misfortune though not even his skill could have saved the missions in the times that were coming."[39]

The image of the mission enterprise was important to Father Payeras, who worried that reports would circulate outside of California about the ease with which the Franciscans lived. His belief in an austere lifestyle was demonstrated by his opposition to the use of fancy carriages by his associates. More important to Payeras was the mortality of mission neophytes, who continued to die at an alarming rate. Even though he was dutiful in strict adherence to Franciscan rules, he had the courage to question mission methodology. Despite his concern over neophyte mortality and the image of the missions, Payeras tried to work within the framework of the College of San Fernando. Never would he publicly compromise the position of his order, his missionaries, or the secular government.

Not long after the death of Payeras in 1823 came what he had worked so hard to push back—the secularization of the missions. Payeras's anxiety that the mission Indians would suffer terribly at the hands of civilian officials proved well-founded. Administrators quickly stripped the mission Indians of their lands; and, in part because the Franciscans were unable to adequately acculturate their neophytes, the former mission residents found themselves to be a landless people. Although the padres had held the mission lands "in trust" for the Indians, those natives who did receive plots were unable to hold on to them after mission secularization. They received little support from Mexican Californians, who believed that mission lands should not be held for "rude Indians" when "good patriots" could become productive *rancheros*.[40] Once the mission lands were broken up, most of the mission converts went to work as *vaqueros*, agricultural laborers, and household servants. "Former mission Indians also migrated to towns, where they lived in *rancherías* located on the outskirts and served as a pool of temporary laborers."[41]

This kind of *patrón* system during the Mexican period of California history was likely preferable to the Anglo version of peonage and free labor that was implemented in the 1850s, brought on by the gold rush. According to historian Albert Hurtado, "Despite abuses by Mexican *hacendados*, Indian *peones* were permitted to live in their own communities and retain tribal customs. When Anglo-Americans adapted peonage, however, they usually broke up native communities and families, thus contributing to Indian demographic decline."[42] The partially acculturated Indians could not return to traditional lands that no longer existed in their precontact form, nor did other Indians embrace them.

Father Mariano Payeras would have been saddened to see his former charges left without what he considered to be a guiding hand.

Notes

1. Adapted from the letters of Mariano Payeras. See specifically Mariano Payeras to Juan Norberto de Santiago, La Purísima, August 6, 1816; in Donald Cutter, ed. and trans., *Writings of Mariano Payeras* (Santa Barbara, 1995), 97.

2. Mariano Payeras to Father Procurador Pedro Martinez, April 11, 1812, Historia de México, Primera Serie, tomo 2, Archivo General de la Nación, Mexico.

3. Adapted from the letters of Mariano Payeras. See Cutter, *Writings of Mariano Payeras*, 337.

4. Cutter, *Writings of Mariano Payeras*, 16, 26.

5. In this paper we use the term "Indian" when referring to the Native American population of early California. Although the designation is frequently viewed as contentious, trying to identify each indigenous group by its tribal name is more problematic, given the vast heterogeneous aboriginal population. By the same token, we refer to the non-Franciscan population as "Spanish," even though few had true Spanish origins. The Franciscans, on the other hand, almost to the man were recruited in Spain. "Neophytes" were Indians brought into the missions for Christian training and eventual baptism.

6. For a good analysis of these problems, see William Simmons, "Indian Peoples of California," in Ramón Gutiérrez and Richard Orsi, eds., *Contested Eden: California before the Gold Rush* (Berkeley, 1998), 48–77.

7. The two areas, Alta and Baja California—today's state of California and both Mexican states of Baja California—were designated in 1772. The Jesuits missionized Baja California and had plans for further expansion north. After the Jesuit expulsion in 1768 the mission field was divided between the Dominican and Franciscan orders. Given their preference of location, the Franciscans opted for the northern zone, giving the Dominicans Baja California.

8. See especially Zephyrin Engelhardt, *The Missions and Missionaries of California*, 4 vols. (San Francisco, 1908–1915); Finbar Kinneally, *Writings of Fermín Francisco de Lasuén*, 2 vols. (Washington, DC, 1965); and Maynard Geiger, *The Life and Times of Junípero Serra* (Washington, DC, 1959) and *Franciscan Missionaries in Hispanic California, 1769–1848: A Biographical Dictionary* (San Marino, CA, 1969).

9. On the life of Mariano Payeras, see Douglas Cutter, "The Life of Mariano Payeras: A Study in Church/State Relations" (Master's thesis, University of San Diego, 1996); Cutter, *Writings of Mariano Payeras*; and Richard H. Dillon, "Father Payeras, O.F.M., at San Rafael," *The Americas* 11 (July 1954): 79–86.

10. Hubert Howe Bancroft, *Works* (San Francisco, 1882–1900). Much of the source material for the Spanish era is housed in the Archivo General de las Indias in Seville, Spain, and the Archivo General de México in Mexico City. The best source for California mission research is the Santa Barbara Mission Archive Library, which is both extensive and easily available to historians. The Bancroft Library at the University of California at Berkeley holds microfilm from Spanish and Mexican archives, mission records, and government correspondence as well as a series of interviews called *recuerdos*,

of *californios*, which were collected between 1877 and 1878. The Huntington Library in San Marino also contains a number of important sources on Spanish and Mexican California.

11. For a particularly biased attack against the Franciscan missions, see Rupert Costo and Jeannette Henry Costo, *The California Missions: A Legacy of Genocide* (San Francisco, 1987). The title is especially misleading, and we agree with James Axtell, who writes that "only the rare certifiable homicidal maniac sought to commit 'genocide' upon the Indians. . . . *Genocide* was coined in 1944 to denote the systematic 'annihilation of a race.' " See Axtell, *After Columbus: Essays in the Ethnohistory of North America* (New York, 1988), 43–44. The missionaries, even more so than settlers in colonial America, had no desire to have Indians die, since their goal was to gain converts and sustain the missions by an assured labor supply.

12. Early historians of California's past tended to bring their Protestant bias to their writing in frequently depicting the Franciscan missionaries as cruel and power-hungry. In 1885, Theodore Hittell stated that the mission fathers treated the Indians with "barbarous cruelties added to the miserably slavish kind of existence which the neophytes were compelled to live at the missions." Bancroft, widely regarded as the father of early California history, was equally unfavorably inclined toward the missionaries, often labeling founding Father Junípero Serra as a bigot. Even though many modern scholars dismiss Bancroft as a biased observer of history, much of the anti-mission scholarship currently in vogue liberally cites him as a source. By the early twentieth century, the Franciscans had taken it upon themselves to write their own history. In what was virtually a one-man campaign to promote the Order of Friars Minor, Zephyrin Engelhardt, OFM, wrote the detailed 4-volume work *The Missions and Missionaries of California*. He also penned histories of sixteen of the twenty-one Alta California missions. Father Engelhardt took every opportunity to castigate historians such as Bancroft for their abysmal portrayal of the missions. Despite Engelhardt's attention to detail, negative aspects of the missions were almost wholly disregarded in his writing. These omissions also characterize the work of his protégé, Franciscan Father Maynard Geiger, whose works include *The Life and Times of Junípero Serra* and the biographical dictionary, *Franciscan Missionaries*.

13. Libro de Bautismos, no. 3 (no. 93, folio 49) de la Parroquia de Santa María la Mayor, Inca, Archivo Episcopal de Palma de Mallorca.

14. Cutter, *Writings of Mariano Payeras*, 3; Libro de Bautismos, no. 3.

15. Geiger, *Franciscan Missionaries*, 184.

16. Francis Guest, *Fermín Francisco de Lasuén (1736–1803): A Biography* (Washington, DC, 1973), 5–6.

17. Bartolome Font Obrador, Presidente de la sección Juniperiana, interview by Douglas Cutter, November 21, 1995.

18. Geiger, *Franciscan Missionaries*, 184.

19. Guest, *Fermín Francisco de Lasuén*, 12.

20. Kenneally, *Writings of Fermín Francisco de Lasuén*, 1:xix.

21. Geiger, *Franciscan Missionaries*, 184.

22. Cutter, *Writings of Mariano Payeras*, 4.

23. Lasuén to Fray Antonio Nogueyra, June 30, 1796 and September 3, 1796. Kenneally, *Writings of Fermín Francisco de Lasuén*, 2:384, 399–400. The insignia was a

scallop shell, symbol of Santiago, Saint James, and accorded to those who had made the pilgrimage to the shrine of Saint James in Compostela.

24. Geiger, *Franciscan Missionaries*, 185.

25. Cutter, *Writings of Mariano Payeras*, 4.

26. Payeras to Fray Juan Buenaventura Bestard, December 31, 1820, Santa Barbara Mission Archives.

27. See Campbell Grant, "Chumash: Introduction," and Roberta S. Greenwood, "Opispeño and Purisimeño Chumash," in Robert F. Heizer, ed., *The California Indians* (Washington, DC, 1978), 505–8, 520–23.

28. Calendarruc or Kalinta-ruk was a *ranchería* of Costanoan Indians located at the mouth of the Salinas River. A. L. Kroeber, *Handbook of the Indians of California* (Washington, DC, 1925), 465.

29. Mutsun or Mutsu-n was another Costanoan *ranchería* located at the present-day mission of San Juan Buenaventura. Cutter, *Writings of Mariano Payeras*, 345.

30. Archive of the Archbishop of San Francisco. Diego de Borica served as governor of California from May 1794 until January 1800. For a biographical sketch, see Donald Nuttall, "The Gobernantes of Spanish Upper Californa: A Profile," *California Historical Society Quarterly* 51 (Fall 1972): 253–80.

31. James A. Sandos, "Neophyte Resistance in the Alta California Missions," in Timothy O'Keefe, ed., *Columbus, Confrontation, Christianity: The European-American Encounter Revisited* (Madison, 1994), 175.

32. Payeras to Estevan Tapis, January 13, 1810, Santa Barbara Mission Archives.

33. Cutter, *Writings of Mariano Payeras*, 11.

34. Payeras to the Apostolic College of San Fernando, February 2, 1820, Santa Barbara Mission Archives.

35. Ibid.

36. Ibid.

37. Iris H. W. Engstrand, "The Enlightenment in Spain: Influences upon New World Policy," *The Americas* 41 (April 1985): 436–45.

38. For nonclerical attitudes toward secularization, see Gerald Joseph Geary, *The Secularization of the California Missions* (Washington, DC, 1934); and Manuel Servín, "The Secularization of the California Missions: A Reappraisal," *Southern California Quarterly* 42 (June 1968): 133–49.

39. Hubert Howe Bancroft, *History of California*, 7 vols. (San Francisco, 1886), 2:489–90.

40. Cutter, *Writings of Mariano Payeras*, 14–15.

41. Robert H. Jackson and Edward Castillo, *Indians, Franciscans, and Spanish Colonization* (Albuquerque, 1995), 94–95.

42. Albert Hurtado, *Indian Survival on the California Frontier* (New Haven, 1988), 3.

Suggested Readings

Archibald, Robert. *The Economic Aspects of the California Missions*. Washington, DC: Academy of American Franciscan History, 1978.

Bouvier, Virginia M. *Women and the Conquest of California, 1542–1840: Codes of Silence*. Tucson: University of Arizona Press, 2001.

Cutter, Donald, ed. and trans. *Writings of Mariano Payeras*. Santa Barbara, CA: Bellerophon Books, 1995.

Guest, Francis. *Fermín Francisco de Lasuén (1736–1803): A Biography*. Washington, DC: Academy of American Franciscan History, 1973.

Gutiérrez, Ramón, and Richard Orsi, eds. *Contested Eden: California before the Gold Rush*. Berkeley: University of California Press, 1998.

Hurtado, Albert. *Indian Survival on the California Frontier*. New Haven: Yale University Press, 1988.

Jackson, Robert H., and Edward Castillo. *Indians, Franciscans, and Spanish Colonization*. Albuquerque: University of New Mexico Press, 1995.

La Pérouse, Jean François de Galaup, Comte de. *Life in a California Mission: Monterey in 1786*. Berkeley: Heyday Books, 1995.

3

Guadalupe Trujillo
Race, Culture, and Justice in
Mexican Los Angeles

Special Feature

Miroslava Chávez-García*

For nearly 300 years beginning in the early sixteenth century, Spain controlled a vast portion of the Americas. Whereas British colonists in North America typically eschewed social relationships with Native Americans, Spaniards intermarried widely, creating a diverse mestizo population. Despite the greater levels of social and cultural assimilation, however, Indian and mestizo communities in New Spain increasingly fought against Spanish colonial leaders and policies. Between 1808 and the mid-1820s, revolutionary discontent spread throughout the region, resulting in a declaration of Mexican independence in 1821.

California, the northernmost Spanish province, escaped almost all of the revolution's turmoil and bloodshed, and for the most part its peoples and leaders embraced the new Mexican government when word of the events first reached the region in 1822. The same social tensions that had launched the Mexican revolution were very much present in California, however, as its population encompassed tremendous social diversity. Among the region's peoples were numerous Native American, mulatto, mestizo, and Spanish communities as well as an increasing stream of American immigrants. At times these groups interacted peaceably, but violence and conflict often appeared. In this essay, Miroslava Chávez-García, a historian at the University of California, Davis, takes us into the Mexican pueblo of Los Angeles to shed light on how Mexican and Indian women related both interpersonally and within the legal system. Professor Chávez-García's analysis of the murder trial of Guadalupe Trujillo exposes how Californians struggled to make sense of shifting and competing interpretations of racial, ethnic, and state identity within the confines of Mexican law.

At approximately eleven in the morning on February 15, 1843, Guadalupe Trujillo and her Indian servant, Ysabel, quarreled over domestic chores. Trujillo and Ysabel, along with other members of the

*A grant from the Institute of American Cultures, University of California, Los Angeles, made the research for this paper possible. I thank Norris Hundley, Judith Ann Giesberg, and the editors of this anthology for their comments and suggestions.

family, resided at Mission San Gabriel, fifteen miles from Los Angeles, a *pueblo* (town) of no more than 2,300 inhabitants. Their verbal argument quickly became heated and led to a physical altercation, prompting Trujillo to grab a large kitchen knife. After a brief struggle, the knife slashed Ysabel's throat and she fell to the floor, gasping for air. Within minutes, she died of her wound. By three o'clock that afternoon, the local justice of the peace had notified Judge Manuel Dominguez and a local doctor about the tragedy. Upon arriving, they found Ysabel's lifeless body covered by a blanket on the floor of the room. They removed the blanket and closely examined her body, identifying the severity of the wound that Trujillo had inflicted. Multiple smaller lacerations, they noted, flanked the main cut, which measured 2 inches deep and 8 in length and severed the artery. The doctor told the judge that the perpetrator had used "repetition and force."

Judge Dominguez's initial inquiry into the incident found no dispute about the central fact: Guadalupe Trujillo had stabbed Ysabel, her Indian servant. Trujillo told the judge that she had killed Ysabel for no other reason than self-defense. Following that initial investigation, the judge ordered a trial to determine if Trujillo had killed Ysabel in self-defense or if she, in fact, had premeditated a murder. Under Mexican law, judges and not juries determined the fate of defendants in capital crimes, and the law made capital crimes against Indians punishable by imprisonment. Throughout the trial, the prosecution as well as other witnesses challenged Trujillo's assertion of self-defense, with the prosecution arguing that Trujillo, not Ysabel, had instigated the fight. Trujillo, the prosecution contended, had grown tired of Ysabel's insolence and finally committed "premeditated murder."[1]

Trujillo's crime, while extreme, was not an aberration in the community. The court records from which this case is taken reveal that Mexican women such as Trujillo perpetrated crimes against members of their community, which included the so-called *gente de razón* (literally, people of reason) as well as their cultural and racial "other," California Indians, and that they were regularly prosecuted for their excesses. These cases also indicate that contentious social and family relations existed among women of different socioeconomic, cultural, and racial groups. Women from landowning families or those whose husbands were prominent political leaders had links to the power structure that their impoverished counterparts did not possess. Moreover, some Mexican women had access to economic, political, and social power that Native American women rarely achieved. Native women's entrance into the Hispanic world—where they learned to speak the Spanish language, worship in the Catholic faith, and follow Spanish cultural and gender prescriptions—did not ordinarily lead Mexican and Indian women to forge ties of sisterhood across cultural and socioeconomic lines. As the court trial would reveal, Trujillo and Ysabel's longtime relationship reflected such unequal and strained relations.[2]

Hierarchical relations between Indians and Mexicans, regardless of gender or social class, dated to the founding of Los Angeles in 1781. Though the population of the *pueblo* came originally from the lower strata of Mexican society and had racially mixed backgrounds of native, African, and Spanish ancestry, the settlers and their descendants distinguished themselves culturally and, later, ethnically from the *gentiles* (unbaptized California Indians) residing in villages and from the *neófitos* (neophytes, or baptized California Indians) living at the missions. That identity—*gente de razón*—also forged a cultural and social bond among them as they downplayed (and forgot) their own mixed heritages and saw themselves as *españoles* and eventually *californios*. They also distanced themselves socially from Indians—males and females, *gentiles* and *neófitos*—by relying on them almost exclusively as laborers in the *pueblo* and at nearby Mission San Gabriel. The *pobladores* (settlers) hired Gabrieleño men, women, and children (Indians living in or near Mission San Gabriel) from nearby villages and, later, *gentiles* from other *rancherías* and *neófitos* from the local mission, not only for the public projects but also for plowing, planting, harvesting, and tending to livestock. In return, *pobladores* paid them, their village chiefs, or the mission friars in kind, usually foodstuffs, blankets, small trinkets, or hides. Later, residents turned to locally brewed alcohol (*aguardiente*) as compensation, a practice, though outlawed in 1812, that led to drunkenness, violence, and other adverse social consequences for the Indians.[3]

Following secularization in the 1830s, when the Mexican government ended the mission system, neophytes left the missions and several hundred drifted into the *pueblo* and replaced the *gentiles* as the main source of labor. When the economy failed to accommodate the oversupply of workers who then became a "nuisance" to the *gente de razón*, city leaders enacted vagrancy ordinances in the late 1830s and 1840s. Those Indians unable to pay the fines found themselves performing forced labor on public works or being auctioned off to others. The result of captivity was often slavery in all but name.[4]

The social and cultural position of Indians vis-à-vis the *gente de razón* in Los Angeles provides the context in which to analyze the murder trial of Guadalupe Trujillo. It also allows us to examine how relations of power, based on gender, social status, and cultural and racial identity, structured and informed social and family relations between Trujillo and Ysabel. Only recently have scholars begun to probe the complex interactions between Mexicans and Native Americans, men and women, in California. These studies demonstrate that violence (including rape), labor (work patterns), fictive kinship links (created through marriage and baptism), family ties (established through intermarriage), and reciprocity (mutual obligations) shaped and characterized bonds between Mexican and native peoples.[5] Though significant to our understanding of Mexican–Indian relations, these studies have largely ignored how the legal system—law and justice in the community—handled cross-cultural relationships that turned sour and, ultimately, led to deadly consequences. The documentation available for this trial also allows us to examine the subtleties and details of the incident surrounding Ysabel's death, providing an opportunity to understand how and why her relationship with Trujillo became strained and led to violence. The testimony discloses that their longtime relationship was tolerant at best and hostile at worst. As we will see, the judge had the sole responsibility for determining if Trujillo, as Ysabel's master and social better, had abused her power over the Indian woman. The evidence will enable us to explore closely the immediate circumstances that caused the women to see each other as adversaries and that drove Trujillo to kill Ysabel.

The trial will also allow us to explore not only how *angeleños* dealt with crime, but also how the local court viewed Trujillo's and Ysabel's relations and roles in the larger society. Everyone familiar with the incident agreed that Trujillo had committed a crime when she killed Ysabel, but disagreed as to the reason for and the severity of the crime. The arguments that the defense and the prosecution presented, while in opposition, disclose that both sides attempted to prove the victimization of their respective clients by invoking their cultural identities and social ranks and by drawing on *gente de razón* values that ascribed the role of master to Mexicans and servant to Indians. Trujillo, most residents agreed, was Ysabel's social better but, as the judge's ruling would demonstrate, Trujillo's socioeconomic status and cultural identity did not bar her from community standards of law and justice. The testimony of key witnesses, the counsels' arguments, and the judge's decision provide clues as to the ways in which the local community viewed cross-cultural social relations between the two Mexican and Native American women.[6]

Guadalupe Trujillo, the woman at the center of the controversy and trial, was not a native of Los Angeles or California. She and her family—which included a husband, a young daughter, and their servant, Ysabel—had originally migrated from their hometown of Abiqui, New Mexico, to the San Gabriel–Los Angeles region sometime after 1839. Their relocation was part of a larger trend of migration from New Mexico to California fueled initially, in the early 1830s, by Euro-American traders who went in search of new markets, goods, and livestock, and later by New Mexican families who removed themselves permanently in search of new opportunities.[7] In Abiqui, a small town of no more than 2,000 inhabitants, Trujillo and her family belonged to the lower-middle class, as they were neither members of the nobility nor *genizaros* nor detribalized Indians, as was Ysabel. When they arrived in Los Angeles, a *pueblo* that served as the nucleus of several dozen outlying *ranchos* (privately held large tracts of land for grazing livestock) and *rancherías* (Indian villages), the family had little economic means with which to acquire or maintain their own property, forcing them to rent a room at the mission and the father to work as a laborer for local proprietors, likely *rancheros* (*rancho* owners). In Mexican Los Angeles, land-based pursuits—livestock raising and agriculture—not only fueled the economy but also structured a hierarchical social class system in which *rancho* holders (most of them former military men) and their families belonged to the elite, while those with smaller holdings, usually within the limits of the *pueblo*, belonged to the middle level of society. Those without any means of support, usually recent arrivals such as the Trujillos and former mission Indians, were among the lowest rank in the region.[8]

Ysabel held a lowly and subordinate position as a servant and an orphaned Navajo who had arrived in Trujillo's largely mestizo household at infancy. Her lack of a surname and of a genealogical tie to others in the community indicated that she was not only a *criada*, or servant, but also a *genizara*. In New Mexico, *genizaros* were captured Indians, most often Navajo and Apache, whom Spanish raiders sold or exchanged for payments in cash or in kind. As spoils of war and as captives, they were pressed into domestic service at a young age. In a society that marked captured slaves and the vanquished as dishonored and disgraced, Ysabel, like other *genizaros*, represented a group of individuals who were viewed as intruders and outsiders. *Genizaros* occupied the lowest social rank and were forced to "perform the community's most menial and degrading tasks."[9]

After Trujillo and her household migrated to Mexican Alta California, Ysabel's role as a servant and a slave who lacked honor, status, or privileges remained the same. Despite the fact that officials in colonial Mexico had outlawed slavery, New Mexicans and *angeleños* allowed this practice to continue by using captured Indians as domestics. In the San Gabriel–Los Angeles region, Indian raiders (sometimes native peoples of different tribes) regularly brought to town Yuma children and young women taken from the Colorado River region and put them to labor in the homes and *ranchos* of local residents. In Ysabel's case, she was, for all intents and purposes, a slave until her death, though the court records fail to disclose the reality of her perpetual servitude. How and why her social and family relations with Trujillo turned bitter and culminated in her death is an issue the criminal court addressed.

Guadalupe Trujillo's murder trial opened with the testimony of Juan Pérez, the manager of Mission San Gabriel.[10] Pérez recalled that on February 15, 1843, after he had returned from his early morning duties, he saw Trujillo with her daughter in the kitchen, and proceeded to his room. Soon thereafter, an Indian child came to him saying, "She's calling you." "Who is calling me?" he asked. "Ysabel," the child insisted. He turned and at that moment saw Ysabel on the floor, seriously injured, and he went to her aid.

"What have you done?" he asked Trujillo.

"Ysabel has insulted me on numerous occasions and this time I could no longer contain myself," Trujillo responded.

"Couldn't you have used a stick and punished her that way?" asked Pérez.

"[I] called to . . . Ysabel," she answered, "and told her to go and wash clothes, as she had yet to complete her chores. Ysabel, who was outside, . . . refused . . . so I pushed her in [the mission]. She then grabbed my rebozo and shirt and tore them." Once inside, "I asked Ysabel, 'Why do you refuse to do what I say? Since you haven't cooked the meal, why don't you go and complete the wash?' " In defiance, Ysabel declared, "I don't want to, I don't want to be with you any longer, I want to go wherever I wish. . . . Why is it that the Indian women of the mission work less than I do and [they] have skirts made of *indianilla* [a fine cloth]?" Ysabel's comments, as noted by Trujillo, reveal that the servant believed her master doled out unfair treatment as compared to the treatment received by other Indian women, who seemingly enjoyed more freedoms.

At that instant, Trujillo claimed, Ysabel grabbed a large kitchen knife. "What are you going to do with that knife?" demanded Trujillo. "You'll see," Ysabel responded. As Ysabel approached Trujillo with the knife, Trujillo took advantage of an opportunity to wrestle the weapon from her. Ysabel then grabbed Trujillo by the hair. In an attempt to force Ysabel to loosen her hold, Trujillo put the knife at her throat, but when that move failed, Trujillo felt she had no other option than to stab Ysabel repeatedly.[11]

The manager's narrative, based on what Trujillo had recounted to him, supported Trujillo's claim that she had killed Ysabel in self-defense. Understandably, his testimony painted a picture of Ysabel as the aggressive and unmindful Indian servant who launched a surprise attack on the unsuspecting Trujillo, who clearly had no choice but to defend herself.

Bernardo Guirado, a worker at the mission, also testified about what he saw and heard following Ysabel's murder. Of all the testimonies in the trial, his proved the most damaging to Trujillo's claim of self-defense. The mission employee told the court what he had witnessed firsthand. He stated that on the fifteenth, he had arrived at the mission at about eleven in the morning in the company of the priest. As they entered, they saw Ysabel on the floor, lifeless. At that moment, he saw the manager of the mission, Juan Pérez—the first witness—enter the room. Guirado heard him declare that Trujillo was responsible for Ysabel's murder. To this comment, Guadalupe Trujillo responded, "It has been done. . . . If [I didn't] defend myself, the *india* would have killed me. And also, at the time she launched her attack against me, with the knife in hand, I managed to take hold of it and to remove it from her grasp."[12]

Guirado then informed the judge about details he knew concerning the incident that he had learned secondhand. (In the Mexican court system and Spanish civil law, hearsay was acceptable as testimony.) Francisco Villa, another field worker at the mission, told him about a rumor concerning Ysabel's death. Villa had overheard the story as it circulated among Indian workers at the mission. According to the rumor, the fight had begun when Ysabel slandered Trujillo's honor. Slurs against one's honor, observes historian Ramón Gutiérrez, constituted "the fiercest fighting words" that could be uttered.[13] The Indians also claimed that Trujillo had used the weight of her body to pin Ysabel to the floor and used her knee to hold Ysabel down while she called to her young daughter to bring her a knife from the kitchen cupboard. Guirado continued his testimony by recounting what another field worker at the mission, Tiburcio López, had informed him about the incident. While standing near an open window at the mission to light a cigarette, López told Guirado, he had overheard Ysabel exclaim in fear, "*No me mates hermana Guadalupe*" (Don't kill me, sister Guadalupe). As he turned to see the source of this cry, he witnessed Trujillo stabbing Ysabel in the neck. "What are you doing?" he yelled to Trujillo. "Go to hell," she retorted. López told Guirado that the scene had so startled him that he left the two women, rather than intervene in the scuffle or assist the victim.[14]

Guirado's testimony indicated that Ysabel's insolence had provoked the fight, thus refuting the idea that Trujillo had premeditated the murder. However, the hearsay evidence he presented on behalf of the Indians, Villa and López, not only placed blame on Trujillo for Ysabel's death but also suggested that Trujillo had callously murdered Ysabel, adding credence to the prosecution's contention that Trujillo had used more than self-defensive measures in killing Ysabel. In other words, Trujillo had planned the murder.

In addition to the manager's and field workers' testimony, Tiburcio López and Francisco Villa furnished their own accounts to the court. López supported Guirado's story that he had heard sounds of a fight coming through an open window of the mission. However, he had not heard Ysabel cry, "Don't kill me, sister Guadalupe." Instead, he claimed to hear Trujillo yell, "Is there not a Christian of God to save me?" Francisco Villa's statements before the judge also raised doubts about Guirado's testimony. Villa denied hearing or knowing anything about the incident. He admitted hearing talk among the Indians but, as he told the judge, he had no interest in their conversations. He only knew that Ysabel had died.[15]

Next, Antonio Arce, a transient from Loreto, Baja California, testified. "About eleven in the morning," he stated, "I went out to light a cigarette with the flame coming from a fire in front of Trujillo's home. At that moment," he continued, "I saw Trujillo come out, looking devastated, and she said to me, 'What do you say, Don Antonio, about what has happened to me with this *india*?'" Arce asked her to explain herself. "Look for yourself, look for yourself," she repeated, and then asked him to find the priest. Arce said that he then noticed blood on her hand and "calculated that a tragedy [*desgracia*] had occurred." He immediately went to get the priest and at that moment the padre arrived with Bernardo Guirado, the witness who had testified earlier. Arce's testimony, while insightful, provided no further clues as to motives behind the murder. The lack of an eyewitness other than Trujillo, who would testify last, only helped to obfuscate the facts surrounding the case and perhaps supported the defense's stance of self-defense.[16]

At the behest of Guadalupe Trujillo's husband, Antonio José Quintana, two former New Mexicans—Santiago Chacon and Miguel García—testified that Ysabel had lived a scandalous life in New Mexico. Quintana wanted the men to tell the court that Ysabel had committed an infanticide in New Mexico so as to tarnish her maternal instincts, humanity, and loyalty, traits that the court and the *gente de razón* at large expected of a woman and a servant. When the court interrogated the two men, they confirmed Quintana's allegations. Quintana also had another witness—Juan Pérez—inform the court that he knew of Ysabel's covert plan to leave the household. A fourth and final witness, Antonio Valenzuela, confirmed the assertion that Ysabel had been seduced by another man who had plotted to take her from San Gabriel. Clearly, Quintana's ploy was to characterize her as a depraved Indian woman and to remind the court of her lowly social position. The New Mexicans' testimony gave Trujillo's defense more ammunition on which to draw in their portrayal of Ysabel as the aggressive Indian servant who had stepped out of line when she challenged her master's orders.[17]

Finally, Guadalupe Trujillo, the only available eyewitness, testified on her own behalf. She claimed that Ysabel had become quite quarrelsome during the past few months. On the morning of the incident, Ysabel had refused to complete her domestic chores and announced, "I am leaving the household." Trujillo had immediately retorted, "You are not free to go anywhere because I have raised you since you were a child." "I am, too, free," Ysabel countered. Trujillo had then used physical force to get Ysabel to obey. Ysabel grabbed a knife from the kitchen and threatened to use it. Alarmed, Trujillo asked, "What are you doing with that knife?" "You'll see," Ysabel responded. Trujillo tried to take the knife away, and in the ensuing struggle the knife lodged itself in Ysabel's body. Trujillo called to her young daughter to find help. Trujillo told the judge she could not remember the details of the incident because she had become quite upset by what had transpired.

Trujillo sought to dispel any notion that her relationship with Ysabel had been stormy until the incident itself. She described their relations in language that drew upon a discourse of sisterhood and family unity. "I have always seen [Ysabel] as a sister," she told the judge, ". . . and I feel deeply for what I did. She was my father's orphan . . . and he gave her to me so that we would recognize each other as sisters."

The judge expressed skepticism.[18] "What do you have to say about causing the death of a woman whom you considered as a sister?"

"I killed her in *defensa propia* (self-defense) and without prior thought," she replied.

"How is it you killed her in self-defense? You took the knife away from the deceased and so wasn't the death unnecessary?"

"I took the knife away from her with the intent to throw it away, but I struck her, and I don't know," Trujillo explained.

"How do you not know how you struck her? The wound was such that it was done intentionally."

Trujillo tried to explain that Ysabel had her by the hair and she could not see what was happening, but the judge persisted.

"What do you have to say about using an illegal weapon in the act?" he asked.

"[I] didn't have it in the first place, the one who used it was [Ysabel], [I] took it from her to throw it away," she responded.

"Did you knowingly provoke the situation when you pushed Ysabel?"

"[I] didn't provoke her; what I wanted to do was to get her inside in order to reprimand her in another way," she explained.

"If you had wanted to correct her in another way, why not wait for your husband to do so; he could have used more prudence."

"[I intended] to correct Ysabel, as a mother does a daughter."

While Trujillo had previously informed the court that she had "always seen [Ysabel] as a sister," implying equality, now she characterized their relationship as hierarchical and unequal. Trujillo's conflicting testimony makes it unclear how they saw their roles in the household and in the larger community. Did they see each other as sisters, as Trujillo testified? Or did they perceive their arrangement as a parent–child relationship? While the case records never make clear how they viewed each other, the evidence reveals that their relations were anything but equal.[19]

The judge's interrogation of Trujillo's motives and actions suggests that he considered it improper for her to take the initiative to reprimand Ysabel. Customarily, the head of the household—the patriarch—held the power to govern and to correct members of the family, including any household servants, when they stepped out of line. In the judge's view, Trujillo had violated not only her role as the master but also her gender role in the family. In other words, she had temporarily usurped her husband's position as the family's head and had abused that power.

With the conclusion of the testimony, the prosecution, representing the people of Mexican Alta California, headed by José del Carmen Lugo, and the defense, headed by Vicente Sánchez, presented their arguments. In all likelihood, the trial took place in the home of a private citizen who rented it to the authorities for official affairs, as Los Angeles did not have a courthouse. The prosecutor, Lugo, began by boldly asserting, "On the fifteenth [February 1843], D[oñ]a Guadalupe Trujillo committed a scandalous murder of the unfortunate Indian woman from New Mexico, named Ysabel. It is true," he acknowledged, "that no witnesses appeared to justify the antecedents of such an attempt, but we must determine what occurred from those who manifest their declarations: the prisoner attempts to evade her crime frivolously, despite the existence of a notable contradiction in the [testimony]. Certainly, [s]he who uses vengeance does not do it without forethought but with premeditation." The prosecution declared that "persuasive evidence exists [of Trujillo's deceit and disdain of Ysabel] to prove that Trujillo had a motive to kill Ysabel," and did so at the moment when no one was present. The plea of self-defense, he concluded, was implausible. For her crime, he asked the court to "sentence her to two years of harsh imprisonment." Crimes against Mexicans undoubtedly brought harsher punishment.[20]

The defense attorney, Vicente Sánchez, responded to prosecutor Lugo by arguing that Ysabel had attacked Trujillo with ferocity. Trujillo had merely defended herself, he declared, "as is natural with any living being." She had not committed a scandalous crime but rather a simple homicide, done without prior thought. The defense reminded the court of the testimony of one of the witnesses, Tiburcio López, in which he heard Trujillo exclaim, "Is there not a Christian of God to save me?"—a declaration demonstrating that Trujillo had no choice but to defend herself. He also recalled for the court the word "*impensadamente*" (unintentionally), which Trujillo used to describe how she had killed Ysabel. The defense concluded by emphasizing the obvious—that Trujillo was a "woman of honor and family," a member of the *gente de razón* in the community. He did not have to remind anyone that Ysabel, as an Indian, was not among the *gente de razón*. To be Indian or, more precisely, a *genizara*, a domestic servant pressed into service, was to be without honor, family, or power.[21]

In his rebuttal, prosecutor Lugo directly challenged the defense's "attempt to excuse the severity of [Trujillo's] crime with the statement that she [is] an honorable woman with family." To argue that "she did not commit a crime" because of her position in the community, declared the prosecution, "insults the public." Lugo reminded the court that no member of the community, regardless of his or her social class, ethnicity, or gender, was above the law and justice. The judge agreed, ruling that Trujillo deserved a lengthier sentence than that suggested by the prosecution. On June 1, 1843, after weighing the evidence, he issued the following judgment: "In the criminal case against Guadalupe Trujillo . . . I sentence [Trujillo] to three years . . . in [the presidio of] Sonoma, or where the Superior Tribunal shall determine." While the judge ruled that Trujillo was at fault for killing Ysabel, he did not state whether he believed that she had killed Ysabel in self-defense or had premeditated the murder. Nevertheless, his decision to banish Trujillo to a sparsely populated and remote presidio northeast of Monterey reveals that he did not tolerate her actions. The sentence of banishment, which a contemporary noted was viewed as "equal to a sentence of death," served as a warning to any *gente de razón*, men as well as women, who contemplated taking such measures against their Indian servants.[22]

The judge's decision then passed to the Superior Tribunal of Monterey, an appellate body made up of three members who reviewed capital cases tried in the local courts throughout Mexican Alta California. The tribunal agreed with the Los Angeles local court that Trujillo had committed a crime but disagreed with the sentence that had been given to her. "It has been proven that Guadalupe Trujillo killed her *criada*, and for such an act she deserves punishment; but as the [punishment] should fit the crime and as the crime Trujillo committed was a homicide done in self-defense . . . [we] revoke the sentence of three years of seclusion." Instead of sending Trujillo to Sonoma for three years, the tribunal ordered her to the port of San Diego for one year, allowing her to remain in a *pueblo* and in proximity to her family in the San Gabriel–Los Angeles region. While it did not completely excuse her actions, the tribunal officially upheld the claim that Ysabel had instigated the fight and that Trujillo had defended herself.[23]

The tribunal's decision also reveals that it did not share the Los Angeles court's views about Mexican and Indian women's social and family relations. While the local judge believed that Trujillo's transgression of acceptable master–servant standards of behavior deserved three years of banishment, the Superior Tribunal believed otherwise. In the tribunal's view, killing an Indian servant who had attacked a woman *de razón* did not merit such punishment. Nor did the tribunal see the malevolence in Trujillo's actions that was detected by the local court. Put simply, the tribunal overruled the local judge's findings and undermined his attempt to carry out justice, as he interpreted and applied that concept.

The local court's standards were further undermined when Guadalupe Trujillo was set free, though by whom or in what court is unknown, and allowed to return to Los Angeles less than a year after the tribunal's sentence. By the middle of 1844, she was living with her husband, Quintana, and daughter, María, within the *pueblo's* limits. Apparently, the murder trial and conviction did little harm to their social mobility in the *pueblo*. Within six years, in 1850, the Trujillo-Quintana family had managed to acquire farmland valued at 2,000 pesos, and likely had become self-sufficient farmers. María, now seventeen, had also obtained her own level of social status, as she had married a local farmer from New Mexico who owned land, though worth only half that of the Trujillo-Quintana household. Thus, the family had managed to walk away from the incident relatively unharmed and rebuild their lives, while Ysabel had no doubt been forgotten.[24]

The murder trial of Guadalupe Trujillo has allowed us to explore an instance in which social and family relations between Mexicans and Indians became strained, and to examine the court's institutional role in the conflict in a larger cultural context. As we have seen, Trujillo's and Ysabel's social relations reflected a hierarchical and unequal distribution of power among women in the community. Despite commonalities of gender and patriarchal oppression, differences of socioeconomic status and cultural and racial identity relegated Ysabel, the Indian servant and "slave," to labor for Trujillo. Indeed, as Trujillo and Ysabel's soured relations indicate, women's material reality and cultural and racial identity drew a sharp distinction between Mexicans and Native Americans in the nineteenth century. Indian women labored for the *gente de razón*, and while the latter considered domestic servants as part of the larger household, the servants did not have the same privileges that their social betters enjoyed. The court case made these adversarial roles and relations clear.

The murder trial also reveals that Mexicans, men or women, regardless of social class, were not above the law even when their adversaries were Indian servants. In this case, the court's purpose was clear: to enforce the law and impart justice in the community, in spite of social, class, cultural, or racial considerations. Notwithstanding the local court's conflict with the appellate body and, ultimately, Trujillo's relatively light sentence, the Los Angeles judge's ruling served as a warning to all that such actions as Trujillo's would not be tolerated. To what extent the outcome of this case had an impact on social relations in Mexican Los Angeles is unclear. What is clear is that Mexican–Indian relationships were hierarchical and yet sometimes contested.

Notes

1. Guadalupe Trujillo's trial is found in the *Alcalde Court Records, 1830–1850*, 9 vols. (hereafter cited as *ACR*) 1:1014–31. The collection is held at the Seaver Center for Western History, Natural History Museum of Los Angeles County. The initial proceedings of the case are found in ibid., 1014–22.

2. On the term *gente de razón*, see George Harwood Phillips, "Indians in Los Angeles, 1781–1875: Economic Integration, Social Disintegration," *Pacific Historical Review* 49 (August 1980): 430; and Gloria E. Miranda, "Racial and Cultural Dimensions of Gente de Razón Status in Spanish and Mexican California," *Southern California Quarterly* 70 (Fall 1988): 265–78.

3. Antonio Ríos-Bustamante and Pedro Castillo, *An Illustrated History of Mexican Los Angeles, 1781–1985* (Los Angeles, 1986), 24–25, 33; Lisbeth Haas, *Conquests and Historical Identities in California, 1769–1936* (Berkeley, 1995), 9–44; Douglas Monroy, *Thrown among Strangers: The Making of Mexican Culture in Frontier California* (Berkeley, 1990), 18–50; David J. Weber, *The Spanish Frontier in North America* (New Haven, 1992), 307; William Mason, "Indian and Mexican Cultural Exchange in the Los Angeles Area, 1781–1834," *Aztlán* 15, no. 1 (Spring 1984): 123–25; Mason, *The Census of 1790: A Demographic History of Colonial California* (Novato, CA, 1998); Miranda, "Racial and Cultural Dimensions of Gente de Razón," 265–78; and Thomas W. Temple, trans. and ed., "Documents Pertaining to the Founding of Los Angeles: Supplies for the Pobladores," *Historical Society of Southern California Quarterly* 15 (1931): 121–34.

4. The sources consulted for the discussion of Gabrieleños include William McCawley, *The First Angelinos: The Gabrielino Indians of Los Angeles* (Banning, CA, 1996); A. L. Kroeber, "Elements of Culture in Native California," in R. F. Heizer and M. A. Whipple, comps. and eds., *The California Indians* (Berkeley, 1965), 1–67; Sherburne F. Cook, *The Conflict between the California Indians and White Civilization* (Berkeley, 1976); and Phillips, "Indians in Los Angeles, 1781–1875," 427–51.

5. See Suggested Readings.

6. This analysis of Mexican and Native American women's relations builds on the work of Antonia I. Castañeda, including "Presidarias y Pobladoras: Spanish-Mexican Women in Frontier Monterey, Alta California, 1770–1821" (Ph.D. diss., Stanford University, 1990); and "Sexual Violence in the Politics and Policies of Conquest: Amerindian Women and the Spanish Conquest of Alta California," in Adela da la Torre and Beatríz M. Pesquera, eds. (Berkeley, 1993), 15–33. Some of the ideas developed in this essay are drawn from Karen Halttunen, " 'Domestic Differences': Competing Narratives of Womanhood in the Murder Trial of Lucretia Chapman," in Shirley

Samuels, ed., *The Culture of Sentiment: Race, Gender, and Sentimentality in Nineteenth-Century America* (New York, 1992), 43; Richard Wightman Fox, "Intimacy on Trial: Cultural Meanings of the Beecher-Tilton Affair," 103–34, in Fox and T. J. Jackson Lears, eds., *The Power of Culture: Critical Essays in American History* (Chicago, 1993).

7. Hubert H. Bancroft, *History of California* (San Francisco, 1886), 3:395; ibid., 4:276–78.

8. For more information about Trujillo and her family, see "Padrón 1844," *Los Angeles City Archives*, 3:666–801, City of Los Angeles, Records Management Division, C. Erwin Piper Technical Bldg., Los Angeles, California. See also Warren A. Beck and Ynez D. Haase, *Historical Atlas of New Mexico* (Norman, OK, 1979), 20.

9. Ramón Gutiérrez, *When Jesus Came, the Corn Mothers Went Away: Marriage, Sexuality, and Power in New Mexico, 1500–1846* (Stanford, 1991), 149–56, 176–94.

10. Mission San Gabriel was secularized in 1833.

11. *ACR*, 1:1024–31.

12. Ibid., 1026.

13. Gutiérrez, *When Jesus Came, the Corn Mothers Went Away*, 205–6.

14. *ACR*, 1:1032–36.

15. Ibid., 1046–57.

16. Ibid., 1037–41.

17. Ibid., 1058–68.

18. Ibid., 1068–76.

19. Ibid., 1085–90.

20. Ibid., 1093–95.

21. Gutiérrez, *When Jesus Came, the Corn Mothers Went Away*, 205; *ACR*, 1:1099–1103.

22. Quote cited in *The Los Angeles Prefecture Records*, Los Angeles City Archives, Los Angeles, California, book 1, part 1:112, 533, 613 (1841). See also *ACR*, 1:1108–9.

23. *ACR*, 1110–13.

24. See "Padrón 1844"; and Maurice H. Newmark and Marco R. Newmark, eds., *Census of the City and County of Los Angeles, California, for the Year 1850* (Los Angeles, 1929), 94.

Suggested Readings

Brooks, James F. " 'This Evil Extends Especially to the Feminine Sex': Captivity and Identity in New Mexico, 1700–1846." In *Writing the Range: Race, Class, and Culture in the Women's West*, ed. Elizabeth Jameson and Susan Armitage. Norman: University of Oklahoma Press, 1997.

Burkett, Elinor C. "In Dubious Sisterhood: Class and Sex in Spanish South America." *Latin American Perspectives* 4 (Winter–Spring 1977): 18–26.

Castañeda, Antonia I. "Sexual Violence in the Politics and Policies of Conquest: Amerindian Women and the Spanish Conquest of Alta California." In *Building with Our Hands: New Directions in Chicana Studies*, ed. Adela de la Torre and Beatríz M. Pesquera. Berkeley: University of California Press, 1993.

Gutiérrez, Ramón A. *When Jesus Came, the Corn Mothers Went Away: Marriage, Sexuality, and Power in New Mexico, 1500–1846.* Stanford: Stanford University Press, 1991.

Haas, Lisbeth. *Conquests and Historical Identities in California, 1769–1936.* Berkeley: University of California Press, 1995.

Hurtado, Albert L. *Indian Survival on the California Frontier.* New Haven: Yale University Press, 1988.

Thornton Dill, Bonnie. "Race, Class, and Gender: Prospects for an All-Inclusive Sisterhood." *Feminist Studies* (Spring 1983): 131–50.

4

Alfred Doten
Diversity and the Anglo Forty-niner

Brian Roberts

James Marshall discovered gold in the Sierra Nevada foothills in February 1848, just one month after the United States acquired California from Mexico in the Treaty of Guadalupe Hidalgo. With the possible exception of World War II, no single event has ever had more impact on the state. By 1849 accounts of vast gold deposits lying untouched in California's fertile soil had reached around the world, and the great gold rush was on. Only 26,000 Europeans, Americans, and Mexican Americans lived in California at the start of 1849, but during the next twelve months roughly 100,000 hopeful gold seekers arrived. By the mid-1850s the richest gold deposits were largely exhausted, but Californians would desperately mine for more through the early 1870s.

The rugged and heroic Forty-niner, the individualistic, masculine figure who ventured west in search of great riches, has dominated popular images of the gold rush to the present day. But in fact, Forty-niners were more often married, middle-class men who expected to return quickly to their wives and children on the East Coast upon securing their fortune. American Forty-niners, furthermore, represented only a part of the immigration stream to California. They were joined by tens of thousands of people from around the world, including Mexicans, British, French, Spaniards, Chileans, Peruvians, and Chinese.

The international nature of the gold rush ensured that California would be a cosmopolitan region from its American start. Multicultural relations were rarely peaceful or happy, however. Chinese miners faced particular hostility, and, in fact, more than one-third of state revenues in the 1850s and 1860s came from a special "foreign miners tax" targeted against the Chinese. In this essay, University of Northern Iowa historian Brian Roberts takes us into the world of the California gold rush—a place of contested boundaries, memories, and rights, where diverse peoples were thrust into a new and tumultuous environment.

In the spring of 1849, 20-year-old Alfred Doten of Plymouth, Massachusetts, did what thousands of other young men of his time and place were doing: he joined up with the Pilgrim Mining Company, a joint stock association bound for the gold regions of California. On March 18 his ship, the *Yeoman*, set sail from Boston Harbor for a 6-month voyage of some 13,000 miles, around Cape Horn to San Francisco. Crowds would have gathered at the city wharves to see Doten's ship off, composed, as another young man wrote of his own departure, of "wives, fathers, mothers, sons and daughters, aunts, cousins from first to forty-second, besides numerous friends and acquaintances." A minister would have addressed Doten's company, asking its members to "take their Bibles in one hand and their New England civilization in the other," stressing their "great moral purpose" in going to California, and urging them to "never forget" their "New England Sabbath" along with their families, firesides, schools, and courts of justice.[1]

Doten would try to remember these elements of home. At sea he joined his fellow Pilgrims in the singing of temperance hymns, harmonizing with them on the evils of temptation, passion, and alcohol. On his arrival he worked hard, both at finding gold and at keeping his association together. Yet within a few years he would undergo a transformation. His company fell apart, leaving him to go it alone in the foothills of California. He would fail—miserably—to find gold. Eventually, he seemed to fall into the raucous bachelor culture of the gold rush. He would play cards, dance, and get drunk on Sundays. He tried to extort money from Chinese miners, lynched Mexicans, and dreamed of killing Indians, all seemingly without the slightest twinge of moral conscience. He became, in other words, a real California Forty-niner.

For generations of historians and readers of history alike, Doten's experience constitutes the great charm of the California gold rush. As Mark Twain would put it not too long after the event, the gold rush was a rollicking good time for Anglo Forty-niners: "They fairly reveled in gold, whiskey, fights, and fandangos, and were unspeakably happy." As one of the first histories of the rush concluded, "the time was the best ever made."[2] According to this standard image of the rush, the Anglo Forty-niner was a typical frontiersman. Young and unconnected, he turned his back on the East, its rules of behavior, its moral repressions, its blue laws, prudes, and traditions. Thus the Anglo Forty-niner has been portrayed as a childlike individual dominated by little more than greed, competitive drive, and desires for immediate and intense physical pleasure. If he engaged in questionable activities—such as drunkenness, the lynching of Mexicans, or the killing of Indians—it was a result of his liberation from restraint, merely the reaction of a free and unfettered "human nature."[3]

Courtesy of Special Collections, University of Nevada-Reno Library

There are many problems with this standard view of the gold rush and of the Anglo Forty-niner. First, the individuals who came to California from states east of the Mississippi were not nearly as socially unconnected as the dominant historical treatments suggest. They were not, as frontier historian Frederick Jackson Turner referred to them, "types of that line of scum that the waves of advancing civilization bore before them."[4] Among those from northeastern states, as many as one-third were married; nearly all had strong family ties; the vast majority who left written records were well educated; and practically none was poor. Second, they were never quite so liberated from their eastern pasts, traditions, or patterns of behavior. They carried their values with them, in their laws, in their commitment to individualism and success, and in their equally felt desire for social harmony and philanthropic reform.

Finally, while the image of the Anglo Forty-niners dominates much of the history of the gold rush, they were not alone in the drive to riches. The standard narrative of the liberated Forty-niner as a charming figure, in other words, is more ideological than historical. It is a myth—developed during the gold rush and repeated by historians ever since—used to justify competition, exploitation, and desires for freedom from big government and moral responsibility. As a model for human nature, it works only if the focus remains on Anglos and away from those who questioned or suffered from their vaunted freedoms. It works only if all others in California, particularly Indians, Mexicans, and Chinese, are removed from the picture. And finally, it works only if we ignore the actual humanity of the Anglo Forty-niner, the fact that he was a complicated person, with motivations, self-doubts, and a moral conscience.

When Alfred Doten's ship sailed out of Boston Harbor, it joined a massive migration to California of worldwide proportions. At the same time, this migration would be limited to certain parts of the world, to areas that by and large were experiencing rapid economic development or acute political instability. Partly because of its proximity to California and partly due to the destruction created by its war with the United States between 1846 and 1848, Mexico would see some 20,000 individuals leave for California. Most would come from the country's northern region, particularly the state of Sonora. Many, along with several thousand Chileans from Pacific Coast ports, would arrive in the gold country before the great wave of Anglo Forty-niners.[5]

In addition to emigrants from France, Hawaii, and Australia, large numbers of Chinese gold seekers would go to California during the next few years, as many as 40,000 by 1854. Most came from the southern region of Guangdong, an area that had seen great increases in trade along with recent wars and rebellion. In 1848 at least 70,000 (and possibly as many as 150,000) Indians lived in California. The region's non-Indian population stood at 14,000, most of them Hispanic *californios*. By the end of 1849 the non-Indian population reached more than 100,000.[6] In the public imagination, the gold rush has remained a story focused on Anglo-Americans from the eastern United States. Early on, these individuals comprised no more than one-half of California's total population.

Some 80,000 Anglo-American Forty-niners joined the gold rush in 1849. Like the emigrants from other parts of the world, the vast majority were men; well into the 1850s, California's non-Indian population would be over 90 percent male. About half of these gold seekers departed from states in the American Northeast, from New York, Massachusetts, Pennsylvania, Connecticut, and New Jersey. These men preferred the ocean route to California: most went by ship, brig, or schooner around Cape Horn; fewer went by steamship to Panama, where they crossed the Isthmus on foot or mule-back to pick up a sailing ship or steamer on the Pacific side. Nearly another half left from the western, or in later terms midwestern, states like Ohio, Illinois, Indiana, and Michigan. Most of these gold seekers took the overland route, traveling nearly the entire 2,000-mile distance of the Oregon Trail from St. Louis to the cutoff that led them through the Sierra Nevada.[7]

The Anglo gold seekers were rarely the unconnected men of many historical accounts. Nor could they afford to be, for the cost of getting to California—either by ship or overland—was staggeringly high, the equivalent of more than a year's wages for the average American in 1849. As one eastern newspaper put it at the time, they were "educated, intelligent, civilized, and elevated men, of the best classes of society." According to another article, they were the "finest portion of our youth, and in all cases such as possess some means—such as are not impelled to emigrate by want."[8] Still, like gold seekers from other parts of the world, these men faced their share of economic and social instability along with many internal tensions.

Alfred Doten was typical in this regard. Like the greatest number of Anglo Forty-niners, he grew up and came of age in the 1830s and 1840s, during a period of rapid change, class formation, and industrialization. Born in 1829 within shouting distance of Plymouth Rock, Doten was an average young New Englander of the region's rising middle class when he sailed in March of 1849. He had his share of advantages: he was well educated, the son of a successful captain in the merchant marine, and a direct descendant of "first Pilgrim" William Bradford.[9] And yet he faced a crucial dilemma. As an adolescent, Doten would have witnessed an enormous growth in middle-class standards for status and success. The problem was that these standards coexisted in sharp opposition. Beginning in the 1830s and increasing in the 1840s, middle-class status stressed "respectability," a host of traits including honesty, self-control, philanthropy, and temperance, and placed a higher value on white-collar employment or "brain work" over physical labor. Middle-class success required competitive drive; often, especially in the cut-throat new world of industrial business relations, it required dishonesty, deceit, and the willingness to actively promote the desires and physical appetites of potential customers.[10]

By the time Doten reached young adulthood, these conflicting stan-dards had created an increasingly dominant middle-class ideology of separate spheres: at home, in the private sphere, the middle-class man was respectable; outside the home, in the sphere of business and com-merce, he did what needed to be done to get ahead in a competitive economy. For young men like Doten, this ideology made the transition from boyhood to manhood a time of enormous stress. Unlike previous generations of Dotens, he could not simply follow in his father's foot-steps and join the merchant marine. For by this time, the physical labor of the sailor seemed vulgar and dirty, more indicative of a working-class type than a refined middle-class man. Like other young men of his time, Doten was supposed to strike out on his own. Much was expected of him—he might be a clerk, a merchant, or even a doctor or a lawyer—but little had been accomplished. By the end of 1848 he was still living at home.[11]

Given this context, once the news of California's gold discoveries reached the East, it made sense for young men like Doten to imagine the region in utopian or escapist terms. Guides to the gold country, published quickly by writers who had never been to California and sold for less than a quarter, drew pictures of streams running over solid beds of gold. Newspapers carried advertisements for magical gold-seeking appliances, from "goldometers" that promised to detect ore beneath the ground to "California Gold Grease," which, if the Forty-niner rubbed it on his body and rolled down a gold country hill, would cover its buyer in precious dust, since "nothing else" would stick to the prod-uct.[12] Individuals like Doten spent time calculating their riches even before they departed; as another seeker put it, $2,000 in gold was "cer-tain," $20,000 was "probable," and $100,000 "possible."[13]

Historians have frequently cited these wild fantasies as examples of dementia and "gold fever" and as evidence of the enormous greed of Anglo Forty-niners. More than mere greed, however, such dreams re-flected the thinking of the time. The decade of the 1840s was marked by a wide variety of social experimentation. Partly in response to the anxieties of early industrialization, utopian communes sprang up in many places throughout the nation, such as Brook Farm in Massachusetts, the Oneida Community in New York, Hopedale in Indiana, and Nashoba in Tennessee. Most of these settlements were utopias of scarcity, places where people pooled their resources, shared them equally, simplified their lives, and attempted to live in harmony outside of the increasingly competitive world of industrial capitalism. California, as many Anglo Forty-niners envisioned it, was perhaps the greatest utopia of the age.[14] The difference was that it was a utopia of abundance. California's supply of gold, claimed one eastern newspaper, was "absolutely inexhaustible"; its promise, according to one gold seeker, was that it would "entirely obliterate all social distinctions."[15]

Thus, as much as greed characterized the motivations of Anglo Forty-niners, so did yearnings to escape competition and desires for a type of social and economic leveling, for fraternity and cooperation. Many, again like Alfred Doten, traveled to California as part of mining and trading associations complete with written codes for good behavior or with rules calling for honesty, temperance, self-control, and the communal sharing of profits. In the words of one historian, the language of these companies reflected "the concept of a socialistic brotherhood." As one young Forty-niner said of his company at the time: "We were a commune—a socialistic order. The sick, and the weak, were to be on one common level with the strong and the well."[16] In a major sense, the gold rush was driven not by competition but by fears of competition. According to these fantasies, competition would not be a factor in California, for once there, everyone would be rich. "According to all accounts there is enough for us all," wrote another young man at the moment of departure. "So Hurrah!!" he concluded in a typical burst of utopian optimism, "For California!!"[17]

Shortly after their arrival in California, Anglo gold seekers experienced a slow destruction of their optimistic visions. First came the experience of actual gold mining, "the hardest work that ever was done," as one described it.[18] Back in the East many had heard that California's gold came in placer deposits, that it was aboveground rather than embedded in solid rock. Many seem to have translated this information to mean that in California, gold could be simply picked up from the ground, that collecting it involved little more than a leisurely stroll among nuggets.

Indeed, much of California's gold *was* aboveground, in streambeds, beneath boulders, along the edges of washouts and gullies. But it could not simply be picked up. It came in small granules, flakes that had to be found and washed, separated from pebbles, dirt, and dust through painstaking effort. Many Anglo Forty-niners had been clerks, students, or merchants; "most of them," said one, were "men who never had done hard work."[19] Now they would labor, digging and moving mountains of dirt, changing the course of rivers to expose the gold grains in their beds, moving boulders in icy streams, stooping over rockers, and building Long Toms, or troughs. And they would suffer from sunburn, blisters, lame backs, chills, and fevers.

Most failed to break even. "It cost us about $2 per day to live," as one put it, "and we did not average more than that washing gold."[20] When they failed, they had to explain to wives, family, and friends back East, to people who still believed in the claims of California's abundance. "I never labored so hard in my life," wrote one to a friend. Digging and washing gold was *"oppressive beyond measure during the excessive heat,"* wrote another to his wife, adding that he "could not stand it long."[21] With failure came a return of competition; with competition came frustration. Nearly all echoed the refrain: California was a "humbug." When family members responded, as one wife did, by asking, "How is it that Mack makes more than you?" many responded with tears, with even more strident calls for sympathy, with drink, and with feelings of anger.[22] Some quickly identified the sources of their problems. The most obvious one seems to have been their "foreign" competitors and "hostile" antagonists, California's Mexicans, Chinese, and Chileans along with the region's many Indian peoples.

When thinking about Anglo Forty-niners, it is easy to fall into the trap of assuming that they were "men of their times" and that at that period, all Anglo-Americans were racists, committed to Indian removal, ethnic hierarchy, and the immediate dismissal of all foreign peoples as inferior. The reality of Anglo-American culture in 1849 is far more complicated. Of the diverse peoples Anglo Forty-niners would meet and interact with in the gold country, the Chinese were viewed as perhaps the most truly foreign. Yet they could hardly be considered inferior without question. By 1849, China had been a major trading partner with the United States for at least a generation and the customs houses of eastern ports were always well stocked with Chinese crockery, dishware, and fabric. In addition to these goods, most Forty-niners probably associated the Chinese with fireworks rather than inferiority, for during Fourth of July celebrations they would have seen their share of what were then called "Chinese fires."

As for Mexicans, the U.S. war of aggression against Mexico between 1846 and 1848 had a dual result. First, with the Mexican Cession of the

Treaty of Guadalupe Hidalgo, it transformed many Mexican citizens, including those living in California, into Americans. Second, it spawned an explosion of romantic accounts and novels portraying "Old Mexico" along with the exotic charms of its people. Most of the resultant images were stereotypes, as these writers filled their novels with predictably hot-blooded characters: Spanish dons, sensual friars, and the "flashing dark eyes" and "raven tresses" of passionate *vaqueros* and *senoritas*.[23] These images may have reflected Anglo racism, but certainly not simple race hatred. Then, as now, they reflected a blend of racism with exoticism and attraction.

The vast majority of Anglo Forty-niners would have been acquainted with Indians, albeit in similarly generic ways. With the rise of new middle-class reform movements in the 1820s, a large number of Americans in the Northeast "discovered" the Indian as a subject for philanthropic aid. As one popular reform circular published in 1829 had it, Indians were "pure and noble," "simple and beautiful," and a "cherished relic of antiquity." They should not be removed from their homelands, claimed the circular's writer in objection to Andrew Jackson's infamous policies of removal, for "who would permit such a race to be swept from the earth?—a nation . . . whose wild and interesting traits are becoming the theme of the poet and novelist." Indeed, by this time, writers such as James Fenimore Cooper and Lydia Maria Child had already made the noble yet vanishing Indian a stock figure in popular American literature. Meanwhile, museums and "cabinets of curiosities" began displaying Indian artifacts and lifeways, while hosting speaking tours of representative "Indian chiefs."[24]

By 1849 these literary images and "Indian shows" had established a firm groundwork for a public fascination with "vanishing Americans" and "noble savages" that, however based in stereotype, would influence reformers in their efforts to protect Indian ways well into the twentieth century. Surrounded by these early statements of cultural diversity and reform, few Anglo Forty-niners would have arrived in California as one-dimensional racists or complete xenophobes. Nor would they have been unaware of the moral problems of Indian removal. Far from reflecting simple patterns of racial hostility, their perceptions of the diverse peoples with whom they shared California seem to have been marked by ambivalence, by a blend of revulsion, attraction, stereotype, and romanticism.[25]

For a time after they arrived, at least, many Anglo Forty-niners reveled in California's ethnic diversity. "Verily," exclaimed one shortly after landing in San Francisco, "we were the Cosmopolis of the world."

Many freshly arrived men, according to one observer, "affected to imitate the costume of Mexican muleteers"; many others purchased *ponchos* and wide-brimmed Mexican *sombreros* as soon as they stepped off their ships.[26] As early as the mid-1850s, San Francisco's Chinatown would become a well-known site for Anglo visitors, a place famous for druggists, dentists, firecrackers, and opium dens. So would the area called Little Chile, as Anglo Forty-niners flocked to partake of its gambling halls, *fandango* parlors, and, because they were frequently cheaper than the more upscale brothels on Portsmouth Square, its houses of prostitution.

In the foothill mining districts, meanwhile, close contacts between Anglo Forty-niners and Indians, Mexican prospectors, and Chinese miners were just as common. This was particularly the case in the southern mining area around Sonora, where beginning in 1848 some 10,000 Mexicans would emigrate, giving the area its distinct flavor, culture, and early spirit of social diversity. Again, the pattern of these contacts suggests that Anglo ways of seeing diversity reflected an ambivalent blend of stereotype, romance, and attraction. Very quickly, Anglos in the southern mines learned to sprinkle their day-to-day talk with Spanish, with references to *compadres, amigos, tortillas,* and *cantinas.* For many, the Mexicans around Sonora were a source of danger. One Anglo wrote to his wife in the East that the region's "murders and robberies" were committed "chiefly by Mexicans."[27] Many Anglos agreed that the area's Chinese were hardworking, serious, and avaricious; or, as one put it, a "strong contrast to the thriftless Mexicans and joyous Gauls." One reported that his fellow tentmates had engaged a Chinese cook and servant, a "coolie," so that "we might live in a Christian manner."[28] From Sonora, one Anglo miner sent his family a lock of "Chinaman's hair," another sent home a detailed description of a Chinese funeral, and still another sent home an account book "lost by some unfortunate Celestial," along with a sample of Cantonese writing (added to the margins of his letter by his "good friend Ah Young") and a Chinese–English dictionary, all as "curiosities."[29]

With the failure of increasing numbers of Anglo Forty-niners along with their discovery that gold mining was extremely hard work, the general pattern of these social contacts appears to have changed in the early 1850s. Two letters from a young Forty-niner from Ohio suggest the shift. In 1853 he wrote to his brother to tell him that "when I return to Ohio I shall take pleasure in showing you a Celestial Costume presented me by some of my Chinese friends." Less than a year later he would write to the same brother in a far different tone. "We are overrun with Chinese," he reported, adding that after "considerable dealings" he had "not formed a very high opinion of them" and that he looked forward to the day when they would be "driven out of the country by the Americans."[30] Within a year, in other words, this young man's friends had become his enemies. What happened was not an upwelling of inherent racism and xenophobia, nor was it a simple assertion of human nature. The source of this change in attitude was a dramatic increase in competition. With this competition would come an equally dramatic increase in cross-ethnic violence.

Alfred Doten's experience in California offers a typical example of these patterns of social and cultural exchange. Doten's company of Pilgrims arrived in San Francisco in October of 1849. By November they had made their way to the southern mines around Sonora. There they went about prospecting and sifting dirt, learning the harsh lesson that mining was hard work. Within a month they were forced to admit that they had failed. During the next few weeks, Doten tried desperately to keep the Pilgrim Company together, pleading with his fellows to hang onto its articles of association, its moral codes, and its promises to share all profits.

He had particular reasons for doing so. The Pilgrim Company was an experiment among experiments: unlike most other companies, its members sailed to California free of charge, supported by stockholders back in Plymouth in exchange for the members' agreement to remit two-thirds of all earnings to their eastern investors. Among these investors was Alfred Doten's father. Despite Doten's efforts, at the end of 1849 his partners voted to disband the company and throw its charter into the fire.[31] Thus, like the vast majority of Anglo Forty-niners, Doten had failed. His failure, in turn, contained a large measure of psychological strain, for not only had he not met his own dreams of escape, but he had also failed his father's expectations. From this point in time, Doten, who had started a diary on the day of his departure, would almost never mention his past again; and his drinking, which began on social occasions, would become chronic.

During this period, Doten interacted with the diverse peoples of the southern mines with a typical blend of ambivalent attraction. He learned to speak some Spanish. He attended a number of *fandangos* held in the tents of his Mexican acquaintances, where he drank the traditional *aguardiente* and where also, because he could play the violin, he supplied much of the music. In February of 1850 he walked to the *cantina*

58 The Human Tradition in California

of a neighboring mining camp to see an Indian scalp that had been posted as a trophy. The scalp had been taken a few days before, as a group of Anglo vigilantes had tracked down several Miwok who had stolen some mules. They found their prey "in too great numbers to drive from their position," according to Doten. The Miwok dared the vigilantes to attack, "using the most insulting gestures" and "slapping their arses." Yet one of them had "exposed himself rather too incautiously" and was shot, thus the scalp in the *cantina*.[32] That night the young New Englander dreamed of joining an Indian-hunting expedition.

Doten, however, like other Anglo Forty-niners, was not a one-dimensional Indian-hater. He may have also dreamed in later days of becoming an Indian. Doten's writings give evidence that he frequently passed the hours in his tent listening to popular tales about the gold-rush era's notorious "white Indian," a man who in these stories went by the name of Savage. "Savage" was one of the most ubiquitous characters of the early gold rush, his fame seemingly the result of a rare confluence of name, calling, and context. According to tales swapped around camp-fires, he was the chief of the Mercedes Indians and had sworn revenge against the Miwok for the killing of his blood brother; he had been kidnapped by Plains Indians as a child and given his evocative name; he commanded 2,700 warriors and had twenty-seven wives, and many of his wives were comely young girls about fourteen years of age.[33]

The actual facts were more mundane. James Savage—it was his real name—was a trader and sometime Indian agent who had come to California from Illinois in 1846. By 1850 he was running several trading posts on the Merced, Mariposa, and Fresno Rivers, where he hired Yokuts to pan for gold and where he formed close bonds with his Indian partners-in-trade by taking several Miwok and Yokuts brides.[34] Yet the stories made him a romantic figure, suggesting a certain level of attraction in the idea of "going native," or "riding with Indians." Indeed, James Savage was not unusual in taking an Indian bride. Although population figures of the time are rough at best, estimates and evidence from the 1850s and later indicate that California would have one of the highest rates of Indian-Anglo intermarriage in the United States.[35]

In the minds of many Anglo Forty-niners such as Alfred Doten, fantasies of killing Indians and becoming Indians could exist side by side. So could friendships and conflicts with other non-Anglo peoples in the gold country. Two years after the breakup of his company, Doten was running his own business in Sonora, operating out of a typical canvas-and-frame structure that was at once a grocery, a provisioning post, a *cantina*, and a *fandango* parlor. Here, toward the end of August 1851, he hosted a drunken dance with five Mexican friends. Several months earlier he had taken part in the lynching of two Mexicans after an argument in a saloon led to the shooting death of one of his Anglo acquaintances. In September, Doten took part in the battle of Yankeetown, during which some 2,000 Anglo miners attacked and destroyed an encampment of nearly 300 Mexicans near Sonora. Five days later, Doten reported another night of drink and diversity: "Evening my four Mexicans from up the gulch came down here and we had quite a big fandango spree."[36]

According to many standard historical treatments of the gold rush, this type of behavior was a natural result of the "lawlessness" of the West, a measure of California's disconnection from eastern standards of repression and government control. Yet law, not lawlessness, created much of California's early ethnic conflict. On July 5, 1852, Alfred Doten walked out of Sonora to visit a camp of Chinese miners. He went, as he wrote in his diary, "to collect some money from the Chinese but did not succeed." Three days earlier the Chinese miners had arrived: "They being," Doten recorded, "the first Chinese who have yet been to this bar to work."[37] Three days was not much time to run up a debt at Doten's store, and it seems doubtful that he would have been willing to extend the newcomers any credit anyway. So what was he doing? Very likely, he was trying to enforce California law—attempting, that is, to extort his personal share of California's Foreign Miners Tax. Passed in 1850 by the recently established State Legislature, the tax called for payment of $20 per year by all foreign miners. At the same time, the legislature did little to create a system of enforcement in the distant mines, leaving collection on a casual or vigilante basis, to be levied by any "American" against anyone defined as "foreign."

Similar patterns of ambivalent contact and competitive conflict existed elsewhere. California's foothill Indians were "diggers," according to Anglo slang, a derogatory term derived, as one miner recalled, "from the fact of their subsistence on roots and acorns." They were the "lowest of all God's creation," noted another Anglo observer.[38] In 1850 a company of Anglo volunteers killed some seventy-five Indians in what became known as the Clear Lake Massacre. Another company killed 150 Indians encamped along the Trinity River in 1852. Other massacres would follow, as would a long list of atrocities committed by Anglos against Indians. Again, it is easy to see these interactions as simple examples of Anglo racism, as evidence of the lawlessness of the West, or as

proof that the Forty-niners, as men "liberated" from eastern moral standards, did not know right from wrong. What these interpretations miss
is the fact that practically all of these atrocities—*nearly every one of them*—
were recorded by Anglo observers.[39] Those who wrote about the events
did so not because they were proud of these acts, but to criticize their
fellows. By 1860, as a writer for the *Sacramento Union* had it, California's
entire policy toward Indians was a source of "shame" and "embarrassment."

Few historians or latter-day observers of the gold rush would take
the complexities of these interactions and confrontations into account.
Instead, many have continued to see these conflicts as indicative of human nature and the gold rush as a series of charming and comic anecdotes on the theme of liberation and masculine high jinks. These views,
as popular as they are, are more ideological and descriptive than inter-
pretive. At the time of the rush, Anglo Forty-niners were quick to embrace the ideal of a depraved human nature. One California minister
put it best in 1853: "Here we see our nature free to develop according
to its leanings . . . downwardly." A Forty-niner remarked that there was
a great difference between "law-loving and God-fearing New England"
and California, "where there is no law, and every man's hand is against
his fellow man."[40] As the "father" of California history, Hubert Howe
Bancroft, would later argue, the gold rush showed the emigrant Anglo
possessed of "a nature wholly different" from what he thought, and soon
"he finds himself in the society of harlots, a gambler, an unbeliever."
Like Doten's frequent drinking bouts, such explanations produced ab-
solution and the evasion of responsibility, and in the end they would
produce a type of cultural amnesia. "Before he came to California,"
added Bancroft, the typical Anglo Forty-niner was "nobody knew
what."[41]

Most Anglo Forty-niners returned to the East after their disappoint-
ment in California. Once there, many reworked their memories of the
rush, excising the failures or conflicts and cutting California's ethnic
diversity from their mental pictures until the event became a tale of
liberated adventure, a masculine campout dominated by the archetype
Forty-niner: dirty, bearded, fun-loving, free, and white. Many historians, along with their readers, would later celebrate this characteristic
view of the gold rush. The diverse peoples most affected by the Forty-
niners' vaunted "freedoms" would not.

Alfred Doten never returned to Plymouth, nor did he seem quite as
capable of reworking his gold-rush experiences. In 1855 he returned to
mining, only to have his legs crushed in a cave-in. He went to live with

his sister, who had arrived in San Francisco, and there his drinking became even worse. In 1863 he followed many California miners to Nevada for the Comstock silver boom. After a brief stint as a mine superintendent, Doten began writing for a series of Nevada newspapers, including the *Territorial Enterprise*. He married in 1873 and had four children, but the marriage did not last.[42] Doten's writing career floundered as the Comstock Lode played out, and bad investments in mining companies forced him once again into bankruptcy. He continued to be a heavy drinker until his death in 1903.

Throughout his life in the West, Doten remained at heart a New Englander, the product of a literary culture, compulsively writing down every shameful act and drinking bout in his diary, a record that would eventually fill seventy-nine leather-bound volumes and amount to 1.5 million words. The record would contain little charm and less romance. In the words of one historian, "Doten seems never to have puzzled out the meaning of the life whose daily passage he jotted down with compulsive regularity."[43] Certainly his was not a tale of liberation. Toward the end of his life, Doten returned to the position of dependence he had fled in 1849. He died in a Reno boardinghouse in 1903. By then he had become a pathetic figure, a real California Forty-niner and a town drunk, begging for money, exchanging romantic tales of the gold rush for nickels and dimes to support his drinking habit.

Notes

1. See Walter Van Tilburg Clark, ed., *The Journals of Alfred Doten, 1849–1903*, 3 vols. (Reno, 1973), 1:xviii; Isaac Halsey, "Day of Sailing, diary entry for 12 March 1849," Halsey Collection, Bancroft Library, Berkeley, California; Reverend Samuel Worcester, *California; Address before the Naumkeag Mutual Trading and Mining Company, Given at the Tabernacle Church in Salem, on Sabbath Evening, January 14, 1849*, pamphlet, Bancroft Library Collections.

2. Mark Twain [Samuel Clemens], *Roughing It* (New York, 1980 [1871]), 309–10; Frank Soule and James Nisbett, *The Annals of San Francisco* (Palo Alto, CA, 1966 [1855]), 244.

3. For examples of this dominant view of the gold rush, see: J. S. Holliday, *Rush for Riches: Gold Fever and the Making of California* (Berkeley, 1999); Malcolm Rohrbough, *Days of Gold: The California Gold Rush and the American Nation* (Berkeley, 1997); Paula Mitchell Marks, *Precious Dust: The American Gold Rush Era, 1848–1900* (New York, 1994); David Goodman, *Gold Seeking: Victoria and California in the 1850s* (Palo Alto, CA, 1994).

4. Frederick Jackson Turner, *The Frontier in American History* (New York, 1920), 33n.

5. For an overview of non-Anglo Forty-niners, see Susan Lee Johnson, *Roaring Camp: The Social World of the California Gold Rush* (New York, 2000); Kenneth N. Owens, ed., *Riches for All: The California Gold Rush as a World Event* (Lincoln, NE, 2001).

6. Ping Chiu, *Chinese Labor in California, 1850–1880: An Economic Study* (Madison, 1963).

7. On the sea route to California see: James P. Delgado, *To California by Sea: A Maritime History of the California Gold Rush* (Columbia, SC, 1990); J. S. Holliday, *The World Rushed In: The California Gold Rush Experience* (New York, 1981).

8. "Emigration to California," *New York Herald*, January 11, 1849; "The Character of the California Emigrants," *New York Herald*, January 17, 1849.

9. Clark, ed., *Journals of Alfred Doten*, 1:xviii.

10. See, for example, John F. Kasson, *Rudeness and Civility: Manners in Nineteenth-Century Urban America* (New York, 1990); Richard Bushman, *The Refinement of America: Persons, Houses, Cities* (New York, 1992); Karen Haltunnen, *Confidence Men and Painted Women: A Study of Middle-Class Culture in America, 1830–1870* (New Haven, 1982).

11. Clark, ed., *Journals of Alfred Doten*, 1:xx.

12. Henry I. Simpson [George Foster], *The Emigrant's Guide to the Gold Mines: Three Weeks in the Gold Mines, or, Adventures with the Gold Diggers of California in August 1848* (New York, 1848), 14–15, 37; advertisement: "California Gold Discovered by Signor D'Alvear's Goldometer," *Newark Daily Advertiser*, January 8, 1849; "California Gold Grease" advertisement cited in Donald Jackson, *Gold Dust* (New York, 1980), 78.

13. George Payson, *Golden Dreams and Leaden Realities* (Upper Saddle River, NJ, 1970), 21.

14. John Humphrey Noyes, *History of American Socialisms* (Reprint: New York, 1966 [1870]); Brian Roberts, *American Alchemy: The California Gold Rush and Middle-Class Culture* (Chapel Hill, 2000).

15. Georgia Willis Read and Ruth Gaines, eds., *Gold Rush: The Journals, Drawings, and Other Papers of J. Goldsborough Bruff,* 2 vols. (New York, 1944), 1:xxix; Rohrbough, *Days of Gold*, 17, 19.

16. Articles of Association of the Mutual Protection Trading and Mining Company, recorded in Henry A. Stevens, diary, California State Library, Sacramento, California; Articles of the Bunker Hill Trading and Mining Association, recorded in Thomas Williams, diary, Bancroft Library; Contract—Indenture for the brig *Ark*, American Antiquarian Society Collections, Worcester, Massachusetts; Articles of Agreement for the Perseverance Mining Company, cited in Samuel C. Upham, *Notes of a Voyage to California* (Philadelphia, 1878), 105.

17. Joseph Chaffee to his parents, New York, March 13, 1850, Joseph Bennet Chaffee Collection, New-York Historical Society Collections.

18. Isaac Annis to Nancy Russell [his daughter], Auburn, California, April 18, 1849, Annis Letters, New-York Historical Society Collections.

19. John Callbreath to his parents, Tuolumne Diggings, August 18, 1849, Callbreath Collection, Bancroft Library.

20. J. A. Hull, "Correspondence of the Empire City," *The Jerseyman* [Morristown, New Jersey], November 15, 1849.

21. Henry A. Pierce to Sidney Bartlett [in Boston], San Francisco, August 28, 1849, Sidney Bartlett Papers, New York Public Library Collections; William Prince to Charlotte Prince, "Junction of Woods Creek with the Tuolumne River," July 17, 1849, Prince Collection, Bancroft Library.

22. William Prince to Charlotte Prince, Sacramento City, December 13, 1849, Prince Collection, Bancroft Library; Margaret La Tourrette to Cornelius Wyckoff La Tourrette, Bound Brook [New Jersey], August 6, 1851, Alexander Library Special Collections and Archives, Rutgers University; Joel Brown to Ann Brown, Jamestown, California, April 20, 1852; Ann to Joel, "Locust Grove," [Ohio], June 17, 1852; Letters of Joel and Ann Brown, Collections of the American Antiquarian Society.

23. For examples of this literature, see Robert W. Johannsen, *To the Halls of the Montezumas: The Mexican War in the American Imagination* (New York, 1985).

24. Circular: *Addressed to Benevolent Ladies of the United States* (Boston, 1829); Songsheet: *Where Are the Poor Indians? Composed by Chief Kanenison* (Boston, 1840s); Broadside: *KAH-GE-GA-GAH-BOWH, A Chief of the Ojibwa Nation of North American Indians, Will Deliver an Address Descriptive of the Worship or Religious Belief of the Indian—His Poetry, Songs, and his Eloquence* (Boston, 1849); Broadside: *Catlin's Indian Gallery* (Boston, 1838); Broadside: *Last Week of the Five Real Indians! At Peale's New-York Museum! Broadway, Opposite City Hall* (New York, n.d., mid-1840s); the above taken from collections of the American Antiquarian Society.

25. Robert F. Heizer, ed., *The Destruction of California Indians* (Lincoln, 1974); Robert F. Heizer and Alan J. Almquist, *The Other Californians: Prejudice and Discrimination under Spain, Mexico, and the United States to 1920* (Berkeley, 1971); Albert Hurtado, *Indian Survival on the California Frontier* (New Haven, 1988).

26. Theodore T. Johnson, *Sights in the Gold Regions and Scenes by the Way* (New York, 1849), 105, 109; Leonard Kip, *California Sketches: With Recollections of the Gold Mines* (Reprint: Los Angeles, 1946), 16.

27. "Edmund Booth, Forty-Niner: The Life Story of a Deaf Pioneer," *San Joaquin Pioneer and Historical Society*, Stockton, California, no. 3 (1953).

28. Frank Marryat, *Mountains and Molehills, or, Recollections of a Burnt Journal* (London, 1855), 330–32; Henry Hunter Peters to Joe Ellicott [in Boston], San Francisco, August 12, 1852, Peters Collection, New York Public Library; Albert Powell to Rachel Powell [in New York], Washington, Yolo County, July 25, 1850, Albert Powell Collection, California State Library.

29. J. M. Alexander to Frances Alexander, Jackson, March 22, 1852, Alexander Correspondence, Bancroft Library; Thomas Forbes to Hezekiah Branard [in Connecticut], On the American River, March 15, 1850, Gold Rush Letters Collection, Bancroft Library; Stephen Wing to Family [in Yarmouth, Massachusetts], Dutch Hill, June 25, 1854, Wing Collection, Bancroft Library.

30. Charles William Churchill, *Fortunes Are for the Few* (San Diego, 1977), 95, 99.

31. Clark, ed., *Journals of Alfred Doten*, 1:60–70.

32. Alfred Doten, diary entry for February 8, 1850, Clark, ed., *Journals of Alfred Doten*, 1:67.

33. John M. Callbreath to his parents, Dry Creek, June 20, 1850, John Callbreath Collection, Bancroft Library; Hiram Dwight Pierce to Sara Pierce, [Merced], April 28, 1850.

34. Johnson, *Roaring Camp*, 220–21.

35. Hurtado, *Indian Survival*, 171–73, 176–77, 207.

36. Alfred Doten, diary entries for December 22, 1851, September 9, 1852, September 14, 1852, Clark, ed., *Journals of Alfred Doten*, 1:98, 124, 125.

37. Alfred Doten, diary entries for July 5, 1852, July 3, 1852, Clark, ed., *Journals of Alfred Doten*, 1:118, 117.

38. Marryat, *Mountains and Molehills*, 78; Charles Ross Parke, diary entry for January 1, 1850, in Charles Ross Parke, *Dreams to Dust* (Lincoln, 1989), 88–89.

39. For this string of atrocities, see Heizer, ed., *Destruction of California Indians*.

40. Reverend Joseph Augustine Benton, *The California Pilgrim: A Series of Lectures* (Sacramento, 1853), 66; John McCracken to William Webster, San Francisco, October 7, 1850, Miscellaneous California Collection, New York Public Library; typescript, "Journal of a Voyage from Boston to California," Henry Hovey Hyde Collection, California State Library.

41. Hubert Howe Bancroft, *California Inter Pocula* (San Francisco, 1888), 274, 591.

42. Clark, ed., *Journals of Alfred Doten*, 1:243, 256; 2:1205, 1491; 3:2172.

43. Kenneth N. Owens, "The Real, Real West: Life on the Nevada Frontier Had Little Romance," *Sacramento Bee*, April 6, 1975.

Suggested Readings

Clark, Walter Van Tilburg, ed. *The Journals of Alfred Doten, 1849–1903.* 3 vols. Reno: University of Nevada Press, 1973.

Holliday, J. S. *Rush for Riches: Gold Fever and the Making of California.* Berkeley: University of California Press, 1999.

Johnson, Susan Lee. *Roaring Camp: The Social World of the California Gold Rush.* New York: W. W. Norton, 2000.

Roberts, Brian. *American Alchemy: The California Gold Rush and Middle-Class Culture.* Chapel Hill: University of North Carolina Press, 2000.

Rohrbough, Malcolm. *Days of Gold: The California Gold Rush and the American Nation.* Berkeley: University of California Press, 1997.

5

Wong Kim Ark
Chinese American Citizens and
U.S. Exclusion Laws, 1882–1943

Erika Lee

In 1848, the same year that California became an American possession, the U.S. government began formally encouraging emigration from China. The first Chinese immigrants arrived in California the following year, and by 1870 they comprised 10 percent of the state's population. Early California history is very much a story of Chinese American history, for the state's 50,000 Chinese residents were crucial players in developing the state's mining and agriculture and in building the Central Pacific Railroad.

Most Chinese immigrants in this period were young men from war-torn and poverty-stricken regions. The United States, widely known in China as Gold Mountain, beckoned with tales of easy riches. But despite the crucial role of the Chinese in the state's early development and prosperity, they were the victims of severe abuse and discrimination from the very start. As early as 1850 the state government began imposing a special tax on "foreign miners," and in subsequent years it would enact a series of additional statutes and judicial decisions limiting Chinese civil rights and economic opportunities.

Anti-Chinese sentiment reached a fever pitch in California in the 1870s when, amid a severe recession, many whites vilified the Chinese as the reason for their economic woes. The recession produced the new Workingmen's Party of California in 1877. Led by Irish immigrant Denis Kearney, the party worked actively for the expulsion of the Chinese from California. So powerful were anti-Chinese feelings that in 1882, Congress formally banned immigration in the infamous Chinese Exclusion Act. The Chinese became the only national population ever specifically banned under U.S. immigration law.

In this essay, Erika Lee, assistant professor of history at the University of Minnesota, traces the impact of the Chinese Exclusion Act and the attempts by many Chinese immigrants to challenge the law in court. Wong Kim Ark's story offers a fascinating example. Born in San Francisco in 1873, he was a U.S. citizen, but when he tried to return to the United States in 1895 from a visit to China, he confronted the scathing anti-Chinese sentiment embedded in American law and practice.

In August 1895, Wong Kim Ark, a 21-year-old Chinese American citizen born in San Francisco, returned home after a visit to China. To his surprise, immigration officials denied him readmission into the United States. Collector of Customs John H. Wise claimed that Wong—though born in California—was not a U.S. citizen and was thus excludable under the Chinese Exclusion Act of 1882. Wong challenged the decision, eventually taking the case to the Supreme Court, which ruled in his favor in 1898.[1] Wong Kim Ark's case made constitutional history by establishing the right of citizenship for all persons born in the United States, as provided in the Fourteenth Amendment to the U.S. Constitution. The fact that Wong had to go to the country's highest court in order to secure his right to reenter the land of his birth, however, reveals

From the Return Certificate Application Case Files of Chinese Departing, 1913–1944, San Francisco District Office, Record Group 85, Immigration and Naturalization Service, National Archives and Records Administration—Pacific Region (San Francisco)

how the Chinese Exclusion Acts, designed to shut out and restrict Chinese immigrants, came to be extended to Chinese American citizens as well.

The Chinese Exclusion Act represented the culmination of a decades-old anti-Chinese movement, a California-grown campaign to restrict Chinese immigration that extended across the nation by the 1880s. It prohibited the immigration of Chinese laborers, restricted entry to Chinese belonging to a few exempt classes (merchants, students, teachers, travelers, and diplomats), and barred all Chinese immigrants from naturalized citizenship.[2] The Chinese thus became the first group to be excluded from the country on the basis of race. Setting the precedent for further exclusionary and restrictive immigration laws, Congress renewed and strengthened the Exclusion Act in subsequent decades. By the time of its repeal in 1943, U.S. immigration laws also excluded other Asian groups and severely restricted immigration from southern and eastern Europe.

The unequal status of Chinese American citizens like Wong Kim Ark resulted from the Chinese exclusion laws and the manner of their enforcement. Nineteenth-century racist stereotypes depicting Chinese as slave-like coolies, dangerous vice-ridden criminals, and devious, unassimilable perils merged with the new exclusion laws to provide the framework by which immigration officials processed both Chinese immigrants and returning citizens. In an environment in which Americans increasingly believed in a hierarchy of race and the heredity of racial characteristics, behavior, and abilities, Chinese immigrants and Chinese American citizens were racialized as one indistinguishable group, considered to be both perpetually alien and dangerous to America itself.

Most scholarship on Chinese immigration and exclusion focuses either on anti-Chinese politics or on Chinese immigration patterns during the exclusion era. This essay on Wong Kim Ark and other Chinese American citizens shifts our attention to the ways in which anti-immigrant policies and movements affect not only immigrants but also entire ethnic communities. In doing so, they help to shape definitions and discourses on immigration, race, and citizenship for all Americans. Under exclusion's shadow, the status of Chinese Americans became inextricably related to that of Chinese immigrants. As unequal citizens, Wong Kim Ark and others found themselves targets of discriminatory legislation and policies that affected their ability to freely travel to and from the United States as well as affecting their citizenship rights within the United States. This has proven to be an enduring issue in California, which has a sordid history of xenophobia including not only the Chinese Exclusion Act (1882), but also the Alien Land Laws (1913, 1920), the forced repatriation of Mexicans and Filipinos (1930s), the internment of Japanese immigrants and Japanese Americans during World War II, and Proposition 187 (1994).

The Trial of Wong Kim Ark

Wong Kim Ark was born in San Francisco in 1873. His parents, Wong Si Ping and Wee Lee, were long-term Californians who, at the time of his birth, lived in San Francisco's Chinatown. Wong Si Ping was a merchant who helped run the Quong Sing Company on Sacramento Street. Most San Franciscans in the 1870s were hostile to Chinese. White workingmen, California politicians, and others rallied behind Denis Kearney, the leader of the anti-Chinese Workingmen's Party, and readily answered his call that "the Chinese must go!" In 1876, San Francisco lawyer H. N. Clement stood before a special state senate committee and declared a crisis: "*The Chinese are upon us.* How can we get rid of them? *The Chinese are coming.* How can we stop them?" he asked.[3] In 1882 the U.S. Congress heeded the call of Californians and other westerners to protect them from the so-called Chinese invasion, and it passed the Chinese Exclusion Act of 1882. As a result of the new law, Chinese immigration plummeted and emigration back to China increased. In 1890, S. J. Ruddell, the Chief Immigrant Inspector in San Francisco, remarked that the number of stores in Chinatown was "decreasing every day." Should the trend continue, he predicted, the Chinese community might "completely disappear."[4]

Wong Kim Ark's family joined the exodus from California. In 1890 all three members sailed for China. While Wong Si Ping and Lee Wee remained in China for the rest of their lives, Wong Kim Ark returned to San Francisco several months later. Like the over 300,000 Chinese admitted into the United States as either first-time immigrants or returning residents and citizens during the exclusion era, Wong Kim Ark found that the employment opportunities were better in America than they were in China. The Chinese continued to refer to the United States as Gum Saan, or Gold Mountain. Moreover, for Wong, the United States was his home and on this first return trip, he was recognized as a native-born citizen and quickly readmitted into the country. He eventually joined an uncle and moved to the Sierra Nevada where he became a restaurant cook.

By the time Wong made a second trip to China in 1894, the politics of Chinese exclusion were quickly moving toward greater restriction, affecting citizens like Wong Kim Ark. Zealous immigration officials and supporters of Chinese exclusion successfully campaigned to broaden its scope. In 1892 the Geary Act renewed the exclusion of laborers for another ten years and required all Chinese residents to register with the federal government for a certificate of residence (a precursor to the contemporary green card.) By 1902, Congress extended Chinese exclusion to the newly acquired territories of Hawaii and the Philippines. In 1904 the Exclusion Act was renewed indefinitely and remained in effect until its 1943 repeal.[5] Although the laws themselves were designed to regulate immigrants, the government's enforcement procedures extended to all Chinese, including those citizens born in the United States who traveled abroad. Because many Chinese immigrants and Chinese American citizens maintained strong transnational ties to families in China, migration between the two countries was common for both groups during the exclusion era. Indeed, from 1894 to 1940, 97,143 Chinese claiming to be native-born citizens like Kim Ark were readmitted into the country. They made up 48 percent of the total number of Chinese admitted.[6]

Wong Kim Ark's case demonstrates how ideologies of race and citizenship in relation to Chinese immigration acted together to extend the exclusion laws to Americans of Chinese descent. This trend was largely driven by the widespread support for Chinese exclusion in general as well as the government's concern over illegal immigration, which often involved Chinese who fraudulently claimed U.S. birth in order to enter the country. However, a third motivation grew from the belief that the Chinese *as a race* were unfit for American citizenship. In the context of the exclusion laws, this translated into attempts to block Chinese born in the United States from birthright citizenship and the government's efforts to use the exclusion laws against citizens. All three of these factors affected how Chinese American citizens were perceived and processed as they traveled back and forth from China. The conflation of Chinese American citizens with allegedly dangerous Chinese immigrant aliens had an especially damaging effect on the entire Chinese community in America. The argument that Chinese would not make good citizens had been a centerpiece of the anti-Chinese movement prior to 1882. In 1875, Representative Horace Page of California argued in Congress that the Chinese were "a class of people wholly unworthy to be entrusted with the right of American citizenship."[7] Other politicians claimed that unlike "Aryan or European races," the Chinese lacked "sufficient brain capacity...to furnish motive power for self-government," having "no comprehension of any form of government but despotism."[8] In 1877 a congressional committee investigating Chinese immigration concluded that the Chinese were "an indigestible mass in the community, distinct in language, pagan in religion, inferior in mental and moral qualities and all peculiarities." Prohibiting them citizenship was not only desirable, the committee concluded, but it was also a "necessary measure" for the good of the public.[9] The Chinese Exclusion Act legitimized this belief by barring all Chinese immigrants from naturalized citizenship, but the question of birthright citizenship for Chinese born in the United States remained an open question until 1898, when Wong Kim Ark challenged immigration officials in the U.S. Supreme Court.[10]

Following the passage of the Chinese Exclusion Act, various politicians and anti-Chinese spokespersons attempted to extend the logic used to bar Chinese immigrants from naturalization to those born in the United States. Because the Chinese were incapable of assimilation, they charged, even those born in the United States would inherit the deficient characteristics that made their parents so objectionable. The first court case to rule on the question of birthright citizenship involved Look Tin Sing, a 14-year-old boy born in Mendocino, California, who attempted to reenter the United States in 1884 after studying in China. As natives were not explicitly listed as an exempt class in the original Exclusion Act, and because Look Tin Sing had no other documentation proving his membership in another exempt class, he was denied entry by immigration officials in San Francisco. Look appealed, and the Northern District Court of California reversed the decision and ruled in his favor. Declaring that the Fourteenth Amendment provided that "all persons born or naturalized in the United States" were citizens, the court ruled that Look Tin Sing was indeed a citizen and that the Exclusion Act did not apply to him.[11]

Dissatisfied with this failure, the anti-Chinese lobby attempted to reverse this decision and the birthright citizenship it granted to the Chinese. The forum they chose was the case of Wong Kim Ark in 1895. Although Wong had been readily readmitted into the country following his first visit to China in 1890, a new customs collector had taken over the job of inspecting and admitting Chinese in San Francisco. In 1895 the notoriously anti-Chinese official John H. Wise denied Wong readmission when Wong returned from a trip to China that began in

1894. He based his decision on his belief that Wong was not a citizen of the United States and was therefore excludable under the exclusion laws. Wong was placed under custody of the U.S. marshal and detained on shipboard for over four months. After 1910, Chinese detainees were housed in the barracks of the immigration station on Angel Island, but at the time that Wong Kim Ark returned to San Francisco, there was no government-run immigration detention or processing center. Most likely he spent the entire four months on board the same steamship on which he had sailed from China. Although we know little about the conditions of detainees like Wong on board the steamships, we can surmise from later accounts that detention conditions for the Chinese during the exclusion era in general were quite abysmal: crowded, dirty, and disease-infested. Moreover, the Chinese, including those claiming to be citizens such as Wong Kim Ark, were treated little better than criminals. The Chinese often referred to the detention centers as "iron cages" or "Chinese jails." Once on Angel Island, the Chinese chose to refer to the immigration station as "Devil Island" in order to better reflect their poor and unjust treatment.[12] While detained on the steamship, Wong Kim Ark was most likely given some poor-quality food and a place to sleep, but very little freedom to do anything else over the four long months.

Like many other Chinese during the exclusion era, Wong Kim Ark refused to accept the immigration official's ruling and challenged his exclusion. Wong hired Thomas Riordan, a prominent San Francisco attorney, and filed a writ of habeas corpus in the federal district court, alleging that he was being unlawfully confined and restrained. He also claimed the right to reenter as a native-born citizen under the Fourteenth Amendment, stating that he had "always subjected himself to the jurisdiction and dominion of the United States, and had been taxed, recognized, and treated as a citizen of the United States."[13]

Henry S. Foote, the U.S. district attorney, argued the case on behalf of the federal government. In his opinion, the question at hand was whether native-born Chinese could be considered citizens if their parents were not and whether they could become naturalized. Foote argued that birth within the United States did not necessarily confer the right of citizenship, especially in the case of the Chinese, who were unassimilable and unfit for citizenship. Foote claimed that Wong had been made a citizen only "by *accident of birth*" on American soil, but his "education and political affiliations" remained "entirely alien" to those of the United States. Since both of Wong Kim Ark's parents were "subjects of the Emperor of China," Foote continued, Wong himself inherited this nationality and was also a "Chinese person and a subject of the Emperor of China." A child born in the United States may "nominally be a citizen" but, raised by alien Chinese parents, the district attorney reasoned, the child remained "an alien loyal to the country of his father and indifferent to the country of his birth." Conflating "Chineseness" with "alienness" and implying that being Chinese and being American were incompatible, Foote declared that Wong could not possibly be considered an American citizen, for he had "been at all times, by reason of his race, language, color, and dress, a Chinese person."[14] Allowing Chinese such as Wong Kim Ark to be recognized as citizens, Foote warned, would be extremely dangerous. Echoing and reinforcing the old anti-Chinese rhetoric of the 1870s, Foote asked, "Is it possible that any Court in the United States will deliberately force upon us as natural born citizens, persons who must necessarily be a constant menace to the welfare of our Country? . . . We submit that such things cannot be without imperilling [*sic*] the very existence of our Country." The district attorney concluded his brief for the court with the position that even if Wong Kim Ark was found to be a citizen by birth, he should still be excluded by the Exclusion Act, because he was a laborer (having worked as a restaurant cook for most of his adult life) and thus came under its provisions.[15]

Judge William Morrow of the federal district court of northern California soundly refuted Foote's arguments. "It is enough that [Wong Kim Ark] is born here whatever the status of his parents," he wrote. "No citizen can be excluded from this country except in punishment for crime. The petitioner must be allowed to land, and it is so ordered."[16] Foote appealed the decision, but lost again in the U.S. Supreme Court. In 1898 the high court's decision in *Wong Kim Ark v. United States* affirmed that regardless of race, all persons born in the United States are, in fact, citizens entitled to all of the rights that citizenship offers.[17]

The "Look of a Citizen"

The rulings in the Look Tin Sing and Wong Kim Ark cases were enormously significant in establishing the legal parameters in citizenship cases. Immigration officials, however, continued to wield a great deal of influence in the actual practice of processing returning citizens' appli-

cations. Despite court-defined standards that citizenship would be determined by birth in the United States, immigrant inspectors established
their own means of measuring "Americanness." In cases of returning
citizens, the ways in which officials interpreted and defined these cat-
egories were inextricably tied to racialized assumptions that positioned
Chinese Americans as fraudulent or inferior.

Chinese claiming citizenship after Wong Kim Ark's case thus still
had to undergo the same lengthy investigative and interrogation process as aliens in order to prove their nativity and reenter the country.
Proof of birth in the United States was not easily verified. Because Chinese infants were often delivered at home, many citizens did not have
birth certificates. After the 1906 San Francisco earthquake and fire destroyed all city birth records, such documents for Chinese or any other
births were nearly impossible to find. The immigration service was thus
forced to accept applicant and witness testimony to prove birthplace,
but the agency also set parameters in relation to the type of witness
required. Beginning in 1892 immigration officials began to require that
two non-Chinese (that is, white) witnesses verify claims of nativity in
Chinese cases.[18]

In this way, relationships with white persons thus became a direct
means of measuring "Americanness" in cases involving Chinese American citizens. In 1890, Wong Kim Ark himself was asked "if any white
men in San Francisco know you were born here" as a means of proving
his nativity. Wong readily produced three white witnesses who remembered him as a young boy on Sacramento Street. H. Selinger, William
Fisher, and F. Benna all came forward to testify and sign affidavits on
behalf of Wong.[19] Yee Kim, returning to the United States in 1900, was
asked the same question and was landed without any delay, largely due
to the affidavits of seven well-known white Los Angelenos in his file.[20]
Nevertheless, this was a particularly large obstacle for most Chinese
Americans, for in the segregated American Chinese communities, white
witnesses to the birth of Chinese children were extremely rare. As one
incredulous immigration official who disagreed with this ruling asked
his superiors, "Who else [but the Chinese relatives of the applicant]
would be likely to have the knowledge required as a witness in a case of
native birth, if not those closely related to the party born?"[21] Over the
course of the exclusion era, this requirement grew increasingly difficult
to fulfill. In 1910 the Chinese American organization known as the
Native Sons of the Golden State complained to the Secretary of Labor

that witnesses were "departing from the country, dying, or removing to parts unknown."[22]

Returning U.S. citizens of Chinese descent were also subjected to additional tests and procedures designed to prove their nativity and to measure their knowledge about the United States, and hence their "Americanness." Citizens were judged according to how well they could speak English, how much they conformed to American customs and dress, and how well they could identify local landmarks and recite basic facts about U.S. history. One of the first questions that immigrant inspectors asked Wong Kim Ark in 1894, for example, was whether he spoke English. Wong was found to speak it fluently.[23] Moreover, it was not uncommon for immigration officials to note favorably that an applicant claiming citizenship dressed in American-style clothing. In recommending that applicant Moy Goon be landed in 1905, immigrant inspector Alfred W. Parker noted that Moy was "an extraordinarily bright, intelligent Chinaman, dresses in American clothes, and speaks good English. By appearances and conduct, I should say that his claim to American birth is quite reasonable." Another inspector reported that Moy used the American name "Charlie" and was "thoroughly Americanized" and "highly respected."[24] Chinese American citizens were also tested on their geographical knowledge, history, and familiarity with San Francisco's Chinatown or their claimed hometown. At times citizen applicants were even asked to give exact addresses for and directions to local landmarks, including which modes of public transportation were available in these areas.

In the eyes of immigration officials and exclusionists, such measures were necessary to ferret out cases in which Chinese aliens falsely claimed U.S. citizenship in order to enter the country illegally. Although some of these tests certainly did help immigration officials expose fraudulent cases, they often required Chinese American citizens to meet high and often absurd standards. The language test was an especially difficult one for many Chinese Americans. Well into the mid-twentieth century, many immigrants of all racial and ethnic backgrounds and their American-born children still resided in segregated ethnic enclaves with little outside contact or opportunity to become fluent in English. Although many Chinese children attended public school and learned English, many others did not. As a result, some Chinese American citizens never learned English fluently and were at risk of deportation under the U.S. government's rigid definitions of "Americanness" and "citizenship."

The Shadow of Exclusion

Classified as citizens under the U.S. Constitution, Chinese Americans such as Wong Kim Ark nevertheless found that their status as citizens offered little protection from government harassment. The exclusion laws and their enforcement reinforced the belief that the Chinese, as a race, were foreign threats to the United States. Chinese illegal immigration and the government's crackdown on Chinese suspected of being in the country illegally continued to cast a shadow on all Chinese, including legal immigrants and Chinese American citizens. Under the deportation clauses of the exclusion laws and the government's zealous efforts, all were vulnerable to frequent immigration service raids, arrest, and deportation.

Chinese Americans organized to protest their unequal status and attempted to distinguish themselves from their immigrant brethren. In 1910 the Native Sons of California, an organization of Chinese American citizens that later renamed itself the Chinese American Citizens' Alliance, issued a formal complaint to the Secretary of Commerce and Labor.[25] Among their many grievances, the group charged that Chinese Americans suffered from constant harassment by immigration officials, both when traveling abroad and when residing in the United States. The Chinese American citizen was "liable to arrest at any time and place by zealous immigration officials upon the charge of being unlawfully in the country. . . . He moves from place to place at his peril," the letter stated.[26] During the 1920s, Chinese immigrants and Chinese American citizens alike charged the immigration service with conducting a reign of terror against Chinese Americans. The Citizens' Alliance complained to California Congressman Julius Kahn that "our unoffending people are being treated with little more respect than animals and every guaranty [*sic*] of the Constitution against unlawful searches is being defied in this ruthless campaign just launched against our people."[27]

In addition to the Chinese exclusion laws, general U.S. immigration laws also had a disproportionate effect on Chinese American citizens. The 1922 Cable Act revoked the citizenship of women who married "aliens ineligible for citizenship," a code phrase that applied to Asians only. The main victims of this law were Asian American women born in the United States as citizens who married Asian male immigrants, who were ineligible for naturalization by American naturalization laws. Once a woman lost her citizenship, her rights to own property, vote, and travel freely were also revoked. Through community activism, the bill was repealed in 1931.[28] Likewise, the 1924 Immigration Act explicitly excluded "aliens ineligible to citizenship," and as such barred alien wives of citizens on the grounds that they were ineligible for citizenship. Chinese American citizens lobbied tirelessly for six years in the courts and in Congress, eventually succeeding in repealing this provision in the law in 1930. [29]

Their precarious status in the United States had long-standing, even generational effects on Chinese American citizens. The shadow of exclusion first led native-born Chinese Americans to be susceptible to the same sense of insecurity and alienation felt by Chinese immigrants during the exclusion era. Moreover, the suspicion and harsh treatment that Chinese Americans endured caused many to reevaluate their status as Americans as well as their place in the United States. Wong Kim Ark, for example, continued to work in the United States but never made it his permanent home. He married and had four sons in China, preferring to visit them periodically rather than bring them to the United States to live. He was with his youngest son, Wong Yook Jim, for only three years, spread out over several years of visits. Eventually, he retired to China at the age of sixty-two and never returned to the United States. Ironically, while Wong Kim Ark's Supreme Court victory is considered a landmark case in constitutional and civil rights history, his own son still had to undergo the same types of rigid and institutionalized suspicion that Wong himself had challenged. When Wong Yook Jim applied for admission into the country in 1926, for example, he was subjected to the same questioning his father had endured in 1895. Yook Jim's stay at the Angel Island immigration station was a relatively short two weeks, but the resentment and bitterness that he felt on behalf of all the Chinese at the immigration station remained vivid for decades afterward.[30]

Other Chinese American citizens also commonly expressed a marked loss of admiration for the United States and a frustrated sense of alienation. "I am an American citizen by birth, having the title for all rights, but they treat me as if I were a foreigner," one explained in 1931. Another observed, "We are American citizens in name but not in fact."[31] The experiences of Wong Kim Ark and other citizens are apt examples of the high personal costs of exclusion to Chinese Americans in the first half of the twentieth century. Born in the United States, they were nevertheless lumped together with other Chinese as "Orientals" or foreigners, and the codification and legitimization of anti-Asian racism in

American immigration laws exacerbated their unequal status as citizens and cast a shadow on the entire community.[32]

Conclusion

Despite the fact that Wong Kim Ark's struggle to reenter the United States is over 100 years old, the lessons from his case remain relevant today. Wong's legal battle ultimately made constitutional history and established the rule of birthright citizenship for all individuals born in the United States. Over the course of California and American history, however, the divisive effects of immigration politics and xenophobia have been borne by other groups. In the 1930s local, state, and national officials launched aggressive deportation and repatriation programs targeting Mexicans and Mexican Americans throughout the Southwest. One recent estimate places the number of Mexicans, including American-born children, who were returned to Mexico at one million.[33] During World War II, 120,000 Japanese Americans, two-thirds of whom were second-generation citizens born in the United States, were incarcerated in remote camps and forced to take loyalty oaths. In 1994, Californians attacked the Mexican immigration "problem" with Proposition 187, which barred state agencies from providing benefits to illegal aliens. The anti-immigrant mood and government crackdown on illegal immigration that has followed has placed the entire Mexican American community at risk, and the treatment of Mexican Americans as perpetual foreigners reverberates with similarities to the Chinese exclusion era.[34] As recently as 1998 a representative from California submitted for Congressional consideration a bill to deny U.S. citizenship to children born in the United States of undocumented immigrants as well as to legal residents who are in the country without permanent resident status, including refugees.[35] Resonating with some of the same arguments attorneys used to deny Wong Kim Ark his birthright citizenship, such laws reveal how anti-immigrant politics continue to revive older, racialized definitions of American citizenship. Unfortunately, California has a long history of leading the country down some of its most divisive anti-immigrant paths—paths that affect not only the immigrants these political and cultural campaigns are designed to target but entire communities as well. Wong Kim Ark's legal battle and experiences under the Chinese exclusion laws serve as important reminders of the perils that these journeys pose for all Americans.

Notes

1. *United States v. Wong Kim Ark*, 169 U.S. 649, 694 (1898).

2. Act of May 6, 1882 (22 Stat. 58).

3. California State Senate, Special Committee on Chinese Immigration, *Chinese Immigration: Its Social, Moral, and Political Effect* (Sacramento, 1878), 275.

4. U.S. Congress, House Select Committee of Immigration and Naturalization, *Investigation of Chinese Immigration*, 51st Cong., 1st sess., 1890, H. Rept. 4048, 270–71.

5. Act of May 5, 1892 (27 Stat. 25); Act of July 7, 1898 (30 Stat. 750); Act of April 30, 1900 (31 Stat. 141); Act of April 29, 1902: Chinese Immigration Prohibited (32 Stat. 176); Act of April 27, 1904 (33 Stat. 428).

6. Madeline Hsu, *Dreaming of Gold, Dreaming of Home: Transnationalism and Migration between the United States and South China, 1882–1943* (Stanford, 2000); "Immigrants Admitted" and "Summary of Chinese Seeking Admission to the U.S." in U.S. Bureau of Immigration, *Annual Reports of the Commissioner-General of Immigration*, 1898–1943.

7. *Congressional Record*, 43rd Cong., 2nd sess. (1875), 1082.

8. *Congressional Record*, 44th Cong., 2nd sess., vol. 5, pt. 3, 1877, 2005; U.S. Congress, *Report of the Joint Special Committee to Investigate Chinese Immigration*, 44th Cong., 2nd sess., 1876, S. Rept. 689, vii.

9. *Congressional Record*, 44th Cong., 2nd sess., vol. 5, pt. 3, 1877, 2005.

10. *United States v. Wong Kim Ark*, 169 U.S. 649, 694 (1898).

11. *In re Look Tin Sing*, C.C.D. Cal., 21 Federal Reporter, 905, 910 (C.C.D. Cal. 1884).

12. See Rhyme No. 5 in Marlon Hom, *Songs from Gold Mountain: Cantonese Rhymes from San Francisco Chinatown* (Berkeley, 1987), 78.

13. Petition for Writ, November 11, 1895, Wong Kim Ark, Folder 11198, Box 594, Admiralty Case Files, 1851–1934, Northern District of California, San Francisco, Records of the U.S. District Court, RG 21, National Archives, Pacific Region.

14. Brief on Behalf of the U.S., November 19, 1895, 3–5; Opinion Rendered *In the Matter of Wong Kim Ark*, January 3, 1896, 5, Petition for Writ, November 11, 1895 [emphasis added]; Petition for Writ, November 11, 1895, and Points and Authorities of U.S. District Attorney, November 11, 1895.

15. Brief on Behalf of the U.S., November 19, 1895, 6; Points and Authorities of U.S. District Attorney, November 11, 1895.

16. Opinion of Judge Morrow, January 3, 1896, 14, Opinion Rendered *In the Matter of Wong Kim Ark*, January 3, 1896.

17. *United States v. Wong Kim Ark*, 169 U.S. 649, 694 (1898); Lucy Salyer, *Laws Harsh as Tigers* (Chapel Hill, 1995), 99.

18. U.S. Department of the Treasury, *Annual Report of the Commissioner-General of Immigration*, 1902, 76–77.

19. Interrogation of Wong Kim Ock (*sic*), July 16, 1890, 12017/42223, Box 458, Return Case Files, San Francisco, NA-P.

20. File 10039/41, Chinese Arrival Files, San Francisco, Records of the Immigration and Naturalization Service, RG 85, National Archives, Pacific Region (hereafter cited as Chinese Arrival Files, San Francisco, NA-P).

21. Collector of Customs to the Secretary of the Treasury, March 30, 1899, File 53108/9-B, Subject Correspondence, Records of the Immigration and Naturalization Service, RG 85, National Archives (hereafter cited as INS Subject Correspondence, NA).

22. S. G. Carpenter to Secretary of Commerce and Labor, September 23, 1910, File 52961/24-B, Box 170, INS Subject Correspondence, NA.

23. Signed Affidavits, November 2, 1894, File 12017/42223, Chinese Arrival Files, San Francisco, NA-P.

24. Report from Immigrant Inspector, October 5, 1905, File 10079/6, Chinese Arrival Files, San Francisco, NA-P.

25. Sue Fawn Chung, "Fighting for Their American Rights: A History of the Chinese American Citizens' Alliance," in K. Scott Wong and Sucheng Chan, eds., *Claiming America: Constructing Chinese American Identities during the Exclusion Era* (Philadelphia, 1998), 95–126.

26. S. G. Carpenter to Secretary of Commerce and Labor, September 23, 1910, File 52961/24-B, INS Subject Correspondence, NA.

27. Native Sons of California to Julius Kahn, October 24, 1923, File 55383/30, INS Subject Correspondence, NA.

28. Sucheng Chan, "The Exclusion of Chinese Women," in *Entry Denied: Exclusion and the Chinese Community in America, 1882–1943*, ed. Sucheng Chan (Philadelphia, 1991), 128–29.

29. The Immigration Act of 1924, Act of May 26, 1924 (43 Stat. 153); Act of June 13, 1930 (46 U.S. Stat. 581). See Sucheng Chan, "The Exclusion of Chinese Women," 126–27.

30. Bill Wong, "Native-Born American," *Asian Week* 19, no. 32, April 8, 1998, 6; "Wong Kim Ark's Legacy," *Asian Week* 19, no. 36, May 6, 1998, 6; "Claiming a Birthright," *Asian Week* 19, no. 39, May 27, 1998, 6.

31. Louis Kit King, "A Study of American-Born and American-Reared Chinese in Los Angeles" (Master's thesis, University of Southern California, 1931), 127.

32. Ching Chao Wu, *Chinatowns: A Study of Symbiosis and Assimilation* (Ph.D. diss., University of Chicago, 1928), 288.

33. Francisco E. Balderrama and Raymond Rodriguez, *Decade of Betrayal: Mexican Repatriation in the 1930s* (Albuquerque, 1995), 122.

34. Kevin R. Johnson, "Race Matters: Immigration Law and Policy Scholarship, Law in the Ivory Tower, and the Legal Indifference of the Race Critique," *University of Illinois Law Review* 2000, no. 525 (2000): 525–57.

35. The bill, known as the Citizen Reform Act of 1997, was introduced by Republicans in the House of Representatives led by Rep. Brian Bilbray, R-San Diego. It was defeated. See "Clarifying America's Citizenship Laws," *San Diego Union-Tribune*, August 17, 1997; "Boxer Hits Bilbray Bill on Automatic Citizenship," *San Diego Union-Tribune*, July 4, 1997; Editorial, *San Francisco Examiner*, April 10, 1998, A-19.

Suggested Readings

Chan, Sucheng, ed. *Entry Denied: Exclusion and the Chinese Community in America, 1882–1943*. Philadelphia: Temple University Press, 1994.

Chan, Sucheng, and K. Scott Wong, eds. *Claiming America: Constructing Chinese American Identities during the Exclusion Era.* Philadelphia: Temple University Press, 1998.

Choy, Philip, Lorraine Dong, and Marlon Hom. *The Coming Man: 19th Century American Perceptions of the Chinese.* Seattle: University of Washington Press, 1995.

Daniels, Roger. *Asian America: Chinese and Japanese in the United States since 1850.* Seattle: University of Washington Press, 1988.

Gyory, Andrew. *Closing the Gate: Race, Politics, and the Chinese Exclusion Act.* Chapel Hill: University of North Carolina Press, 1998.

Hsu, Madeline. *Dreaming of Gold, Dreaming of Home: Transnationalism and Migration between the United States and South China, 1882–1943.* Stanford: Stanford University Press, 2000.

McClain, Charles J. *In Search of Equality: The Chinese Struggle against Discrimination in Nineteenth-Century America.* Berkeley: University of California Press, 1994.

Palumbo-Liu, David. *Asian/American: Historical Crossings of a Racial Frontier.* Stanford: Stanford University Press, 1999.

Peffer, George Anthony. *If They Don't Bring Their Women Here: Chinese Female Immigration before Exclusion.* Urbana: University of Illinois Press, 1999.

Salyer, Lucy. *Laws Harsh as Tigers: Chinese Immigrants and the Shaping of Modern Immigration Law.* Chapel Hill: University of North Carolina Press, 1995.

Saxton, Alexander. *Indispensable Enemy: Labor and the Anti-Chinese Movement in California.* Berkeley: University of California Press, 1971.

Yung, Judy. *Unbound Feet: A Social History of Chinese Women in San Francisco.* Berkeley: University of California Press, 1995.

6

William Hammond Hall
City Water and Progressive-Era Reform in San Francisco

Jessica Teisch

There is much truth behind the oft-heard cliché that present-day California is a geographical accident, for its natural rainfall and resources can hardly support a population of 34 million. Only the northern tiers of the state receive significant rainfall, and the runoff from its various mountain ranges is woefully inadequate to meet the state's needs. Throughout its history, however, Californians have viewed water as the state's lifeblood and have ingeniously devised irrigation systems that have maximized local resources and allowed for the growth of population and industries far beyond expectations.

Early in the modern era, Californians confronted their limited water resources when a devastating drought in the 1860s wiped out large stretches of agriculture and vast herds of cattle throughout the state. The economic calamity began a process of devising irrigation systems that would ultimately transform the Central Valley from a semidesert to one of the world's richest agricultural regions. By the early twentieth century, both the San Joaquin Valley and southern California's Imperial Valley were vast centers of international agribusiness.

The most dramatic chapters in California's history of water management occurred around the turn of the century when rapidly urbanizing San Francisco and Los Angeles both engaged in contentious debates over water rights. Securing adequate supplies for each of these cities entailed not only massive engineering feats but also intense political battles between various regions and constituencies within the state. In this essay, Jessica Teisch, a Kevin Starr Fellow in California Studies at the University of California Humanities Research Institute, uses the life of San Francisco engineer William Hammond Hall to explore the complex history of this city's quest for water, which ultimately pitted city planners, environmental activists, and private developers against each other in a fierce battle that would cost Hall his professional reputation.

> [Hetch Hetchy's] availability for a dam site and reservoir are so marked as to completely hypnotize every civil engineer that sees it, and to render him forever after incapable of a rational consideration of the larger problem of public policy relating to it.[1]

81

William Hammond Hall sought power, status, and wealth his entire life. At the height of his engineering career, however, naive faith in professional conduct and simple hubris stripped him of the last vestiges of power. Hall laced civic duty with personal greed, sundering the professional interests of the expert engineer from the public interests of society. The story of San Francisco's fight for a municipal water supply system in the early 1900s traces Hall's quest for power. Yet as the activities of the private utility company for which Hall fronted eclipsed the stated public good of a city-owned water system, tensions between the engineer and the goals of Progressive Era reform clouded the "rational consideration of the larger problem of public policy" at hand. In the end, Hall's civic vision came back to haunt him, and he merely donned power's facade.

A municipal water and power system was the centerpiece of Progressive reform in San Francisco. The Progressive Era, which spanned the years between the late 1890s and World War I, was distinguished by national efforts to reform politics and ameliorate many of the social problems created by industrialization and urbanization. Many government officials and experts, including engineers and scientists, expressed new concern for the future of land, water, and forest resources in the semiarid West. Some Progressives were also involved in "good government" movements. They wished to clean up city governments by curbing monopolies, quelling the influence of big corporations in local politics, and hence better serving the public. Yet how could experts and government officials eliminate waste in industry, distribute natural resources equitably, and efficiently manage and conserve these resources for present and future generations? Was it possible to prevent large water or power monopolies from burdening citizens with poor supplies or high costs? Municipal ownership of water and hydroelectric power was seen as one logical solution to these problems.

Cities from London to New York and Chicago had already begun to develop extensive water supply systems in the mid-nineteenth century. San Francisco was not far behind these places. Although San Francisco abuts a majestic bay into which the state's largest rivers empty, the water is salty and the surrounding landscape is semiarid. In the 1850s capitalists began to devise ways to provide water for manufacturing and domestic use to San Franciscan residents. But under private water companies—the monopolistic Spring Valley Water Company in particular—the growing gold-rush city suffered inadequate water supplies, poor service, and exorbitant rates. By the 1890s it became clear that San

Courtesy of the Bancroft Library, University of California, Berkeley

Francisco needed to develop a city-owned source of water and electrical power if it would continue to grow. In 1900, as part of its Progressive agenda, San Francisco's city charter mandated the municipal ownership of utilities.

This was no small concept, for San Franciscan politicians and engineers had to look beyond the Bay Area for a suitable river from which to draw water and generate electric power. They chose the Tuolumne River watershed, which stretched fifty miles across the Coast Range, another fifty miles across the San Joaquin Valley, and another fifty miles through the Sierra Nevada foothills, as the premier site for its massive project. Approximately 90 percent of the watershed lies above 6,000 feet, creating a powerful natural staircase as the river descends from the Sierra Nevada crest and merges with the San Joaquin River west of Modesto. A dam at Hetch Hetchy Valley in Yosemite National Park was to be the linchpin of the project. A U-shaped glacial valley lying approximately 170 miles east of San Francisco, Hetch Hetchy could hold enough water and generate enough hydroelectric power to furnish most of San Francisco's needs for many years. Yet opposition to damming this protected valley by preservationist John Muir and the Sierra Club, which viewed a dam as the devil in Eden, stalled San Francisco's water supply project for almost two decades. San Francisco politicians thus chose Lake Eleanor, a shallow glacial lake eight miles northwest of Hetch Hetchy, as an alternative site for its great dam.[2]

Little did city officials realize that this decision would further embroil San Francisco in conflict—not with wilderness groups such as the Sierra Club, as Hetch Hetchy did, but with Hall and a private company. In 1902, Hall, a well-known civil engineer and vocal advocate of public power and water, speculated in land and water rights along Cherry Creek and Lake Eleanor. He held dear to these rights as the federal government repeatedly denied the use of Hetch Hetchy to San Francisco. For almost a decade, Hall and the private San Francisco–based utility corporation for which he fronted, Pacific Gas and Electric Company (PG&E), obstructed the city's so-called Progressive agenda. In 1910, Hall exacted more than $1 million for the sale of PG&E's Tuolumne River land and water rights to San Francisco. In so doing, Hall put into question the basis of Progressive Era reform—and the values that had instilled most of his life's work.[3]

Why did Hall thwart the city's agenda for more than a decade? Hall had devoted his career to trying to maximize California's resources for the general good of society. He embraced many of the principles of Progressivism, including conservation, expert management, long-range planning, and government intervention in resource development. From the 1870s to 1890s, Hall attempted to develop California's scenic areas for tourism and recreation, rid the state of its water monopolies and reform its antiquated water laws, reconcile mining and farming interests, and encourage planned, democratic agrarian settlement. He sought to curb the depredations of private enterprise in a time legendary for its indifference to the public welfare. Yet in his dealings with San Francisco over Lake Eleanor and Hetch Hetchy, Hall put his personal interests above society's general welfare.

Hall's inconsistent notion of the public good reveals what it meant to be an engineer in the late nineteenth and early twentieth centuries. Engineers measured stream flows, mapped watershed areas, and dammed rivers. As mediators between the natural environment, technology, and industry, engineers necessarily dealt with the larger issues of business and public policy. "By his training," one engineer noted, "the engineer will bring a broader mind to bear on public problems than will the lawyer, financier, or merchant."[4] Indeed, engineers designed and constructed many of the nation's great works of the nineteenth century, including the Erie Canal and the transcontinental railroads. Yet Hall, like most engineers of his time, shared very little of the power and wealth that his business and politician colleagues enjoyed. The realization that he was a classic middleman who bowed to his employers' wishes goaded him for his entire life.

Hall was born in Hagerstown, Maryland, in 1846. His family migrated to California and settled in Stockton when he was seven. Hall had a sportsman's habits as a young boy and only reluctantly gave up his horse and guns for surveying instruments. He intended to go to West Point to study engineering, but the Civil War, as well as his families' Southern sympathies, curtailed these plans. Instead, by his own admission, he received his engineering education in California, "by bits or small chunks and irregularly." Hall's self-education left him slightly arrogant and ever on the alert for the financial advances that a lack of formal education had denied him.[5]

Vast opportunities for engineers arose in the mid-nineteenth century. These opportunities followed the advance of settlement west of the Mississippi Valley, the Mexican War that produced a vast new American territory, California's gold rush, and plans for a transcontinental railroad. The end of the Civil War in April 1865 initiated a flurry of federal engineering activity on the Pacific Coast. The postwar army took up surveying the West with renewed vigor. New government agencies, including the U.S. Board of Military Engineers and the U.S. Geological Survey, began to link the acquisition of scientific and technical knowledge to the commercial future of the nation.[6]

At age twenty-one, Hall began his career as a draftsman for the U.S. Corps of Engineers in Oregon. From 1866 to 1870 he worked as a field engineer for the U.S. Board of Engineers for the Pacific Coast. During that time he surveyed locations for lighthouses, military posts, and harbors from southern California to Puget Sound. Hall's topographic survey of San Francisco's Golden Gate Park in 1870 led to his appointment as superintendent and chief engineer of the park in 1871, a post he held for five years. Hall worked with Frederick Law Olmsted, the famed architect of New York City's Central Park, and John McLaren to design the layout. Together they wrested the park away from the encroaching sand dunes and sea and created an isolated, public retreat from the city.[7]

Hall's design of Golden Gate Park, as well as his irrigation work for politically influential businessmen in the San Joaquin Valley, cemented his professional reputation. In 1878, Hall was appointed by Governor William Irwin as California's first state engineer. He faced his biggest professional challenges during his eleven years at this post. He tried to implement a statewide irrigation and drainage system, improve the state's navigable waterways, and clear hydraulic mining debris from Sacramento Valley rivers. He sought to monitor private enterprise for the benefit of the larger public, using the government as a tool to resolve issues between competing interest groups. Yet Hall accomplished little of what he set out to do during this time. His contempt for compromise and his tendency to take advantage of personal opportunities made him an unpopular figure. Hall was also a visionary whose ideas preceded their time. His progressive notions about long-range technical planning as well as his belief that only state control of rivers could produce a practical scheme of irrigation for California met with resistance by policymakers, farmers, ranchers, and miners from all parts of the state. To top it all off, Hall consistently lacked government funding and political support. After more than a decade of futile efforts to piece together a statewide water system, he resigned as state engineer. The state legislature abolished the office in 1889.[8]

Hall first saw Yosemite in 1881, during his third year as state engineer. Scientists with the U.S. Geological Survey had compared the Sierra's snowcapped peaks and rushing waterfalls to those of the Swiss Alps. Their descriptions influenced President Abraham Lincoln, who ceded Yosemite Valley and the Mariposa Big Trees to California in 1864. The Southern Pacific Railroad, realizing the potentially high profits of tourism, also played a significant role in expanding Yosemite from its original grant of the valley and big trees to its inclusion of other lands surrounding the valley. Yosemite became a national park in 1890, a trust for the whole nation to enjoy.[9]

In 1881, Hall examined Yosemite Valley and advised its Board of Trustees on matters pertaining to the "preservation and opening out" of its attractions. In this "gem of topographical carving," Hall wrote, "with its sparkling settings of snow-covered peaks, polished granite knobs, and verdure-clad ridges, the Creator has provided a magnificent jewel." Although Hall wished to protect the valley's watersheds and "grand and beautiful" landscape, he nonetheless held a utilitarian view of nature. He believed that nature existed for human use, and grounded his obligations toward the public in the principle of the greatest good for the greatest number. He recommended building roads, stone dwellings for visitors, and a hotel. "There [was] no reason," Hall even mused, that the valley's natural meadows "should not be converted into grass meadows of the most productive description, and while adding to the charm of the landscape, augment the revenues of the State, and enhance the pleasure of the visitor, by furnishing abundant forage at low rates, and consequently cheap and good transportation in and about the valley."[10]

Hall's recommendations, although not adopted, were intended to engineer nature for the greatest good of society. This utilitarian belief contrasted with the philosophy held by preservationists. John Muir and his Sierra Club followers, for example, valued nature for its inherent ecological, aesthetic, and spiritual qualities. They thought that Yosemite should remain free from human influence. According to Muir, for example, a man-made lake at Hetch Hetchy was a lesser order of beauty than an ancient glacial canyon. These differences in how nature should be valued formed the heart of the conflict over transforming Hetch Hetchy Valley into an electricity-generating reservoir for San Franciscans.

Hall did not see Yosemite again for more than a decade. In 1891, as head of the California division of the U.S. Geological Survey, Hall again visited Yosemite and the high Sierra. This time he laid eyes on Lake Eleanor and Hetch Hetchy, remote mountain gorges in Yosemite National Park. Lake Eleanor, eight miles northwest of Hetch Hetchy Valley, forms the northwest boundary of Yosemite National Park. Hall later recalled that on seeing Hetch Hetchy, a deep, grassy valley enclosed by steep granite walls, General John Wesley Powell, head of the U.S. Geological Survey, had advised Hall that "such a wonder spot of nature" should not be developed until absolutely essential.[11]

That time soon came. In 1900, San Francisco mayor James D. Phelan directed City Engineer Carl E. Grunsky to study fourteen possible water sources for a municipal water supply project. Grunsky established the superiority of the Tuolumne River watershed because of its great hydroelectric power possibilities, amount and quality of water available, and freedom from complicating water rights. Hetch Hetchy, with Lake Eleanor as a substitute site, offered San Francisco an alternative to the monopolistic Spring Valley Water Company's supplies.[12]

How could San Francisco claim water inside of Yosemite National Park? Federal acts passed in 1901 allowed individuals to claim rights-of-way over public lands, forests, and other reservations for general improvements such as reservoirs and telegraph lines. That year, Phelan posted notices of water appropriation for the city on the Tuolumne River at the outlet of Hetch Hetchy Valley and on the Eleanor Creek branch of the river near Lake Eleanor. But the federal government, heeding its duty to preserve Yosemite's natural curiosities and scenery, denied Hetch Hetchy to San Francisco in 1903 and again in 1905. With Hetch Hetchy in question, Phelan prioritized acquiring Lake Eleanor, a less spectacular but nonetheless suitable reservoir site.[13]

In 1901, Hall again visited the high Sierra. This time he came not as a civil servant but as a private speculator. He investigated the area and, one year later, posted water rights notices and filed claims at Phelan's Lake Eleanor site and along Cherry Creek. Hall reasoned that the city did not need Lake Eleanor because Hetch Hetchy, whose status as use for a reservoir was then in question, could store enough water to supply San Francisco for fifty years. Moreover, according to state statute, the city had not yet put its Tuolumne water to good use by beginning construction of its planned water supply system. Legally, the city thus forfeited its claims. Hall then designed a reservoir site, acquired more land from private owners, and bought a local water company to keep his water rights active. At this point, Hall had no intention of becoming embroiled in city politics by pitting his claims against San Francisco's. Rather, he simply wished to build a water and power network that would supply water for irrigation to surrounding farmlands and sell its excess power to San Francisco.[14]

Hall's plan was soon complicated by three of San Francisco's gas and electricity barons: Frank G. Drum, Eugene de Sabla, and John Martin. Drum had learned of Hall's Sierra holdings. He soon convinced Hall to use his several hundred acres of land and reservoir rights around Lake Eleanor and Cherry Creek for his own "broad scheme of water-power." This plan agreed with Hall, for Drum also intended to supply water to irrigators in outlying agricultural lands and sell electrical power to San Francisco. The businessmen would supply the necessary capital and Hall the engineering expertise. In 1902, Hall conveyed his Tuolumne land and water rights to Drum, who subsequently hired him to map, acquire more rights for, and design a comprehensive 9-reservoir water and power system along the Cherry-Eleanor branch of the Tuolumne River. Drum agreed to pay Hall $10,000 for his services and one-tenth of all the proceeds derived from any future sale of the properties.[15]

In 1905, Drum incorporated the Sierra Ditch and Water Company (SD&W). He transferred all of the properties around Lake Eleanor and Cherry Creek valleys to the new company and hired Hall as chief engineer and agent. SD&W, however, was a dummy corporation that served to conceal the identities of its wealthy owners. That same year, Drum and de Sabla, backed by some of the most influential men in California, had also incorporated another utility company, PG&E. This new company in effect owned SD&W. Drum hid this relationship between the two companies from the public. He knew that he and his partners had possibly preempted San Francisco's plans for use of the same land and water. They did not wish to be seen as conspirators against the city's municipal water and power project.[16]

Hall, who had been appointed by Drum as SD&W's agent, entered the public spotlight. This position gave him some measure of power, yet it also made him put into question the public-spirited ideals that had, up to that point, guided his career. As state engineer in the 1870s and 1880s, Hall had supported public ownership and distribution of water. He had staunchly opposed private water monopolies. On principle, Hall thus valued San Francisco's future municipal water and power system. Yet at the same time, the city's project interfered with SD&W's own plans. Hall's new position with the private company thus put him in a bind: would he adhere to his principles or let his desire for power and money guide his actions? Hall's internal conflict did not last long. He was loyal to his employers and wished to gain influence in the business community. More important, he could not stand to lose an opportunity to line his pockets with the promised commission.

If Hall did not see conflicts between his actions and ideals, others did. Phelan, who was still active in the fight to dam Hetch Hetchy, saw an inevitable dispute over the Tuolumne River water supply between San Francisco and Hall, between public and private interests, and between corporate profit and municipal reform. In 1908 the former mayor, unaware that he was really dealing with the growing corporation PG&E, expressed interest in purchasing the holdings that Hall represented for use as part of the city's municipal water and power system. Drum had appointed Hall as the exclusive agent for the sale of SD&W's properties on the condition that he offer them at a minimum price of $300,000. Phelan, shocked at the exorbitant price, refused the offer. Phelan still hoped that the federal government would grant the use of Hetch Hetchy to San Francisco. Hall nonetheless defended his offer in the name of the public interest. "I was giving Mr. Phelan my inside opportunity," he claimed.[17]

Phelan's refusal meant that San Francisco still had no municipal water and power supply system. But acquiring a water supply source soon became the city's first priority. The 1906 earthquake and fire had destroyed much of the city and its existing electrical power distribution system. Spring Valley Water Company's supplies had failed to curtail the widespread destruction caused by the three days of fire following the great shake. The city government realized the dire necessity of constructing a municipal system and reducing San Francisco's dependence on private companies.

Yet certain events delayed the development of San Francisco's water and power project. First, the federal government repeatedly denied the use of Hetch Hetchy Valley to San Francisco. Second, the city refused to purchase its alternative reservoir site, Lake Eleanor, from Hall. Circumstances were just as unfavorable on the local level. In 1906, San Francisco's government exploded in scandal. As "good government" movements spread across the country as part of the nation's Progressive agenda, San Franciscans began to question how certain business interests had unduly influenced city politics. In the early 1900s many members of the city's Board of Supervisors had dealt illegally with city officials in the interests of several of the great public utilities corporations. In 1906, for example, PG&E directors Drum, de Sabla, and Martin had bought off the Board of Supervisors in order to keep the gas rate low. They were indicted, along with other well-known businessmen and politicians, one year later. The graft proceedings and trials dominated San Francisco's politics for most of 1907 and 1908, stalling the city's Tuolumne River project.[18]

Hall, however, was moving ahead with his plans. Shortly after Phelan refused his offer, Hall proposed to sell the Lake Eleanor and Cherry Creek holdings to his wealthy younger cousin, John Hays Hammond, one of the nation's preeminent mining engineers. Hall offered the company's holdings to Hammond at the same price he had offered them to Phelan. "I would rather have sold the whole proposition to the City," Hall mourned, "for I was a believer in the Tuolumne source for City main supply." But Phelan had refused what Hall believed was a generous proposal. In 1908, Hammond joined into partnership with SD&W and bought its holdings. Luckily, Hammond's purchase of SD&W's holdings protected Drum, de Sabla, and Martin from further political humiliation by masking their association with a project that stood in direct opposition to the city's.[19]

After the graft proceedings, San Francisco officials reopened negotiations with Hall. In the fall of 1908, Hall once again offered to sell the 960 acres on the floor of Lake Eleanor Valley and 1,000 acres along Cherry Creek to the city. But as the new owner of SD&W, Hammond told Hall to severely restrict the conditions of the sale. Hammond wished to strike a deal whereby SD&W would supply water and power to San Francisco but retain ownership over the power supply. Private interests would still control the public power supply.[20]

The conflict between Hall's offer and the city's needs, as well as between Hall's words and actions, further fueled the battle between private and public interests. It also signified the turning point in Hall's career. As he became enmeshed in city politics, the previously public-spirited engineer who only years earlier had struggled to allocate California's resources for the general good became a private capitalist. Hall was now more interested in enriching himself and portraying himself as a man with supreme power over the fate of San Francisco's water system than he was in working toward civic ends. The politics surrounding the development of San Francisco's municipal water and power supply system show that Hall's dealings with the city belied the views he once espoused.

Yet Hall was not as powerful as he thought. His altered notions of Progressive reform began to reflect his dwindling control over the land and water rights that he had painstakingly acquired years earlier. Not surprisingly, Hammond's new restraints took away some of Hall's power within SD&W and also marred Hall's public reputation. Learning that Hall would offer the properties he represented to the city only under certain conditions, the local press accused him of "posing as a public benefactor" in his offer to sell the Tuolumne holdings to the city.[21] "I was," Hall admitted, "shielding [Hammond, Drum, Martin, and de Sabla], and I did all I could to conceal their identity."[22] The public still did not know for whom Hall was fronting: PG&E directors and his cousin Hammond. Despite the local press's speculation that Hall was merely an "agent without credentials," Hall continually voiced his support for San Francisco's municipal project.[23]

At the same time, Hall realized that he and the properties he represented were indispensable to the city's plans. He could thus use his position to blackmail the city. Angered at Hammond's restrictions on the sale of the lands and the water rights to the city, Hall resorted to public threats. If the city did not like his offer, he warned in the *San Francisco Call*, he would "turn right around" and sell the properties to the Spring Valley Water Company. Then, he threatened, "let's see the city touch it." If San Francisco officials did not comply with his terms of sale, San Francisco faced the prospect that PG&E, still the hidden power behind SD&W, would collude with Spring Valley Water. Hall had the power not only to jeopardize the city's municipal water supply project but also to collude with the city's notorious water monopoly. He used this knowledge to his advantage.[24]

Hammond and PG&E directors, however, increasingly began to view Hall as a political buffoon and financial liability. Hall's unprofessional conduct and threats to sell the holdings he represented to the Spring Valley Water Company had already weakened his position within the company and in the public eye so much that Hammond and Drum secretly discussed firing Hall and replacing him with someone more agreeable. They could not rid themselves of Hall, however, without fear of having him publicly expose PG&E as the real power behind the throne.[25]

Hall decided to play hardball. Although he had caved in to Hammond's restrictions for the sale of the properties, he still had control over one thing: the price tag on the Tuolumne holdings. Hall's dealings with the city over the cost of these lands exemplified just how far he had diverged from his earlier career, which had been built on public works. Hall nonetheless justified his actions by arguing that he was working in the public interest. City officials, for example, had agreed to pay $165,800 for lands in Hetch Hetchy Valley that private owners had sold to the city. These lands, according to Hall, were decidedly less important than those around Lake Eleanor.[26] Hall asked at least double $165,800 for the Lake Eleanor lands. He argued that Lake Eleanor's 1,050-foot greater elevation than Hetch Hetchy would allow waters to begin their "long journey colder, and arrive in San Francisco purer." According to Hall, there was "no cheaper development to be found in this State."[27]

Of course, Hall's offer to supply the city with clean and cheap water did not exclusively benefit the public, as he claimed. Hall would sell only those lands and rights "which might legitimately form a part of [San Francisco's] water supply system." He maintained that his plan of selling water and power to local agricultural lands, with Lake Eleanor as the center of a large system, "was initiated without any idea of a conflict with the City." Hall still believed that Phelan's original claims of 1901 were invalid. Unfortunately, the city could not condemn Hall's lands for power purposes. Hall stressed, moreover, that San Francisco's utilization of the Lake Eleanor site would very seriously impede *his* enterprise. Hence, the lands that he chose to sell to the city should reflect that cost.[28]

During the summer months of 1909, Hall increased Lake Eleanor's value in each communication to San Francisco's Board of Supervisors, but neither the city nor Hall would abandon their respective Tuolumne projects. Already, too much was at stake: for San Francisco, a reliable supply of water and power; and for Hall, money, pride, and loyalty to his employers.[29] Lake Eleanor's value continued to rise through 1909. By the end of the year, the cost of the lands and water rights Hall represented had increased sixfold—from double the original $165,800 to more than $1 million, a "friendly concession," in Hall's opinion, to the city. Had Phelan taken up Hall's original offer of $300,000, the city would have saved hundreds of thousands of public dollars—an ironic twist to the meaning of the public good.[30]

Nobody wished to bow to Hall's exorbitant demands. But most San Francisco officials and citizens believed that it was better for the city to pay Hall's price than to go through a long course of litigation for the Lake Eleanor lands and water rights. In April 1910, Hall and San Francisco officials finally closed a deal. The city bought the Lake Eleanor and Eleanor Creek properties for $400,000 and took an option to buy the Cherry Creek properties for an additional $600,000. The latter holdings had been assessed in 1908 for only $14,890. One year later, San Francisco citizens passed a bond sale of over $1 million. This measure authorized city engineers to begin construction of the dam at Lake Eleanor.[31]

In 1913, after a bitter fight that destroyed the efforts of John Muir and the Sierra Club, the federal government finally granted San Francisco permission to dam Hetch Hetchy Valley. San Francisco could now build its long-awaited municipal water and power system. Citizens approved $45 million in bonds for a hydroelectric reservoir at Hetch

Hetchy, which would form the linchpin of the city's system. The entire project was begun in 1914 and completed in 1934. It drew together the highest engineering talent available—city engineers, private consultants, and world-renowned engineers. The system was designed to produce 400 million gallons of water per day and generate immense quantities of electrical power for industrial and domestic use in San Francisco. One of the first dams to be built was along Eleanor Creek, which transformed Lake Eleanor from a shallow glacial lake into a reservoir capable of holding 28,000 acre-feet of water. O'Shaughnessy Dam at the outlet of Hetch Hetchy Valley was built shortly afterward. By 1934—thirty-four years after San Francisco's city charter mandated municipal ownership of utilities as part of its Progressive Era agenda—a series of powerhouses, tunnels, reservoirs, and aqueducts finally carried Sierra water and power to San Francisco and its environs.

San Francisco's Hetch Hetchy system heralded many of the goals of Progressive Era reform. It fulfilled the Progressives' ideals of conservation, utilitarianism, and long-range planning. The construction of reservoirs at Hetch Hetchy and Lake Eleanor amounted to victories for those who wished to use, instead of preserve, a mountain valley. The project also showed the importance of government intervention in private industry and of public control and ownership over resources like energy and water.

Progressive Era reform in San Francisco also fell short of many of its goals. Public ownership and distribution of water and electric power came at a cost that belied many of the original principles of Progressives. In 1925, after a long controversy, the San Francisco Board of Supervisors turned over the power from Hetch Hetchy to PG&E, which by that time was the largest commercial developer of power in northern California. This deal was carried out even though in 1913 the U.S. Congress had forbidden San Francisco to let a private company dispose of its power. But the arrangement worked so well that rather than adhere to federal restraints, PG&E purchased the remaining Hetch Hetchy power for $2.4 million annually. It promptly turned around and sold this power to city residents for $9 million.[32]

What happened to the engineer? Hall's cohorts profited handsomely from his wheeling and dealing with the city, and their identities were never discovered. Yet Hall's plans for status, power, and wealth had taken many disappointing turns. He had sold the Lake Eleanor lands to the city for a lucrative sum, but at the expense of his professional pride and public reputation. He also fell into disfavor with his employers, who, according to Hall, had failed to compensate him for his services. In May 1910, Hall demanded 10 percent of the $1 million paid by the city in addition to his salary and the $30,000 seller's fee. PG&E's attorney refused to honor this request, even when Hall once again threatened to expose the company owners.[33]

Unfortunately, PG&E directors viewed Hall as a powerless middleman. All Hall cared for was money, one of the directors claimed, "and would sell you out in a minute."[34] Hammond stated that Hall spent a good part of his job "faking up reasons for additional compensation."[35] Hall was, after all, a mere appendage to a complex project, by his own admission a regular employee whose place could have been filled by any engineer. He emerged as PG&E's puppet and co-conspirator at best, a deceitful extortionist at worst. He cohered neither with the profile of the objective scientific expert nor the professional, public-spirited engineer heralded during this time.

One final incident exemplified Hall's last, futile grasp at power. In April 1913 he sued Hammond for $150,000 for libel. Hall claimed that his cousin had injured his reputation, disturbed the peace of his household, and impaired his credit with local banks. Hammond had also publicly voiced disgust at Hall's surly, money-grubbing temperament and political incompetence. One year later, Hall experienced a small victory. Local courts dismissed the suit and Hammond renounced all charges against Hall's character. Anything that detracted from Hall's reputation, Hammond admitted, discredited their common family name. Despite the bad feeling that the entire Lake Eleanor project had caused, Hall began to work on the city's Hetch Hetchy system as a consulting engineer.[36]

The Lake Eleanor incident gave Hall's career a tragic ending. His career was, at best, a reminder of the engineer's brilliant and often prophetic understanding of society's problems. At its worst, it signified Hall's great personal fallacies. His Lake Eleanor dealings revealed a shortcoming in a man who had otherwise shown great energy, foresight, and commitment to identifying and proposing solutions to California's water problems and serving the public good. Hall, a forgotten figure in California history and an embittered man, died in 1934, the first year that Tuolumne River water poured out of the taps in San Francisco homes. In the end, Hall likely rued the day that he had ever entered city politics.

Notes

1. William Hammond Hall, "The Story of Hetch Hetchy," ms., folder 18, carton 6, William Hammond Hall Papers, 1803–1979, Bancroft Library, University of California, Berkeley, p. 63.

2. Warren D. Hanson, *San Francisco Water and Power: A History of the Municipal Water Department and Hetch Hetchy System* (San Francisco, 1994), 23–25.

3. Donald J. Pisani, *From the Family Farm to Agribusiness: The Irrigation Crusade in California and the West, 1850–1931* (Berkeley, 1984), 154–90; Charles P. Korr, "William Hammond Hall: The Failure of Attempts at State Water Planning in California, 1878–1888," *Southern California Quarterly* 45.4 (December 1963): 305–22; Jessica B. Teisch, "Engineering Progress: Californians and the Making of a Global Economy" (Ph.D. diss., University of California, Berkeley, 2001).

4. John Hays Hammond, *The Engineer* (New York, 1921), 192–93.

5. William Hammond Hall, "Recollections of Early California Engineering," undated ts., folder 14, carton 7, William Hammond Hall Papers, 2.

6. See A. Hunter Dupree, *Science in the Federal Government: A History of Policies and Activities to 1940* (Cambridge, MA, 1957).

7. Hall, "Recollections of Early California Engineering," 7–8; William Hammond Hall et al., *The Development of Golden Gate Park* (San Francisco, 1886).

8. Pisani, *From the Family Farm*, 154–90; Korr, "William Hammond Hall," 305–22; William Hammond Hall, *The Irrigation Question: A Memo* (Sacramento, 1886).

9. William H. Goetzmann, *Exploration and Empire: The Explorer and the Scientist in the Winning of the American West* (New York, 1971), 377.

10. Quotes from William Hammond Hall, *To Preserve from Defacement and Promote the Use of the Yosemite Valley* (Sacramento, 1882), 4, 5, 10, 26; Alfred Runte, *Yosemite: The Embattled Wilderness* (Lincoln, NE, 1990), 39–44.

11. Runte, *Yosemite*, 176; Powell quoted in Gray Brechin, *Imperial San Francisco: Urban Power, Earthly Ruin* (Berkeley, 1999), 101.

12. Marsden Manson, "Outline of History of the Water Supply of the City of San Francisco," in Board of Supervisors, *Reports on the Water Supply of San Francisco California. 1900 to 1908, Inclusive* (San Francisco, 1908), 7–8.

13. Marsden Manson, *Efforts to Obtain a Water Supply for San Francisco* (San Francisco, 1907), 17–23; Hanson, *San Francisco Water and Power*, 24.

14. Hall, "Hetch Hetchy," 14; William Hammond Hall, Memo book for 1901–02, folder 15, carton 2, William Hammond Hall Papers; William Hammond Hall, *In the Matter of Water Storage and Utilization on the Tuolumne River, California* (San Francisco, 1907), 2–3.

15. Quote from "Agreement between Wm. Ham. Hall and Frank G. Drum, September 15, 1902," folder 27, carton 10, William Hammond Hall Papers; Hall, *In the Matter of Water Storage*, 5–8; Hall, "Hetch Hetchy," 10, 16, 20–21; Charles M. Coleman, *P.G.&E. of California: The Centennial Story of Pacific Gas and Electric Company, 1852–1952* (New York, 1952), 124–37, 173–74, 343–67.

16. "Agreement between William Hammond Hall and Frank G. Drum, Eugene J. de Sabla Jr., and John Martin, Jan. 14, 1905," "Agreement between Drum, Martin, and Joseph C. Love, March 14, 1905," "Agreement between PG&E and William

Hammond Hall, June 1, 1908," folder 27, carton 10, William Hammond Hall Papers; Coleman, *P.G.&E.*, 154, 363–67.

17. "Hall Defends Terms of Offer," *San Francisco Bulletin*, September 12, 1908; "Power Combine Seeks to Kill Sierra Water Project," *San Francisco Call*, September 13, 1908; quote from Hall, "Hetch Hetchy," 75.

18. William Issel and Robert Cherny, *San Francisco, 1865–1932: Politics, Power, and Urban Development* (Berkeley, 1986), 32, 156–61; Walton Bean, *Boss Ruef's San Francisco: The Story of the Union Labor Party, Big Business, and the Graft Prosecution* (Berkeley, 1952), 88–90, 140–44; Coleman, *P.G.&E.*, 174–75.

19. John Hays Hammond, *The Autobiography of John Hays Hammond*, 2 vols. (New York, 1935), 2:735, 739–40; quote from Hall, "Hetch Hetchy," 32.

20. "Hall's Offer Has Balking Condition," *San Francisco Post*, September 12, 1908; "Ham Hall Asked to Name Owners," *San Francisco Call*, December 9, 1908.

21. "Power Combine Seeks to Kill Sierra Water Project," 18.

22. Hall, "Hetch Hetchy," 34.

23. "Ham Hall Asked to Name Owners."

24. "Mr. Hammond Hall's Impudent Proposal," *San Francisco Call*, September 15, 1908.

25. John Coffee Hays, letter to John Hays Hammond, May 19, 1910, folder 20, carton 14, William Hammond Hall Papers.

26. *Proceedings before the Secretary of the Interior in re Use of Hetch Hetchy Reservoir Site in the Yosemite National Park by the City of San Francisco* (Washington, DC, 1910), 2–3.

27. William Hammond Hall, letter to C. D. Marx and John D. Galloway, May 20, 1909, Galloway Papers 96.1, Water Resources Center Archives, University of California, Berkeley.

28. William Hammond Hall, letter to the Public Utilities Committee of the Honorable Board of Supervisors, City and County of San Francisco, September 11, 1908, Galloway Papers 96.1, Water Resources Center Archives.

29. "Ham Hall Has Poor Title to Water Flow," *San Francisco Examiner*, April 7, 1911; Marsden Manson, letter to John D. Galloway, July 18, 1909, Galloway Papers 96.1, Water Resources Center Archives; "Agreement between SD&W, the California Gas and Electric Corporation, and William Hammond Hall, September 28, 1908," folder 27, carton 10, William Hammond Hall Papers; Hall, "Hetch Hetchy," 23.

30. William Hammond Hall, letter to C. D. Marx and John D. Galloway, May 20, 1909, Galloway Papers 96.1, Water Resources Center Archives.

31. "Long Cannot Fix Price of Ham Hall lands," *San Francisco Examiner*, March 18, 1910; "M'Carthy Will Pay $1,000,000 for Hall Lands," *San Francisco Examiner*, December 11, 1910; "Cherry Creek Deal Is Closed," *San Francisco Examiner*, December 28, 1911; "All Hall's Rights Included in Offer," *San Francisco Examiner*, March 5, 1910; "Hall Explains His Reservoir Offer," *San Francisco Examiner*, September 13, 1910; "Will Take Up Option on Ham Hall Property," *San Francisco Chronicle*, April 6, 1911.

32. Coleman, *P.G.& E.*, 342–62; Norris Hundley, *The Great Thirst: Californians and Water, 1770s–1990s* (Berkeley, 1992), 184–92; Michael M. O'Shaughnessy, *Hetch Hetchy: Its Origin and Story* (San Francisco, 1934), 105–9.

33. John Coffee Hays, letter to John Hays Hammond, May 19, 1910, folder 20, carton 14, William Hammond Hall Papers; William Hammond Hall, letter to A. F. Hockenbeamer, April 25, 1910, folder 27, carton 10, William Hammond Hall Papers; William B. Bosley, letter to A. F. Hockenbeamer, San Francisco, April 27, 1910, folder 27, carton 10, William Hammond Hall Papers; Jesse W. Lilienthal, letter to John Hays Hammond, March 2, 1914, folder 37, carton 15, William Hammond Hall Papers.

34. John Coffee Hays, letter to John Hays Hammond, June 10, 1910, folder 12, carton 14, William Hammond Hall Papers, p. 2.

35. District Court of the United States, Northern District of California, Second Division. *William Hammond Hall, Plaintiff, vs. John Hays Hammond, Defendant*, April 15, 1913, pp. 3–4.

36. "J. Hays Hammond Sued for $150,000 for Libel," *San Francisco Bulletin*, May 7, 1914; "John Hays Hammond Makes Apology to Wm. Ham. Hall," *San Francisco Bulletin*, November 20, 1914; John Hays Hammond, letters to William Hammond Hall, November 20, 1914, and September 28, 1916, folder 8, carton 14, William Hammond Hall Papers.

Suggested Readings

Bean, Walton. *Boss Ruef's San Francisco: The Story of the Union Labor Party, Big Business, and the Graft Prosecution*. Berkeley: University of California Press, 1952.

Deverell, William, and Tom Sitton, eds. *California Progressivism Revisited*. Berkeley: University of California Press, 1994.

Goetzmann, William H. *Exploration and Empire: The Explorer and the Scientist in the Winning of the American West*. New York: Knopf, 1971.

Hays, Samuel. *Conservation and the Gospel of Efficiency: The Progressive Conservation Movement, 1890–1920*. Cambridge, MA: Harvard University Press, 1959.

Hundley, Norris. *The Great Thirst: Californians and Water, 1770s–1990s*. Berkeley: University of California Press, 1992.

Muir, John. *The Yosemite*. New York: Century, 1912.

Pisani, Donald J. *From the Family Farm to Agribusiness: The Irrigation Crusade in California and the West, 1850–1931*. Berkeley: University of California Press, 1984.

Runte, Alfred. *National Parks: The American Experience*. Lincoln, NE: University of Nebraska Press, 1979.

Smith, Michael L. *Pacific Visions: California Scientists and the Environment, 1850–1915*. New Haven, CT: Yale University Press, 1987.

Starr, Kevin. *Americans and the California Dream, 1850–1915*. New York: Oxford University Press, 1973.

Feminism

7

Caroline Marie Seymour Severance
Activist, Organizer, and Reformer

Judith Raftery

Over the course of the nineteenth century, America shifted from a largely rural nation of small farmers, sharecroppers, tenants, and slaves to a significantly (urban) nation of wage laborers, factory workers, small business owners, and office employees. For most Americans the movement from family farms and towns to cities entailed an entirely different form of life as they *Etc* struggled to make sense of new urban environments. Historians have often labeled the period surrounding the turn of the century the Progressive Era, because the need to deal with the challenges and problems of massive industrialization and urbanization created a broad new political movement devoted to modernizing the nation's social and political structures. While Progressives were a diverse group, most shared the general goals of using social science and reason to improve working conditions, the democratic process, and civic life.

California's powerful Progressive movement enjoyed many political victories, including women's suffrage in 1911, the regulation of public utilities in 1913, and a statewide initiative, referendum, and recall system as well as a host of workers' safety and public education programs. Critical to these achievements were hundreds of women's clubs, which became key sites for social and political activism during the decades around the turn of the century. In this essay, Judith Raftery, a professor of history at California State University, Chico, traces the life of Los Angeles reformer Caroline Severance. Severance's involvement in political culture prior to suffrage included founding the Friday Morning Club, one of the nation's largest and most influential women's clubs in the early twentieth century. Her experiences illuminate the broad range of civic activities that filled the daily lives of many American women during the era in which they won their right to enter the nation's formal political sphere.

In June 1895, James Seymour Severance wrote a series of letters from San Francisco to his mother, Caroline Seymour Severance, in Los Angeles. Susan B. Anthony and Anna Howard Shaw had just arrived in San Francisco from Los Angeles on their most recent suffrage campaign drive in the Golden State, and son Seymour, as he was called, wanted to keep his mother informed. Among other things, he told her that two of

99

the city's major newspapers, the *San Francisco Call* and the *San Francisco Examiner*, had reported Anthony and Shaw's visit to her Los Angeles home, Red Roof, and the eastern pair's enthusiastic recounting of their stay. Seymour used the occasion to caution his 75-year-old mother against overexertion in this, the latest and largest of the campaigns for women's suffrage, and in most of her socializing, no matter how important the cause. Now that Anthony and Shaw had left Los Angeles, Seymour, concerned about his mother's welfare, warned her to take it easy. "I hope you will call a halt" to "the usual Los Angeles entertainment," he wrote, suggesting that she "patronize them lightly."[1]

Caroline Seymour Severance was one of California's notable women activists and organizers. There would be little chance she would pay much attention to her eldest son's urgings. Her life would span nearly a century, and for most of those years she worked for reform. She was a woman of privilege and she used her social position to benefit those causes she found compelling. She participated in the major reform movements of the antebellum period—abolition, temperance, and women's rights—and she lived to initiate many of the reforms associated with the Progressive Era—suffrage, peace, purity, and municipal and school reform. Severance represents the first full generation of American women to enter the public arena. She founded the New England Woman's Club in Boston in 1868 and the Friday Morning Club in Los Angeles in 1891 to expedite reforms. Years later, friends gave her the sobriquet, "Mother of Women's Clubs."[2]

Severance's club work put her in the forefront of reform and, as California became a major site of Progressive activity, her role in it took on greater significance. She lobbied for women's increased education and participation in the professions. Women's clubs became the center for these activities and they thrived in the Golden State. Through her leadership, Severance modeled a more public role for women with shared political and civil rights. In 1911, California became the largest state to pass women's suffrage legislation. Its action preceded the national amendment by almost a decade.

Eastern Beginnings

Severance was born in Canandaigua, New York, in 1820 to a family of some means. Her father, Orson Seymour, was a banker, and she was named after her mother, Caroline Maria Clark. Her childhood was

Courtesy of the Huntington Library, San Marino, California

marred by her father's death when she was four. Her own sorrow and her mother's deep bereavement left a lasting impression that she claimed made her a serious and overly sensitive girl often haunted by fears of personal damnation. Shortly after Orson Severance's death, Caroline's mother gathered her eight children and returned to her family's home in Auburn. Caroline would later remark that she thought that her uncle's fearsome Presbyterianism caused much of her childhood anxieties. She sought solace in the religious revivals of the Second Great Awakening that were lighting fires all around her region to the extent that her area of western New York acquired the epithet of the Burnt or Burned-Over District. Caroline came under the sway of the great revivalists Charles Grandison Finney and Jedediah Burchard, whose emotional preaching stressed perfection of mankind and the attainment of millennial happiness.[3] These two principles guided her life's work, although her religious fervor waned.

Caroline had a quick mind and her family soon recognized her abilities. When she was in her early teens, she was encouraged to attend Elizabeth Ricord's female seminary in Geneva, twenty miles or so from Auburn. She graduated as valedictorian in 1835 and taught school for a few years, not an uncommon occupation for well-educated, middle-class young women of her time. In 1840 her life changed. She married Theodoric Cordenio Severance, a banker, and settled in Cleveland. Theodoric's father was well known in Cleveland for his abolitionist views. Theodoric shared his family's abhorrence of slavery and Caroline quickly adopted his principles. She later wrote that her marriage into the Severance family freed her from the bondage of "authority, dogma, and conservative ideas."[4] The Severances appear to have had a loving and compatible relationship. In 1890, after fifty years of marriage, Theodoric's only complaint was of being left alone for three weeks that fall while Caroline went gallivanting. Addressing her as Carrie, he wrote that he promised to be more "husband-like" when she returned.[5]

Although her early Cleveland years were busy with childbearing—she had five children in seven years, four of whom survived to adulthood—Caroline became active in the three causes that would occupy her for many years: abolition, temperance, and women's rights. She and Theodoric worked in tandem, sharing many of the same beliefs and social goals. He joined the Liberty Party and, along with fellow Ohioan Salmon P. Chase, was an early supporter of the Republican Party. Caroline helped found the Ohio Woman's Rights Movement and in 1854 she and Theodoric were elected officers of the Fourth National Woman's Rights Convention held in Cleveland. Her ideas received wider coverage after the Mercantile Library Association of Cleveland asked her to prepare and present a tract on a woman's right to retain inherited property and her own earnings. She delivered her views before the Ohio legislature, the first woman to do so.[6]

The second important move for Caroline came in 1855 when Theodoric accepted a position in Boston. Caroline claimed that the move was undertaken so that their sons could attend Harvard College, but the prospect of living in Boston must have electrified her. Historian Joan Jensen notes that Caroline plunged into activities immediately. William Lloyd Garrison invited the Severances to a reception as soon as Caroline had "unpacked her bonnets." Caroline became a convert to Theodore Parker's Unitarianism and the first woman officeholder in the Parker Fraternity Course. She also become the first woman to give a lecture at the Boston Lyceum Association. Caroline worked with Garrison in the New England Abolitionist Society, and in 1859 she became president of the New England Woman's Rights Convention.[7]

During the last years of the Civil War, Theodoric served as customs officer at Port Royal, South Carolina. Caroline, who worked with the Sanitary Commission and helped to establish the Freedman's Bureau in Boston, accompanied Theodoric to the South where, as a member of the New England Freedmen's Aid Society, she assisted in teaching freed slaves. Her son Seymour also served under the same auspices as a school superintendent in Beaufort.[8]

Returning to Boston after the war, Caroline resumed her activities, but now that slavery had ended she turned her attention to two new areas: education and broadening women's options. Severance's interest in education led her to join the faculty of Dio Lewis's school. Lewis taught unorthodox subjects, including physical training to female students, and hired Caroline to teach practical ethics. Her own ethics were tested when an African American girl asked for admission. Over the objections of faculty and students, Lewis rejected the girl's application. Whether Severance left the school in protest or for other reasons is not clear, but Jensen suggests that her experience in that situation may have turned her to other reforms. She took a keen interest in the first English-speaking kindergarten in America, a tuition program for middle-class children opened in Boston in 1860 by Elizabeth Peabody, whose work inspired Severance to establish kindergartens in Los Angeles a few years later.[9]

Severance's longtime interest in women's issues resulted in the formation of the New England Woman's Club (NEWC) in 1868. That same year, Jane Cunningham Croly, a journalist and women's rights advocate in New York, founded Sorosis, and the two clubs are considered the earliest formal women's clubs in American history. To form the NEWC, Severance gathered reform-minded friends who had worked to improve their society and the role of women within it. All were white, Protestant, educated, and from well-situated, socially prominent families. Most were married. They designed their clubs exclusively for women, fearing that if men became active members they would take the clubs over, as had been the case in other organizations. The NEWC sought to provide its members with the appropriate tools, information, and education to enable them to initiate successful reform campaigns. Severance served as president until 1871, when Julia Ward Howe succeeded her.[10]

Under Severance's adroit leadership the NEWC raised funds for many projects. It lent support to Boston's first hospital run and officered by women, New England Hospital for Women and Children. The NEWC set up scholarships for college-bound girls, raised money to support a tuition-free kindergarten for the city's poor children, and funded archaeological expeditions in Greece and Egypt. It established a horticultural school for women, lobbied for the Massachusetts law changing "age of consent," put police matrons in institutions where girls and women were held, and worked for dress reform. It helped elect women to Boston's School Committee, paving the way for women to have a voice and a vote in city government before they attained state or federal suffrage.[11]

It was through her women's clubs (known at the time as woman's clubs) that Severance achieved her most far-reaching reforms and set up the mechanism that would be associated with female political culture. Her greatest political commitment was to women's suffrage, and many of her other activities were ancillary to that goal. She considered herself a poor platform speaker and rarely gave public lectures after 1855, a decision that caused suffrage leaders to criticize her. In a letter to Henry Blackwell in 1906 she wrote that she recalled a "friendly rebuke" from his wife, Lucy Stone, several years earlier. Stone had called her a "back slider from the suffrage ranks" because she no longer spoke for it "on the platform." Severance explained that she "had no platform gifts as had the others but was confident that my club efforts would bring the cause vastly more numerous recruits than all my efforts on the platform."[12]

Not all of her actions found appreciative audiences, even within the suffrage movement. During the conflicts over strategies in the late 1860s, Severance and others, including Howe, Stone, and Blackwell, decided that the Fifteenth Amendment, even though it failed to include women, should pass. They were "willing" to let black men vote first.[13] They formed the American Woman's Suffrage Association in 1869 and focused their attention on getting the franchise for women in individual states rather than on a national level, and they included men in their organization. Elizabeth Cady Stanton and Susan B. Anthony formed the women-only National Woman's Suffrage Association and continued to work for a national amendment. It may have been more than coincidental that when Anthony made her symbolic attempt to vote in 1873, resulting in her arrest, she did so in Severance's birthplace of Canandaigua.[14]

The California Years

Some time in the early 1870s the Severances decided to leave Boston and relocate to southern California. Two of their four children had already moved to California, and the middle-aged couple also thought the salubrious climate would prove a welcome relief from harsh Eastern winters. The Severances were in the vanguard of millions of Americans who migrated west, seeking year-round sunny skies and mild temperatures. The family arrived in Los Angeles in 1875, just ahead of the Southern Pacific Railroad. Theodoric had purchased property in San Bernardino in the hope of growing oranges, but Caroline insisted on living in town. They settled into a modest but pleasant home, Red Roof, or "El Nido" (the nest) on a new street they named Severance, just off exclusive West Adams Boulevard. To the sophisticated Severances, Los Angeles with a population of less than 11,000 must have seemed a frontier town, but one wide open for the reforming pair to mold.

The Severances stood out in any setting, but because they arrived in Los Angeles at the beginning of its transformation from village to metropolis, their—and particularly her—presence loomed large. Utilizing their considerable talents, they brought some eastern amenities to the far western semidesert community. They organized the Unitarian Church by inviting Quincy, Massachusetts, minister John D. Wells to preach in the parlor of their new home, and they set about raising money for a church.[15]

Building on the NEWC model, in 1878 Caroline organized the first women's club in Los Angeles. The small group held its organizational meeting in the newly constructed Unitarian Church. The gathering of affluent matrons appeared too radical for many Angelenos, and the *Los Angeles Herald* warned that intellect and virtue were not compatible in women. Some of the criticism stemmed from the clubwomen's neglect to include a prayer to begin their meeting.[16] Criticism aside, women's clubs began to flourish both as cultural clubs for self-betterment and as agencies of reform in cities across America. Those clubwomen who came to support reform did so as a means of reordering a society they perceived as corrupted by modernization and its concomitants: industrialization, immigration, and urbanization. Many also hoped to create a more public role for women whereby they would share the same civil and political rights as men. Drawing on ideas that political culture encouraged women to become the moral guardians of their homes, many clubwomen saw themselves as municipal housekeepers: they transferred their responsibilities of domestic feminism to work for civic betterment. As municipal housekeepers, they initiated reform on local, state, and national levels.[17]

Severance's first Los Angeles club was short-lived, but while it functioned its members focused on social and intellectual reforms. Their projects included protecting shade trees from destruction, electing a woman to the school board, bringing about the appointment of a female superintendent of schools and a female librarian, funding a kindergarten, and establishing a juvenile court. In the middle of this activity, Caroline left for an extended visit to the East. She was still there when she heard that one of the club's projects, having a qualified woman placed as school superintendent, had failed. Chloe B. Jones had been appointed in 1880 after serving as principal of Los Angeles High School. After one year she was relieved of her administrative duties and sent back to the classroom, apparently because she had begun to superintend in too modern a manner: changing the curriculum, choosing textbooks, and assigning teachers. These privileges were thought to belong to the Board of Education. Severance wrote from Massachusetts to a friend of her "indignation" upon hearing of Jones's "removal."[18]

By the time Severance returned to Los Angeles in 1881, the women's club had fragmented. She set about founding another one but it also floundered, again in part because of her extended absences. Nevertheless, the second club, as had the first, inspired many of it members to work for particular reforms. Club member Anna S. Averill, for instance, became the first woman elected to the Los Angeles school board, in 1887.[19]

Club members also organized into a Work Committee and began investigating the wages of the city's working women. Industrialization provided the catalyst for urban growth throughout the United States, and Los Angeles had attracted a number of single young women. Concerned for the welfare of these newcomers, elite women tried to provide a modicum of safety in the often-threatening urban landscape. Using data garnered from their study, a group calling itself the Women's Cooperative Union decided to build a boardinghouse for working women. To raise funds they organized a flower festival, which took on such a positive cachet that the group renamed itself the Flower Festival Society. Beginning in 1885, before the real estate boom in southern California bottomed out, the society succeeded beyond its goals. It gave money to the fledgling Orphans Home, the first Protestant orphanage in the city, founded in 1885 by clubwoman Mary Simon Gibson and her mother-in-law. In 1887 the society opened the newly constructed boardinghouse, a 3-story building with thirty-six apartments. It housed the Women's Exchange to help women find buyers for their wares and the Bureau of Information to assist them in finding jobs.[20]

When Severance returned to Los Angeles in 1887 after another extended absence, she did so with renewed determination to organize a strong women's club. In 1891 she and twenty other women founded the Friday Morning Club (FMC). The city was ready to embrace the new institution.[21] Los Angeles's population had grown to over 50,000 by 1890, a size able to support a thriving women's club. Ten years later, in 1900, over 100,000 people cast their fortunes there, and many more active women were eager to participate in Los Angeles club work. The FMC also benefited from national and state coordination of clubwomen: in 1890 national clubwomen organized the General Federation of Women's Clubs (GFWC) and California women formed the California Federation of Women's Clubs (CFWC).[22] The affiliated members mirrored the members of the NEWC, although some clubs such as the FMC accepted Catholics and Jews. Black women's clubs were excluded after a bitter debate in Los Angeles in 1902.[23]

Severance had done her work well. The FMC became the most effective lobbying organization in the city. For many members, suffrage remained the primary goal, but those who found suffrage too controversial could join and participate in the club's various literary and other purely social activities. Committees were established for specific reforms such as health care, juvenile courts, pure milk legislation, immigrant education, and changes in school programs to provide school lunches, after-school playgrounds, and kindergartens.[24]

Severance nearly served on the school board herself. The opportunity came in August 1891. A board member resigned and Severance and three others, including Margaret Hughes, were nominated to fill the position. At one point Severance had the majority of votes, but a consensus could not be reached. In late September, Hughes appeared the winner, but a contentious argument over the issue of women's eligibility kept the issue up in the air for months. In the end, Hughes took the matter to court and won. An 1874 California state law permitted women to hold school offices, and Hughes took her seat. Whether Severance had aspirations to serve herself or whether she allowed her name to be forwarded in order to assure a woman would be elected is unclear. Whatever the case, clubwomen rejoiced at Hughes's victory.[25]

Severance had more success in bringing kindergartens into the public schools. Her campaign illustrated her driving spirit and organizing skills. It also exemplified her ability as one of the city's elite to use her position to further her causes. Elizabeth Peabody had initiated kindergartens for middle-class children to relieve what freer-thinking, educated people saw as the austerity of most childhood schooling. By the 1870s reformers had begun to view kindergartens as instruments of amelioration and Americanization for poor children, particularly immigrant children. Through the pioneering work of St. Louis superintendent of public schools William Torrey Harris and kindergarten promoter Susan Blow, in 1873 kindergartens reached into slum areas as part of public schooling.[26]

Severance began her Los Angeles kindergarten project for middle-class children before her permanent move there. In 1874 she had arranged with a Boston textbook dealer, a relative, to have a set of German books shipped to California for the kindergarten. Then, in 1876, she enticed Emma Marwedel, a German kindergartner who had studied with Friedrich Frobel and had been brought to the United States by Peabody, to move to Los Angeles. Marwedel had a kindergarten in Washington, DC, where future president James A. Garfield and his wife, Lucretia, Cleveland friends of the Severances, sent their three children.[27]

With Marwedel on her way west, Severance began her search for prospective students for the training college as well as for parents willing to send their children to the new school. She traveled to Santa Barbara and convinced the impressionable Kate Douglas Smith (later Kate Douglas Wiggin) that she was "born" to do pioneer service. Severance made all the arrangements. She found two other young women to sign up for the college, convinced families to put their children in the care of the German teacher, and opened the class with twenty-five children aged five to seven.[28]

The kindergarten itself lasted only two years, but the training school continued its independent operations until the kindergarten curriculum became part of teacher training at the State Normal School at Los Angeles in the 1890s.[29] The failure of the kindergarten class did not discourage Severance from trying again. She changed her tactics so that kindergartens might appeal to middle-class parents as well as to school officials who would incorporate them into city schools.[30] She proposed new kindergartens that would reflect American culture rather than the German traditions of Frobel's schools.

Severance's work for kindergartens fit nicely with her campaign for women's rights. As we have seen, she wanted to put women in policy-making posts in city government and help those few women already in positions to retain them.[31] Severance carried out her political strategy through the women's club. As she had done for the kindergarten training school, she chose the club's key committee members with care. Jane E. Collier was on the Education Committee in 1885 and Caroline wanted her to remain there. Recognizing that there was a "clamor" for Collier on the literature committee, Severance wrote, "I think your place in the Education Committee is equally important" because of "the matter of women on the school board by another election." Moreover, she needed someone she could trust "to take up" some of the "shortcomings" of both private and public kindergartens.[32]

Severance now embarked on her campaign to provide kindergartens to the city's poor through a program of cooperation with public schools. Los Angeles's growth astounded most observers. The number of poor and immigrant children grew apace and made apparent the scarcity of institutions available to assist needy families. To fill the void, the Los Angeles Woman's Club established the Free Kindergarten Association. The Association sponsored a tuition-free kindergarten, supported by donations, in a Protestant church in the poorest area of town. The Los Angeles version was based on San Francisco's Silver Street model, organized in 1878 and superintended by Kate Douglas Wiggin. Reformers saw kindergartens as opportunities to provide the essentials of food, child care, and clothing along with moral training to needy children. Americanized kindergartens also created greater interest among middle-class parents who could afford tuition classes.

Working through the women's club during the summer of 1886, Severance intensified her efforts. She had begun raising funds and had brought wealthy patrons to the "cause," and she began "educating" the public. Dr. Dorothea Rhodes Lummis, a newly arrived physician and wife of the flamboyant newspaperman and self-promoter Charles Lummis, offered her office as a meeting place for the "cause of kindergarten." Severance invited prominent visitors to speak before clubwomen. The speakers included Dr. Horatio Stubbens, the highly regarded minister of San Francisco's First Unitarian Church and a supporter of kindergartens in San Francisco, and Miss Nettie Stewart, a student with Wiggin at Marwedel's school in Los Angeles and later a kindergarten teacher at the state school for the deaf in Berkeley. Severance knew that these speakers would create the publicity to win supporters. Other groups began to follow the FMC's lead in promoting kindergartens. The Woman's Christian Temperance Union, for instance, opened its own tuition-free kindergarten.[33]

Through correspondence with Wiggin, Severance knew of the difficulties in persuading the Board of Education to finance kindergartens. During the past three years, the San Francisco board had cut back the number of public school teachers and reduced their salaries. Yet Wiggin sent her old friend encouragement: "I think you can do more with (the) public school question in Los Angeles than we can here."[34] Wiggin may have been correct because shortly thereafter, Los Angeles initiated a program that provided for public kindergartens in some of the city's poorer districts. This came about because of Severance's work behind the scenes to create willingness at the city level to assume the responsibility for funding such a project.

Severance had kindergarten supporters on the school board. Frank A. Gibson, kindergarten advocate and husband of Mary S. Gibson, served as president. In this capacity Gibson had authority to ensure that, in 1889, a new city charter granted the board power to establish kindergartens. That same year, city bond sales provided the funding.[35] Severance could not hide her pleasure. "We gather once more to congratulate ourselves," she wrote in 1891. Kindergartens were no longer an "experiment rather a natural course of human development."[36]

After the success she had achieved in establishing kindergartens, Severance spent her last years still pushing and prodding through her women's organizations. Women's clubs flourished in California; in fact, nowhere in the entire nation did they prosper more than in Los Angeles. The Friday Morning Club grew into one of the most influential women's clubs in the country. Its more than 2,000 members made it the largest, and it was able to construct an impressive headquarters building near downtown. Severance also founded Los Angeles's second-largest woman's club, the Ebell Club, and served as honorary president of the Equity League and on boards of the Protestant orphanage and settlement houses. A new group, which included men as well, called itself the Severance Club and became a meeting place for the city's Progressives. Severance was in the forefront of a campaign to raise money for a home for the nearly destitute Jessie Frémont and her daughter Elizabeth, much as New England clubwomen raised money to support Harriet Tubman in her old age.[37] She continued her suffrage work and organized and lent support to younger, more vigorous women. She had earlier reconciled with Susan B. Anthony and critics from post–Civil War era suffrage campaign battles, and in 1891 helped to start a new, united effort to enfranchise women, the National Women's Suffrage Association.[38]

Severance's racial views have been called into question concerning the 1902 decision of the General Federation of Woman's Clubs to effectively exclude African American women. The issue was whether to have a general policy for admitting clubs or to allow each state to determine which clubs would be admitted to the federation. The GFWC, with Severance's support, chose the latter. Her decision that the time was not right for social equality makes it hard to spare her criticism, particularly since her record might have led us to expect otherwise. Her abolitionist affiliations in the North, particularly with Garrison, and her work in South Carolina put her with a small segment of white Americans who actively sought to emancipate slaves prior to the Civil War's end. Also, we shall assume for lack of contrary evidence that, as a member of the faculty, she supported admitting the African American child to the Lewis school. We do know that she supported the Fifteenth Amendment even though it would provide African American men but not women the franchise. She took this position over the objections of former allies within the women's movement, in particular Stanton and Anthony, who argued that educated, cultured white women such as themselves deserved the franchise before unlettered black men.[39]

During her years in California, Severance strongly defended Chinese Americans and Japanese Americans against agitators who wished to deport them and ban further immigration from Asia. She extolled their virtues as excellent workers, "faithful, skillful, and greatly needed." Our nation's treaties, she continued, pledged to treat the Chinese and Japanese with the "same right and privileges which we extract from them for ourselves." She questioned the use of the popular cry "America for Americans" as a justification for exclusion: "How soon and how easily we make the most patriotic Americans of these masses when justly treated. Justice and love conquer all men without bloodshed."[40] There is no evidence as to how she treated or regarded the Mexican population, nor what her feelings were toward Jews. Jewish women belonged to the FMC, and she readily accepted banker Isaias W. Hellman's kindergarten sponsorship and later worked with Meyer Lissner on civic matters. Yet in an 1892 letter, Seymour told his mother of his "pleasant month in Santa Cruz though the place was quite crowded with Hebrews."[41] Caroline might not write such things but she may have been in agreement.

In the midst of the GFWC discussion on admitting black clubwomen, Severance might have consulted Ida B. Wells Barnett, well known by 1902 for both her suffrage and antilynching work, but no evidence exists that she did. Instead she wrote to Booker T. Washington, whose stated views on social equality seem not too different from her own. Washington wrote that he refused to discuss the matter since his concerns were with the "larger aspect of the problem of race." Severance may have been concerned with the larger aspects of women's issues, and in 1902 her concerns were with suffrage. Almost all southern clubs and many elsewhere threatened to pull out of the GFWC if African American clubs were admitted. For tactical purposes, Severance would not alienate potential suffrage supporters at this crucial stage of the battle. When the GFWC publicly discussed race and membership of "colored" clubs in 1902, Caroline sided with the majority, and against her daughter, to exclude black women. African American women, now excluded, formed their own organization. They also worked for suffrage but their major focus was on antilynching legislation.[42]

Writing about a different age, but so prophetically, Willie Lee Rose noted that in order for African Americans to achieve full social and civil rights, white Americans would have had to "assume a moral obligation which, in the final event," the majority were "unwilling to discharge." Rose might have been speaking of Severance and most former abolitionists when she wrote of the lack of interest in black Americans at the end of the nineteenth century. The cause of "Negro equality" became "less fashionable." By 1902, Severance had moved beyond the issue to other ones she found more pressing or perhaps more in vogue.[43]

During these years many of Severance's political views had changed. She had rejoiced over Ohioan James A. Garfield's victory in 1880 and after his assassination she remained in contact with his widow. But by the close of the century she grew wary of Republican leadership and moved leftward. It has been suggested that after Theodoric's death in 1894, Caroline became more radical.[44] It may be more accurate to say that a series of circumstances turned her away from conservatives within the Republican Party. By 1906 she endorsed William Jennings Bryan and began referring to herself as a Christian or "opportunity socialist."[45] She spoke out against the city of Los Angeles hosting the naval fleet in 1907 and contended that the $25,000 the city spent on that fete would be better served to feed the unemployed. She detested Theodore Roosevelt's bellicose stance, and openly criticized his views on "race suicide," noting that "when there is peace" women would consent to have children and not fear that their sons "will be cut down in budding manhood."[46] She did not support the national Progressive ticket in 1912, but it is not clear if she supported Woodrow Wilson. She endorsed Cleveland mayor Tom Johnson's plan to help the homeless by giving them city land on which to support themselves by growing food for city institutions. Indeed, she thought well enough of the plan to encourage its implementation in Los Angeles. She worked with Los Angeles Progressives John Randolph Haynes and Meyer Lissner on local reform issues and relied on them to support her projects.[47] Yet it is not clear whether she promoted Hiram Johnson's gubernatorial bid in 1910; his support for women's suffrage was never more than lukewarm. When California women did win the vote in 1911, suffrage leaders honored Severance. She became the first woman in Los Angeles to register to vote and the first woman in the city to vote in a federal election. Friends and supporters throughout the country sent their congratulations for her nearly sixty years of continuous effort for the cause.

Caroline Severance achieved success for many of her most cherished causes and became a living icon of the motherly female reformer. Out of admiration, she was universally addressed as Madame Severance. The clubs she founded, in particular the Friday Morning Club, became centers for a new political culture that bound women together for collaborative goals. Moreover, her activities helped propel California to become a leader of Progressive reform. From the vantage point of the twenty-first century, however, we can see that she was not a perfect model: we find some faults, some lapses. Nevertheless, she came to Los Angeles with an agenda for reform, much of which she executed through her network of women. She died in Los Angeles in 1914, a remarkable woman who should be remembered for her organizational and social skills as well as for her perseverance.

Notes

1. James Seymour Severance to Caroline Severance (hereafter cited as CS), June 19, 1895, Severance Collection, box 1, The Henry E. Huntington Library, San Marino, California (hereafter cited as HEH). Also see Susan B. Anthony to CS, August 29, 1890, Severance Collection, box 14, HEH.

2. Ella Giles Ruddy, *The Mother of Clubs: Caroline M. Seymour Severance* (Los Angeles, 1906), 22–23.

3. Bella Rankin, "Caroline Marie Seymour Severance," *Dictionary of American Biography*, 2 vols. (New York, 1997), 16:599–600; Gayle Gullett, *American National Biography*, 24 vols. (New York, 1999), 19:661–62; Whitney Cross, *The Burnt-Over District: The Social and Intellectual History of Enthusiastic Religion in Western New York, 1800–1850* (Ithaca, 1950), 3, 154, 163.

4. Joan M. Jensen, "After Slavery: Caroline Severance in Los Angeles," *Southern California Quarterly* 48 (June 1966): 178; Ruddy, *The Mother of Clubs*, 55.

5. Theodoric Severance to CS, October 2, 1890, Severance Collection, box 11, HEH.

6. Jensen, "After Slavery," 178.

7. Ibid., 176–77.

8. Willie Lee Rose, *Rehearsal for Reconstruction: The Port Royal Experiment* (New York, 1964), 148–49; Ray Billington, ed., *Journal of Charlotte Forten* (New York, 1964), 149–50, entry for Sunday, December 21, 1862; New England Freedmen's Aid Society, "Extracts from Letters of Teachers and Superintendents of the New England Education Commission for Freedom" (Boston: David Clapp, 1864), 15; Karen Blair, *The Clubwoman as Feminist: True Womanhood Redefined, 1868–1914* (New York, 1980), 34. Blair's book remains the seminal work on women's clubs.

9. Jensen, "After Slavery," 179; Blair, *The Clubwoman as Feminist*, 15–38.

10. Ruddy, *The Mother of Clubs*, 15, 25–26; Blair, *The Clubwoman as Feminist*, 31–38. Julia Ward Howe, the wife of Samuel Gridley Howe, founder of the Perkins Institute for the Blind, is best remembered for writing "Battle Hymn of the Republic."

11. Blair, *The Clubwoman as Feminist*, 31–38; Sara M. Evans, *Born for Liberty: A History of Women in America* (New York, 1989), 105–6.

12. CS to Henry Blackwell, June 22, 1906, Severance Collection, box 26, HEH. Severance had asked Elizabeth Cady Stanton to speak at the Parker Fraternity Association and when Stanton was unable to make it, Severance spoke in her place. She was less than pleased with her performance and later said she suffered "from want of gift of voice." Ruddy, *The Mother of Clubs*, 14

13. Ellen C. DuBois, *Feminism and Suffrage: The Emergence of an Independent and Separate Women's Movement in America, 1848–1869* (Ithaca, 1978), 57, 188–89.

14. Jensen, "After Slavery," 179–80.

15. Ibid., 180–81.

16. Ibid., 181.

17. Judith Raftery, *Land of Fair Promise: Politics and Reform in Los Angeles Schools, 1885–1941* (Stanford, 1992), 14–46.

18. Jensen, "After Slavery," 180–81; CS to M. C. Graham, September 27, 1881, Graham Papers, box 24, HEH; Raftery, *Land of Fair Promise*, 14–46; Gayle Gullett,

Becoming Citizens: The Emergence and Development of the California Women's Movement, 1880–1911 (Urbana, 2000), 28–30.

19. CS to Margaret Collier Graham, July 15, 1885, CS to Jane E. Collier, June 26, 1885, Graham Papers, box 24, HEH; Sherman H. Freeman, "Board of Education-Superintendent Relationships in the Los Angeles City School System, 1853–1920" (Ph.D. diss., University of California, Los Angeles, 1951), 2:661.

20. Gloria Ricci Lothrop, "Strength Made Stronger: The Role of Women in Southern California Philanthropy," *Southern California Quarterly* 71 (Summer–Fall 1989): 144–47; Gullet, *Becoming Citizens*, 27–29.

21. Jensen, "After Slavery," 182; Gullett, *Becoming Citizens*, 29.

22. Mary S. Gibson, compiler, *A Record of Twenty-Five Years of the California Federation of Women's Clubs, 1900–1925* (Los Angeles, 1927), 5.

23. Rosalyn Terborg-Penn, "Discontented Black Feminists: Prelude and Postscript to the Passage of the Nineteenth Amendment," in Kathryn Kish Sklar and Thomas Dublin, eds., *Women and Power in American History: A Reader*, 2 vols. (Englewood Cliffs, NJ, 1991), 2:132–45.

24. Dora Haynes to CS, n.d, n.p., Severance Collection, box 18, HEH; Judith Raftery, "Los Angeles Clubwomen and Political Reform," in William Deverell and Tom Sitton, eds., *California Progressivism Revisited* (Berkeley, 1994), 148.

25. Freeman, "Board of Education-Superintendent Relationships," 1:244–49, 2: 662–65. Hughes served until 1895. It was not until 1910 that another woman was elected to the board. Gullett, *Becoming Citizens*, 30.

26. Raftery, "Los Angeles Clubwomen and Progressive Reform," 147–53; Ruddy, *The Mother of Clubs*, 31–32; Michael Steven Shapiro, *Child's Garden: The Kindergarten Movement from Froebel to Dewey* (University Park, PA, 1983), 29–63.

27. Henry Ivison to CS, January 1, 1874, Severance Collection, box 42, HEH; Fletcher Harper Swift, *Emma Marwedel, 1818–1893: Pioneer of the Kindergarten in California* (Berkeley, 1931), 153–55, 161, 167.

28. Kate Douglas Wiggin, *My Garden of Memory: An Autobiography* (Boston, 1923), 88–105, quote on 91.

29. Swift, *Emma Marwedel*, 153–55, 161, 167; Seymour Severance to CS, November 20, 1893, Severance Collection, box 1, HEH; *History of the Los Angeles State Normal School, Quarter Centennial, 1882–1907*, p. 7, HEH.

30. Shapiro's *Child's Garden*, 1–105, provides a good account of the reasons kindergartens met with resistance prior to the Progressive period.

31. CS to Margaret Collier Graham, September 27, 1881, CS to Margaret Collier Graham, July 15, 1886, Margaret Collier Graham Papers, box 24, HEH. Margaret Graham was a teacher in Los Angeles.

32. CS to Jane E. Collier, June 26, 1885, Graham Papers, box 24, HEH.

33. Ibid.

34. Kate Douglas Wiggin to CS, October 7, 1885, Severance Collection, box 24, HEH.

35. Sherman H. Freeman, "Board of Education-Superintendent Relationships," 1:154, 223. Superintendent of Schools William Friesner had visited a tuition kindergarten his niece attended and apparently had been impressed by what he observed. The bond provided $200,000 to build classrooms, some of which could be used for

kindergartens. Over the next several years ordinances were passed that made it simpler for supporters to organize kindergartens in middle-class school districts as well as in schools for the poor, and the movement flourished. With the signing by Governor Hiram Johnson of the Petition Law in 1913, kindergarten supporters statewide succeeded in the formal incorporation of kindergartens in public schooling by petition. In 1920 kindergartens became part of the state constitution and part of the public school system, thereby obviating the need for a petition. Barbara Greenwood, *History of the Kindergarten Movement in the Western States, Hawaii and Alaska* (Washington, DC, 1940), 23–24.

36. 1891 Kindergarten Meeting, n.p., Severance begins "Dear Friends," Severance Collection, box 26, HEH.

37. Pamela Herr, *Jessie Benton Frémont* (Norman, OK, 1988), 441–42, 446, 450. The Severances were close family friends of Jessie and her daughter. When Jessie died, Seymour Severance acted as pallbearer.

38. Evans, *Born for Liberty*, 152–53. During the years before the groups were reunited, Severance had a cordial relationship with Anthony. CS to Caroline Dall, April 18, 1867 (or April 8), Caroline Dall Papers, Massachusetts Historical Society, Boston, Massachusetts.

39. DuBois, *Feminism and Suffrage*, 174–79.

40. "Casual Comment," n.p., n.d., Severance Collection, box 42, HEH.

41. James Seymour Severance to CS, July 8, 1892, Severance Collection, box 1, HEH.

42. Booker T. Washington to CS, March 5, 1902, Severance Collection, box 24, HEH; Terborg-Penn, "Discontented Black Feminists," 2:132–45; Jensen, "After Slavery," 182–83.

43. Rose, *Rehearsal for Reconstruction*, 433, 409.

44. Jensen, "After Slavery," 183; fifteen letters from Lucretia Rudolph Garfield to CS, 1908–1914, Severance Collection, box 17, HEH.

45. *Los Angeles Record*, May 2, 1906, Severance Collection, box 42, HEH.

46. Clipping file, n.p., n.d., Severance Collection, box 42, HEH.

47. Meyer Lissner to CS, December 23, 1909, Lulu Pile Little to CS, September 9, 1896, Severance Collection, box 20, HEH; Tom Sitton, *John Randolph Haynes, California Progressive* (Stanford, 1992), 30–33, 44; Mari Jo Buhl, *Women and American Socialism, 1870–1920* (Urbana, 1981), 77–78. Buhl refers to Severance as a "proselytizer for Christian Socialism." Severance was one of many vice presidents of the Socialist Reform Union. Severance probably voted against the Socialists in the 1911 Los Angeles election. In that election Republican George Alexander defeated Socialist Job Harriman for mayor.

Suggested Readings

Blair, Karen. *The Clubwoman as Feminist: True Womanhood Redefined, 1868–1914*. New York: Holmes & Meier, 1980.
Deverell, William, and Tom Sitton, eds. *California Progressivism Revisited*. Berkeley: University of California Press, 1994.

DuBois, Ellen C. *Feminism and Suffrage: The Emergence of an Independent and Separate Women's Movement in America, 1848–1869.* Ithaca: Cornell University Press, 1978.

Gullett, Gayle. *Becoming Citizens: The Emergence and Development of the California Women's Movement, 1880–1911.* Urbana: University of Illinois Press, 2000.

Jensen, Joan M. "After Slavery: Caroline Severance in Los Angeles." *Southern California Quarterly* 48 (June 1966).

Lothrop, Gloria Ricci. "Strength Made Stronger: The Role of Women in Southern California Philanthropy." *Southern California Quarterly* 71 (Summer–Fall 1989).

Raftery, Judith. *Land of Fair Promise: Politics and Reform in Los Angeles Schools, 1885–1941.* Stanford: Stanford University Press, 1992.

Sitton, Tom. *John Randolph Haynes, California Progressive.* Stanford: Stanford University Press, 1992.

8

Transforming the "White" Frontier
Cecil B. DeMille and the Origins
of the Hollywood Home

Lary May

When the United States acquired California in 1848 its population encompassed only about 200,000 persons. One hundred and fifty years later, the state boasted 34 million residents. California's phenomenal growth represents, in large part, the extent to which people from around the world have perceived it as a place to better their lives. For some this view has meant greater economic opportunities, for others, better weather, and for still others, a more modern and liberal atmosphere.

Much of California's prominence in both American and global imaginations has resulted from the self-conscious efforts of regional boosters who have skillfully flooded the world with images of "the California dream." Probably the most important factor in the state's cultural power, however, is that since the 1920s, Los Angeles has been home to the nation's film industry. In this essay, University of Minnesota professor of history Lary May explores how the nation's filmmakers came to settle in southern California and build an industry known today simply as "Hollywood." The life and work of one of the great early filmmakers, Cecil B. DeMille, was central to this effort. May argues that the success of DeMille, and of Hollywood itself, came from the way DeMille and his fellow directors were able to promote a new American national identity through their films in the 1910s and 1920s. The DeMille formula suggested that Americans could escape the degradation of work in a corporate society and the threats of social disorder posed by massive immigration and class tensions through participation in a revolution in morals and a new consumer culture. In other words, individual freedoms and republican ideals could be realized through a luxurious private life.

By the 1920s an unprecedented institution—the American film industry—had entered the lives of millions of viewers through lavish theaters in all the major cities of the United States. As fans watched their favorite stories in sumptuous movie houses, they did not simply sit in an oasis of luxury. Rather, with the rise of the consumer economy it was now possible to emulate the life-styles of their favorite actors in the comfort of their own homes. Yet filmgoers needed experts to show them how. In response to that need, the motion picture industry built a film capital in southern California. Other countries had centralized film studios, but in America the site was surrounded by a community where the stars lived the happy endings in full view of their fans. In Hollywood, moviedom became far more than something seen on the screen or touched in the theater. Out West, celebrities refashioned their lives free of Victorian confinements of work and the genteel home, while audiences learned of a new American life-style that modernized the frontier myth itself.

Few people were more important to the rise of Hollywood than Cecil B. DeMille, whose life and work provide a portrait of the film industry in the early twentieth century. From the teens through the 1920s, the man who became known as Mr. Hollywood helped make the film industry big business as he directed more than twenty formula films that modernized and transformed Americans' ideals of individual freedom.

DeMille's origins differ from those of many early Hollywood elites. DeMille was born in the small town of Ashfield, Massachusetts, on August 12, 1881. His father, Henry DeMille, was descended from Huguenot planters in South Carolina. Coming north to New York City, Henry graduated from Columbia University and took orders in the Episcopal priesthood. By the 1880s he had shed his clerical collar and turned to a much wider pulpit of university teaching and the stage. On Broadway, Henry wrote melodramas geared to the Fifth Avenue rich and joined in partnership with the Broadway impresario, David Belasco. After gaining much success on the stage, he married a young woman named Beatrice from a German Jewish family, who soon converted to Christianity. Henry and Beatrice had two sons, William and Cecil. They raised their sons in the Christian faith, including daily Bible readings as well as wide exposure to art and politics. Reformer Henry George, known nationally for his advocacy of a single tax on land, visited frequently, and Cecil's brother William ultimately married George's daughter.

As a boy, Cecil tried to enlist to fight in the Spanish-American War but was rejected because he was too young. His mother then enrolled him in an art school in New York City where he would meet his future wife, Constance Adams. At the age of eighteen, Cecil began an acting career. It was in his role as an actor that Cecil met Jesse Lasky, who began to turn his interests toward the new art form of moving pictures. In 1912, DeMille and Laskey founded a movie company and went west to Los Angeles. There they joined with Adolph Zukor in founding Famous Players, which became the foundation for Paramount Pictures, the major film studio of the 1920s.

DeMille's influence on the rise of the film industry proved legendary. At a time when writers and politicians alike feared that the rise of

From the *Los Angeles Examiner*, Hearst Newspaper Collection, Department of Special Collections, University of Southern California Library. *Courtesy of the University of Southern California on behalf of the University of Southern California Specialized Libraries and Archival Collections*

big business was undermining individual economic independence, when social moralists complained that immigrants of eastern and southern European stock threatened the nation's cultural unity, when urbanites experimented with a revolution in morals, and when civic leaders feared that class conflict threatened the nation's social and political stability, Hollywood, best epitomized in the films of DeMille, offered a utopia where these problems could be overcome. DeMille's answer in film after film was that liberty and happiness could continue to be found in modern society, but they were now best realized in leisure rather than work.[1]

Los Angeles provided an ideal locale for linking DeMille with others to develop a new understanding of American national identity. By the time the film industry developed in Los Angeles, California had already become a central symbol in American culture as the nation's rich and expansive frontier. Ever since the nineteenth century, the West had symbolized for most whites a virgin landscape where liberation from the Old World occurred. In fact, as white Americans moved west and displaced Indians, they acquired vast tracts of cheap land that allowed many to become independent producers, free of monopoly capitalism. In this environment, according to the prevailing myth, men could realize the dream of a virtuous republic where the class and racial conflicts that plagued Europe and the eastern United States were put aside for a more glorious future.[2] Yet late in the nineteenth century a crisis occurred in the republican ideal of democracy. To begin with, many observers feared that the frontier was disappearing. Over the formerly sacred landscape, ominous forces threatened what many Americans believed to be a homogenous Anglo-Saxon republic. As big corporations acquired seemingly invincible power and a rich elite flaunted what seemed to be grotesque wealth, middle-class Americans responded by forming the Progressive movement to break up business trusts and restore republican ideals.

The conflict between economic and cultural reform, however, yielded a paradox. Although on economic issues Progressives sympathized with the polyglot working class, their nativism and ethnocentrism prevented any real alliance across the racial divide. Instead, their cultural aversion to immigrants and persons of color meant that the middle classes aligned with the wealthy to protect the nation's Anglo-Saxon character by repressing class conflict, by passing Prohibition, and by enacting a series of racially biased restrictions on immigration.[3] In the end, many Progressives thus allied with what they had initially set out to reform—

corporate interests and the social elite. Americans thus found themselves even more ensconced within a stifling new corporate order.

Amid this dilemma, Hollywood filmmakers such as DeMille directed middle-class ambitions for individual freedom away from the economic or public spheres and toward a moral revolution through mass culture. This culture, however, had its roots in the lower classes, and thus it was no easy task to make this a new middle-class ideal. In the Victorian codes that DeMille's middle-class characters inherited, the private life centered in the white citizen's home provided the basis for self-control. Expressive sexuality and desire were linked to the degraded world of racial and ethnic minorities. In order to avoid fears of "mongrelization"— the mixing of the races that presumably lowered the quality of Western civilization—DeMille encouraged audiences to redefine private life to uplift and whiten the forbidden "black" impulses. Whatever the economic and political perils of the modern age, his characters showed how white Americans could focus their quest for pleasure on refined homes modeled on aristocrats' visions of play and leisure. And the place where that became real unfolded in the new film capital. Yet what was Hollywood, and how did DeMille give form and meaning to this merger of art and life?

Los Angeles Progressives and the Myth of the West

Before turning to DeMille's creative work and exploring how he and the larger community of Hollywood aided in the creation of a new national identity, it is crucial to understand why DeMille and other filmmakers set up shop in Los Angeles and found it such an ideal locale for solving the crisis of Progressive reform. First, there was nothing predetermined about the move of the industry from east to west, since movie producers had been centered in the East ever since the 1890s. In explaining the magnitude of this change, some writers stress that filmmakers found in Los Angeles the mild weather and diverse topography that provided numerous venues for year-round film production. Others argue that to escape an eastern trust that monopolized patents on cameras, rebel producers came to the West to avoid court orders and escape prosecution, if necessary, by crossing the border to Mexico. Still others suggest that producers involved in building large, integrated corporations were attracted by Los Angeles's antilabor policies, which allowed them to crush unions and minimize labor costs.

A sober second look, however, suggests that none of these factors alone determined the move. For one thing, film producers had survived eastern weather for well over twenty years, and when conditions required, they had easily traveled to Florida, the Caribbean, and western states. In addition, the first movie makers to relocate were not independents fleeing the patent trust, but established trust members. And if proximity to Mexico had been the factor, independents would have settled in San Diego, a good 200 miles closer to the border. Further, while there is no doubt that the producers appreciated the favorable antiunion climate in Los Angeles, hostility to unions was by no means unique to the area. It also existed in the East.[4]

No, something else drew moviemakers to Los Angeles: the region provided a locale to link moviemaking with revitalizing the frontier myth in the twentieth century. To gain perspective it is well to remember that in Los Angeles, as in the nation, a Protestant middle class equated the West with forging the ideal of republican freedom in work and politics. Carrying that ideal to the West, they saw themselves improving the natural environment. City leaders used technology to overcome the acute problems of the lack of a natural harbor and lack of water by building the Owens River Aqueduct and the San Pedro Harbor in 1913. As technology made it possible for local business to expand beyond its agrarian roots, boosters lured people with the promise of escape from the problems of the East. "Here were 50,000 people," wrote a promoter, "suddenly gathered together from all parts of the union, in utter ignorance of one another's history. It was a golden opportunity for the fakir and the humbug and the man with a past he wished forgotten."[5]

Once in Los Angeles, the newcomers worked to create an Anglo-Saxon republic free of the markers and memories of earlier settlers. While the Mexican population had once dominated civic affairs and sponsored workers' saloons and festivals like the Day of the Dead and carnival, white newcomers used their political power to attack these traditions and practices. Since well over 60 percent of Los Angeles's population by 1910 came from the Midwest, these newcomers quickly gained political control. A local elite aligned with the Protestant churches used the Republican Party to pass laws closing the lowbrow saloons and legitimizing public recreation focused around segregated suburbs, parks, and beaches. Running parallel with these uplift efforts, reformers initiated nonpartisan elections that undercut Mexican and working-class wards, ensuring recreation and citywide organizations that institutionalized Anglo-Saxon practices as the universal norm.[6]

The promotion of institutions to forge an Anglo-Saxon polity also converged with reformers' goals of saving the democratic West from the threat of big business and labor strife. Similar to Progressives nationwide, Los Angeles leaders desired to retain the control over work that lay at the heart of republican ideals and the mythic West. To restore that vision, reformers mobilized against the Southern Pacific Railroad, which dominated City Hall. Yet as they took power, the Anglo community followed national trends in that they did not form cross-class coalitions with labor unions or with Mexican politicians. Instead they pointed with scorn toward San Francisco, where immigrants and labor unions controlled politics. Seeking to "Americanize" Los Angeles, reformers coalesced with corporate leaders to wage militant war against unions, Socialist parties, and working-class politicians. That battle climaxed when two radicals admitted to bombing the *Los Angeles Times* building in 1910. Civic leaders used the ensuing panic to attack strikers and impose antiunion codes. By the 1920s the Chamber of Commerce proudly boasted that the area had weak unions and low labor costs.[7]

Within this context, filmmakers moving west found Los Angeles Progressives' efforts a perfect shield to advance their economic interests. A prime example of how these converging political and economic factors interacted with the emerging film industry can be discerned in the career of a local reformist politician, landholder, and head of the state real estate board. As the population grew sixfold, Harry Culver accumulated a fortune by encouraging land speculation and moviemaking. The formula was quite simple: Culver saw that movies brought more people who bought more homes from his company. To this end, Culver initially gave real estate tracts to a member of the moviemaking trust, Triangle Studios, headed by Harry Aitken. When independent companies like Metro-Goldwyn-Mayer bought the old Triangle studios, they constructed an enormous complex complete with a Corinthian gate and huge Grecian facades. As the ambitious Harry saw no contradiction in naming the new area Culver City, moviemakers found the partnership ideal. It did not matter to them that Los Angeles lacked an industrial base. Making reels of celluloid did not require nearby mining, steel mills, or even processing plants. All moviemakers of ambition needed were a good camera, a location site, laborers, and an intercontinental railroad system that allowed them to ship the product to the East. Little wonder that Samuel Goldwyn explained that he came west because "Los Angeles is more efficient for us, more cheap. In Manhattan the movie waits on the community and not the community on the movie. Los Angeles has no other interest save real estate and climate. The climate takes care of itself, and we keep the real estate booming, so Los Angeles gives us all her interests and resources."[8]

Los Angeles also provided moviemakers with the opportunity to Americanize what many saw as a disreputable industry. To begin with, the producers who founded Hollywood were mainly the children of Jewish immigrants who saw that free land, low taxes, and an antiunion environment allowed them to build large, monopolistic firms. And since in the East the film industry had been associated with lowbrow entertainment, unfit for the middle class, Los Angeles provided a place where the immigrant producers linked the industry with the ideals of Progressive reform. Along these lines, William McAdoo, former secretary of the treasury in Woodrow Wilson's cabinet, was named the president of United Artists. Similarly, Joseph Tumulty, Wilson's key aide, became the counsel for the Motion Picture Producers and Distributors Association, while Will Hays, the Republican Party chairman in 1920, became the industry's chief executive, charged with both coordinating the industry and enforcing censorship. As the strict censor for the industry, Hays eliminated images of class conflict and made what he called "passionate but pure" films. As an example of the industry's increasing respectability, the major film star of the day, Mary Pickford, was known to entertain President Wilson's daughter at her Hollywood home, "Pickfair."[9]

On another level, however, Los Angeles offered a new vision of the West to overcome a dilemma that reformers repressed in their public rhetoric. One could discern that ambiguity at a conference held at the Harvard Business School to celebrate the film industry's arrival into the new economic order. Sponsored in the mid-1920s by Joseph Kennedy, a film executive and father of the future president, the conference featured several studio leaders who explained how they created large firms that furthered the goals of progress. However, an actor, Stephan Stills, noted that it would be a mistake to believe that movies were like previous business enterprises. On the contrary, movies made money because they satisfied psychic needs unaddressed in public. The people felt stifled, explained Stills, because "monotonous work" pervaded their lives. In response, the movies had become an "indispensable industry" because "never before in the history of civilization has there been felt such a need for entertainment. It is a disquieting fact that very few of the men and women who do the world's work find compensating joy in that work. Sadly enough, it lacks enjoyment. It has become standardized and specialized. The jobs of the factory workers and the shop girls, the clerks and the miners, are all routine jobs; they represent so much drudgery."[10]

DeMille and the Crisis of the Democratic Ego

Exactly how could these anxieties be placated? What form and style emerged on the screen to address these issues? Hollywood developed so rapidly and in such stunning fashion during the 1910s and 1920s because it provided Americans answers to these pronounced cultural dilemmas. And no one in Hollywood did more in this regard than Cecil B. DeMille. His first film, *The Squaw Man* (1914), began one of the most prolific and successful careers in moviemaking history. During the silent era, he would direct at least one film per year, ultimately creating fifty-two silent films between 1913 and 1928.

DeMille and his studio, Paramount Pictures, where he did most of his work, helped to construct a new corporate order in public life. DeMille's films showed how the middle class could recover freedom within the private domain—a process that set the tone for the concern with life-style that would inform twentieth-century culture. Over and over, DeMille's heroes and heroines were the model Victorian man and woman who provided, in the eyes of middle-class opinion makers, the moral order for the nation. They believed in the rational domination of nature and self-control over animal instincts. In private life they validated a domesticity whereby Caucasian women remained virgins or mothers, free of sensuality. Carrying these moral ideals into politics, DeMille's protagonists labored to eliminate corrupt politicians associated with racial and ethnic minorities and decadent businessmen.

Nonetheless, if DeMille's characters embodied the model citizen, they also gave clear expression to the repressed anxiety lying at the core of reform. The problem was that as his protagonists exerted considerable business and political power, they found that they built their own cage. In response to the loss of power, they sought freedom in pleasures that the middle-class moralists associated with the degraded bodies and low amusements of racial minorities and the working class. In the Progressive Era, that situation was highly problematic. Take DeMille's *The Squaw Man*. It charted the discontent of a man bored with his refined home and increasingly routinized office work. The protagonist goes west for freedom. But while in the past the good citizen could find on the frontier the opportunity to master nonwhites and exert control over work, the DeMille hero looks across racial boundaries for personal freedom by falling in love with an Indian maiden. Why? She offered him far more "red-blooded" primitivism than his genteel sweetheart. Yet his move also threatened his psychic equilibrium. Only when the squaw man marries his lady Diana, after all, does stability return. When he leaves behind his Indian maiden, the native girl then commits suicide, eliminating traces of race mixing. In this way, DeMille's early films dramatized that to attain success, men had to restore white Victorian codes.

After World War I and the end of reform, DeMille's productions showed how one might sanction dark desires within what he called the "the bonds that the Bible has lain down." That is, normative marriage could be the vehicle for learning that "the breaking of the law . . . comes from adultery, not sex."[11] With titles like *Old Wives for New* (1918), *Don't Change Your Husband* (1919), *Male and Female* (1919), *Why Change Your Wife* (1920), and *Forbidden Fruit* (1921), DeMille's films showcased characters who inherited the fruits of reform and material success. Increasingly restless in a business world ruled by the boss, they turned to mass amusements where the moral heroes encountered "jazz babies" and Asiatic lovers and asked their wives to become more sensual and playful in the home.

Around that axis, however, lay peril and promise. At first the wives rejected the men's "Oriental ideas" and "physical music." Soon the frustrated husbands left, proclaiming, "I want a sweetheart, not a governess." In answer, modern wives scurried to dressmakers, declaring, "I've been foolish enough to think a man wants a wife decent and honest. Make my dresses sleeveless, backless, and transparent. Go the limit—thank God, I'm still young." With that choice, the characters found that the dangers multiplied. As husbands and wives altered their appearance with stylish clothes, they learned that mingling in mass amusements is a "Golden Calf which makes the feast of Babylon look like a cafeteria." Alienated men fell prey to dark nightclub dancers like Satin Synne, who told her lovers that the "Devil is not a man but a woman, and that's what every woman knows but is afraid to tell." Similarly, wives found that their attraction to foreign and Asiatic gigolos, as in *The Cheat* (1915), led to mongrelization.

The key to the DeMille formula film was that the characters eventually sanctioned their desires in the white home, a process seen in *The Affairs of Anatol* (1921). Once again a married couple frequents nightclubs where the "management is not responsible for lost husbands." There the husband meets an old school chum, "sweet as a flower" in the old days, but now a hot "jazz baby" with bobbed hair, short skirts, and a loving smile. Since Anatol's wife cannot get into the "swing of it," he tries to liberate the "jazz baby" from a big-spending, dark businessman who is a "man of iron downtown, but a man of dough in the night-clubs." Yet no sooner does the husband succeed with the "jazz baby" than he finds that, try as he may to build a "temple to God," he finds one built "by the Devil nearby." Anatol discovers that his young lover reverts to smoking, partying, and dancing to black music. In a fit of anger, he tells her that she "can have blue-black diamonds" but her soul is "as black as ink." To restore order, Anatol proclaims that "if this is the gay life, I'm going back to my wife." This is not the wife of old, how-ever. Anatol finds his former wife in a nightclub where she has become sexually alluring. As they fall in love again, the finale shows them enjoy-ing the new style at home. There the wife puts a jazz record on a phono-graph and dances the Charleston in a refined, private home uplifted to include play.[12]

The happy ending thus advances a fresh code of success. The mod-ern hero will continue to pursue success within a large organization that stifles creativity but supplies the money for consumer goods. Eman-cipation of the opposite sex means that the woman finds a prosperous man who will purchase the luxury items necessary for raising sexuality from its association with degraded minorities. Best of all, if they had envied the wealthy, they now find that the acquisition of goods mod-eled on the styles of the rich also allows them to become the equal in leisure, if not in work or political power, to the rich.

The Twentieth-Century Frontier: Hollywood and Its Discontent

What made the DeMille formula so important was that the happy ending did not remain a screen fantasy alone. It also became real on the new frontier of Hollywood. Here the film industry was far more than a business enterprise in quest of free land, cheap labor, and low costs. On the contrary, studio publicists proclaimed that the stars found in Los Angeles the ideal locale for sanctioning a revolution in morals modeled on the styles of the rich. In areas like Brentwood and Beverly Hills, the heroine in DeMille's epics, Gloria Swanson, married a European aristo-crat, emulating the patterns of the eastern elites. Mary Pickford told reporters gathered around the tennis courts at Pickfair that "maybe this summer I will take a vacation, but if I do it will be right here in Los Angeles. I can't see why anyone would leave Los Angeles for a vacation."[13]

DeMille's life at times seemed as glamorous as the lives of his stars. He and his wife Constance had four children, three of whom were adopted, and together they enjoyed enormous status and wealth. In addition to his filmmaking, DeMille engaged in numerous other business pursuits. He founded an aviation company, held executive positions at two major banks, and headed a lucrative real estate syndicate in the San Fernando Valley that earned him millions.

Fan magazines spread the glitz of the Hollywood life-style to millions of fans with articles like "Everybody's Doin' It Now." A photograph accompanying the article showed a young star, Bessie Love, dancing in her luxurious Hollywood home to jazz and the rhythms of the Charleston. As Bessie gyrated wildly to black music in a tight-fitting dress, her lavish home signaled that money and elegant taste made it all right. Capturing the appeal of the new West, a scenarist of immigrant, working-class background noted that in Hollywood she suddenly found: "My lifelong hatred of the rich and successful turned to servile gratitude for their friendliness. In my eagerness to be like them, with the ardor of a convert to new faith, I repudiated all that I had been. The poor I thought were too submerged in their own fight for bread to indulge in the amenities of life. This was Zion on earth."[14]

We should remember, however, that the attraction of Zion did not emerge from a vacuum. It interacted with the birth of a mass-production economy geared to the promotion of consumer goods. As the working world for workers and the bourgeoisie became more rationalized, moviemakers and advertisers became aware that popular films set styles for the purchase of goods in department stores and from mail-order houses worldwide. This transformation was not part of a deep conspiracy, nor had the populace in the most racially diverse society in the Western world given up on the hard struggle to earn a living. The rise of Hollywood, however, signaled that for the successful, fulfillment could be found in the private domains of sex and consumerism. Commenting on the wider implications of that process, the president of the industry's major trade association, Will Hays, noted in the mid-1920s: "More and more is the motion picture being recognized as a stimulant to trade. No longer does the girl in Sullivan, Indiana, guess what the styles are going to be in three months. She knows because she sees them on the screen. . . . The head of the house sees a new golf suit. The housewife sees a lamp of new design and down they go to the dealers to ask for the new goods."[15]

Despite the views of businesspeople and civic leaders, it is well known that frontiers have also been known to generate their own counter-narratives that turn upside-down the wishes of those in power. Hollywood in the 1920s proved no exception to that rule. Famed sociologists and historians such as Helen and Robert Lynd and Charles and Mary Beard charged that movies masked the growing inequalities of power and wealth in the 1920s. Others claimed that highbrow models of Western civilization promoted by Hollywood meant that America remained a cultural colony of Europe. At the grass roots, those critics willing to look could find hope. Young women in New York City purchased high heels and extravagant hats popularized by film stars, but they also launched strikes against factory owners to seek higher wages with which to obtain the goods promoted on the screen. Similarly, immigrants and Americans of color in large cities reinterpreted film images to serve their own resistance to Anglo-Saxon nativism. Within Hollywood itself, Charlie Chaplin's *City Lights* (1929) dramatized how a poor tramp finds that the wealthy, as in a DeMille film, turn to lower-class amusements for revitalization. But as the wealthy find liberation in nightclubs and play, they also reject the economic needs of the people, a process that reveals the limits of the consumer ethos.[16]

Once the even starker limits of the new economy were revealed in the Great Depression, however, the subversive potential centered in Hollywood came into full flower. With the old order in disarray, DeMille's films went into a sharp decline. Audiences quickly turned to stars like the part-Cherokee Indian Will Rogers, who embodied a counter-narrative of the frontier in his real life. Rogers's films attacked the high-brow consumer ideals to show that "equality" with the rich was a farce. His characters reinvented republican codes to restore control over work and form alliances between the middle and the working classes. Without rejecting the desire for a revolution in morals or the desire for affluence, Rogers linked moviemaking with an alternative American identity rooted in the vernacular arts of a polyglot people. Soon others followed suit with productions that laid the foundation for a more inclusive New Deal culture and labor movement in Hollywood and the nation. How that shift accomplished what DeMille saw as impossible—the attainment of a more just and inclusive society—is another story for another time. What is of note here is that the modern frontier of Hollywood created in the 1920s continued to be a focal point for struggles over the quality of national identity and politics throughout the century.[17]

While DeMille did not enjoy the same level of success in the sound era as he had in the silent era, he was one of the few major directors to enjoy a long and active career in each. He ultimately produced eighteen sound films, most of which were major historical or biblical epics. His most noted sound films include *Cleopatra* (1934), *The Greatest Show on Earth* (1951), and *The Ten Commandments* (1954), which was DeMille's last film. He died five years after making it, at the age of seventy-seven, and for many of us he remains Mr. Hollywood to this day.

Notes

1. Full descriptions and analyses of DeMille's films can be found in Sumiko Higashi, *Cecil B. DeMille and American Culture: The Silent Film Era* (Berkeley, 1994); Steven J. Ross, *Working-Class Hollywood: Silent Film and the Shaping of Class in America* (Princeton, 1998), 173–211; and Lary May, *Screening Out the Past: The Birth of Mass Culture and the Motion Picture Industry* (Chicago, 1983), 200–236.

2. For discussions of the frontier as myth in American life, see David W. Noble, *The End of American History: Democracy, Capitalism, and the Metaphor of Two Worlds in Anglo-American Historical Writing* (Minneapolis, 1985). For "whiteness" as central to the frontier and national identity, see Alexander Saxton, *The Rise and Fall of the White Republic: Class Politics and Mass Culture in the Nineteenth Century* (London, 1991); and David Roediger, *The Wages of Whiteness: Race and the Making of the American Working Class* (London, 1991).

3. George Mowry, *The California Progressives* (Berkeley, 1951).

4. Arthur Knight, *The Liveliest Art: A Panoramic History of the Movies* (New York, 1957), 51–54. For an economic interpretation, see Robert Sklar, *Movie Made America: A Cultural History of American Movies* (New York, 1975), 67–69; Ross, *Working-Class Hollywood*, 312–40.

5. Robert M. Fogelson, *The Fragmented Metropolis: Los Angeles, 1850–1930* (Cambridge, 1968); Carey McWilliams, *Southern California Country* (New York, 1946). The quote is from Charles D.Willard, *A History of the Chamber of Commerce of Los Angeles, California* (Los Angeles, 1899), 25.

6. Mowry, *The California Progressives*, 6–7; Gregory Singleton, "Religion in the City of Angels: American Protestant Culture and the Urbanization of Los Angeles, 1850–1930" (Ph.D. diss., University of California, Los Angeles, 1976).

7. Mowry, *The California Progressives*, 87, 90–97. A discussion of these trends nationally can be found in James Weinstein, *The Corporate Ideal in the Liberal State, 1900–1918* (Boston, 1968).

8. See Harry Culver's obituary, *Los Angeles Times*, August 18, 1946; the Goldwyn quote appears in *The Motion Picture Herald*, October 19, 1918.

9. Ross, *Working-Class Hollywood*,114–43; May, *Screening Out the Past*, 167–236.

10. Joseph Kennedy, ed., *The Story of the Films* (New York, 1927), 55–58, 175–90.

11. Plot descriptions and the DeMille formula can be gleaned from Gene Ringgold and Dewitt Bodeen, *The Films of Cecil B. DeMille* (Secaucus, NJ, 1969), 27, 41, 95,

99; Adela Rogers St. John, "What Marriage Means, As Told by Cecil B. DeMille," *Photoplay* (December 1920): 29–31.

12. All the cited films can be found in Ringgold and Bodeen, *Films of Cecil B. DeMille*, and at the Museum of Modern Art Film Library, New York, New York.

13. "Movie Royalty Homes in California," *Photoplay* (June 1915): 123–28; George Ade, "Answering Wild-Eyed Questions about the Movie Stars in Hollywood," *American Magazine* (May 1922): 52.

14. "Fannie Ward's New Home," *Photoplay* (January 1919): 78–79; "Everybody's Doin' It Now, Bessie Love Shows You How," *Photoplay* (October 1925): 32–34; Anzie Yezerska, *Red Ribbon on a White Horse* (New York, 1950), 51.

15. William Harrison Hays, "Supervision from Within," in Kennedy, *The Story of the Films*, 33–40.

16. Robert S. Lynd and Helen Merrell Lynd, *Middletown: A Study in American Culture* (New York, 1929), 251–315. *City Lights* (1930) is available on video; see Leonard Maltin, *1999 Movie and Video Guide* (New York, 1999), 244. On blacks using films to suit their own purposes, see Mary Carbine, "The Finest Outside the Loop: Motion Picture Exhibition in Chicago's Black Metropolis, 1905-1928," *Camera Obscura*, 23 (May 1990): 284–99; and for immigrants see Lizabeth Cohen, *Making a New Deal: Industrial Workers in Chicago, 1919-1939* (New York, 1990), 99–159; Junko Ogihara, "The Exhibition of Films for Japanese Americans in Los Angeles during the Silent Film Era," *Film History* 4, no. 2 (1990): 123–42. On women, see Nan Enstad, *Ladies of Labor, Girls of Adventure: Working Women, Popular Culture, and Labor Politics at the Turn of the Century* (New York, 1999), especially 161–205.

17. On the change in Hollywood culture and politics in the 1930s, see Lary May, *The Big Tomorrow: Hollywood and the Politics of the American Way* (Chicago, 2000).

Suggested Readings

Enstad, Nan. *Ladies of Labor, Girls of Adventure: Working Women, Popular Culture, and Labor Politics at the Turn of the Century.* New York: Columbia University Press, 1999.

Higham, Charles. *Cecil B. DeMille.* New York: Charles Scribner's Sons, 1973.

May, Lary. *Screening Out the Past: The Birth of Mass Culture and the Motion Picture Industry.* Chicago: University of Chicago Press, 1983.

———. *The Big Tomorrow: Hollywood and the Politics of the American Way.* Chicago: University of Chicago Press, 2000.

McWilliams, Carey. *Southern California Country.* New York: Duell, Sloan & Pearce, 1946.

Noble, David W. *The End of American History: Democracy, Capitalism, and the Metaphor of Two Worlds in Anglo-American Historical Writing.* Minneapolis: University of Minnesota Press, 1985.

Ross, Steven J. *Working-Class Hollywood: Silent Film and the Shaping of Class in America.* Princeton: Princeton University Press, 1998.

Be free

9

John Steinbeck
On the Road to The Grapes of Wrath

Charles Wollenberg

When the U.S. stock market collapsed in October 1929, California investors were as stung as any in the nation. Wild speculation in California oil shares had been one of the market's most active sectors in the 1920s, and its collapse hurt thousands of investors. The ensuing Great Depression similarly hit the state hard, with unemployment there often surpassing the national average in the early 1930s.

Californians responded to the catastrophe with numerous social and political crusades, several of which caught national attention. Long Beach physician Francis Townsend started a campaign to provide every American with a retirement pension; muckraker Upton Sinclair ran a celebrated though ultimately unsuccessful gubernatorial race in 1934 on the pledge to End Poverty in California (EPIC); and farmworkers throughout the Central Valley organized powerful unions that became models for those in other states.

The depression witnessed a recurring theme in California history: in times of economic distress, wealthy and middle-class whites have often targeted other groups as objects of blame. One-half million Mexican Americans, of whom many were U.S. citizens, were forcibly repatriated to Mexico during the depression, Filipino farmworkers experienced tremendous violence and even deportation, and poor migrants from the country's Dust Bowl region in the Southwest were often vilified and at times turned away. In this essay, Vista Community College professor of history Charles Wollenberg explores the life of John Steinbeck, whose 1939 novel *The Grapes of Wrath* focused on the Okies' desperate plight. Few novelists have been able to claim such immediate political impact for their work. Steinbeck's powerful text brought considerable attention to the Okies' situation and reshaped policy debates about the problems of all people scarred by the depression.

John Steinbeck wrote his masterpiece, *The Grapes of Wrath*, in 1939, dedicating it to "Carol, who willed this book," and to "Tom, who lived it." "Carol" was Carol Henning Steinbeck, the author's wife; "Tom" was Tom Collins, manager of a federal migrant labor camp in the California Central Valley.[1] Steinbeck had met Collins three years earlier, in

1936, shortly after the *San Francisco News* hired the author to write a series of articles entitled "Harvest Gypsies" (originally published in the *San Francisco News*, October 5–12, 1936). While accompanying Steinbeck on a tour of the Hoovervilles and Little Oklahomas of rural California, Collins provided him with much of the in-depth knowledge that makes this series compelling reading even fifty years after the fact. In the process, Tom Collins helped launch John Steinbeck on a personal and literary journey that would lead to the publication of *The Grapes of Wrath*, the most important novel of the Great Depression.[2]

As both a novel and a popular movie, *The Grapes of Wrath* seared the American consciousness. The book followed the fictional Joad family and their fellow Okies on their epic migration from the Dust Bowl state of Oklahoma to the agricultural valleys of California. It described the family's desperate struggle to survive as migrant farmworkers and portrayed the Okies as members of a heroic rural proletariat. The story of John Steinbeck's collaboration with Tom Collins gives us a unique perspective on the making of this major and enduring American novel. It also provides a look at the life and times of California's most famous author and an insight into the social and political reality of rural California during the very hard times of the 1930s.

Steinbeck received the *News*'s offer to chronicle the "harvest gypsies" just as he was experiencing some long-delayed fame and fortune. Born in Salinas in 1902, he grew up in a solid middle-class household. His father was a businessman who eventually became the elected treasurer of Monterey County. His mother was a former schoolteacher, and she introduced young John to the world of books at an early age. Steinbeck dreamed of becoming a writer while still at Salinas High School. He followed that dream at Stanford, eventually leaving the university in 1925 without a degree.[3]

In the years that followed, Steinbeck failed to make a living as a writer and was forced to take short-term jobs and accept financial support from his family. For much of this period, he lived at his parents' weekend cottage in Pacific Grove, often hanging out with members of the Monterey Peninsula's literary bohemia. He cultivated a friendship with Ed Ricketts, who operated a marine biology laboratory on Monterey's Cannery Row. Ricketts had a major influence on Steinbeck's life and intellectual development and appears in three of his novels as the character "Doc." By the early 1930s, Steinbeck had matured into a big, rough-hewn man who masked his considerable sensitivities and insecurities behind a gruff, hard-drinking exterior.

Courtesy of the Bancroft Library, University of California, Berkeley

With the publication of *Tortilla Flat* in 1935, Steinbeck's fortunes finally changed. In this funny, satirical novel about a group of down-and-out Mexican Americans, Steinbeck turned to his roots in the Salinas Valley and Monterey. The book was immensely popular, although it was criticized by middle-class Monterey burghers who objected to its offbeat depiction of their community and, in later years, by Chicano activists who believed it played on unfavorable Latino stereotypes.

By the time *Tortilla Flat* was published, Steinbeck was at work on a far more serious book. He had met an organizer for the Communist Party's Cannery and Agricultural Workers Industrial Union, which in 1933 had launched an ambitious though ultimately unsuccessful attempt to organize California farm laborers. Steinbeck used the organizer's experiences as the basis for *In Dubious Battle*, a grim story of a farmworkers' strike. The book was generally well received, in spite of growers' criticisms of its pro-worker perspective and radicals' unease at its less-than-flattering portrayal of Communist organizers. *In Dubious Battle* established John Steinbeck's reputation as a serious writer with expertise on farm labor matters.

Steinbeck had met George West, an editor for the *San Francisco News*, some years earlier at the Carmel home of the noted radical journalist, Lincoln Steffens. After *In Dubious Battle* was published, West asked the writer to do a series on the Dust Bowl migration then sweeping through rural California. From 1935 to 1938, between 300,000 and 500,000 Okies arrived in California. Poverty, land foreclosures, and drought forced them out of Lower Plains states such as Texas, Arkansas, Missouri, and, of course, Oklahoma. Ironically, federal programs designed to help farmers also contributed to the migration. The government paid property owners to take land out of production, thus displacing thousands of unneeded tenant farmers and sharecroppers.[4]

Steinbeck eagerly accepted the offer to chronicle the Okies' plight and in the summer of 1936 began touring the state's agricultural valleys in an old bakery truck. The federal Resettlement Administration, a New Deal agency that was beginning to establish camps for migrant workers, was looking for favorable publicity and assigned a staff member to accompany the author. It was at the agency's Weedpatch Camp at Arvin, in Kern County, that Steinbeck first encountered Tom Collins.

Collins became the model for the fictional Jim Rawley, manager of the government's Wheatpatch Camp in *The Grapes of Wrath*. Ma Joad, matriarch of the Okie family whose experiences form the core of the novel, saw Rawley as a "little man dressed all in white . . . a man with a thin, brown, lined face and merry eyes. He was lean as a picket. His white clean clothes were frayed at the seams."[5] Steinbeck described the real-life Collins similarly, adding that he looked "tired beyond sleepiness, the kind of tired that won't let you sleep even if you have time and a bed." Collins had previously been a teacher on Guam, the director of a school for delinquent boys, and a social worker for the Federal Transient Service, which dispensed emergency relief in the early depression years. He joined the Resettlement Administration in 1935, managing the agency's first migrant camp at Marysville. When Steinbeck met him, he was in the process of establishing the Resettlement Administration's second facility, at Arvin. Jackson Benson, Steinbeck's major biographer, called Collins "an idealist, a utopian reformer, a romantic, yet also a good administrator."[6]

Steinbeck stayed at Weedpatch Camp for several days, talking to residents, attending camp committee meetings and dances, and watching Collins tactfully promote his concept of limited and guided self-government. Steinbeck and Collins traveled in the old bakery truck to nearby farms and ditch-side migrant settlements, and the author read the manager's regular reports to the Resettlement Administration's regional office in San Francisco. The reports, which included social and cultural observations on migrant life and individual anecdotes sometimes told in Okie dialect, were extraordinary documents. The *News* had already published excerpts from them, and Steinbeck eventually mined them for material for *The Grapes of Wrath*. In 1936 he used them to get beneath the surface of migrant life, to understand the deep despair and hopelessness that poverty and homelessness had created.

When Steinbeck returned from Arvin to his Los Gatos home, he wrote to Collins to thank him "for one of the very fine experiences of a life." The two men remained in contact for another three years, Collins occasionally visiting Los Gatos and Steinbeck returning to the Central Valley for additional joint expeditions in what Collins called "the old pie wagon." The relationship was based as much on mutual advantage as on personal friendship. Steinbeck used the camp manager's observations for real-life material, the grist of a writer's mill. And Collins used Steinbeck to publicize a deeply felt cause, to awaken the citizenry to the migrants' plight. Jackson Benson wrote that Collins's most important contribution to *The Grapes of Wrath* was "to the spirit at the heart of the novel rather than to the details and color of its surface." Much the same can be said for Collins's influence on the 1936 *News* articles. Steinbeck recognized the camp manager's passion and promised, "I shall be very careful to do some good and no harm."[7]

Steinbeck's articles were not only descriptive but also contained specific policy recommendations, which clearly showed Collins's influence. For example, Steinbeck called for a vast expansion of the federal camp program. In both the articles and *The Grapes of Wrath*, the camp experience was the one bright exception to an otherwise gloomy account. Only in the camps does Steinbeck portray the migrants as somewhat in control of their lives, surviving with some dignity and self-respect. But by themselves, the camps were little more than palliatives. In *The Grapes of Wrath*, the Joads are forced to leave the almost idyllic atmosphere of Wheatpatch Camp to find work. "We hate to go," Pa Joad explained. "Folks been so nice here—an' the toilets an' all. But we got to eat."[8] Beyond the camps, Steinbeck advocated the establishment of a state agricultural labor board to protect and promote the migrants' rights to organize unions. Most important, he urged federal and state authorities to begin a program of resettling the Okies on small family farms, perhaps on public land.

Both Steinbeck and Collins viewed the migrants as displaced Jeffersonian yeomen who needed and deserved their own small plots of land. Unfortunately, this stance ran counter to the whole direction of California agricultural history. Jeffersonian yeomen small farmers had never dominated the state's rural economy. Instead, the gold rush allowed commercial producers to grow cash crops for instant urban markets in San Francisco and the mining camps. Completion of the transcontinental railroad in 1869 promoted a wheat boom in the Central Valley with large "bonanza farms" producing for international markets. By the 1870s, though a majority of California farms were small or middle-sized operations, a relatively few very large farms, mostly controlled by San Francisco businessmen, produced the bulk of agricultural output. The shift to intensive fruit, vegetable, and other specialty crop cultivation in the late nineteenth century did little to change that situation. If corporate agribusiness is a fairly new phenomenon in most of the United States, in 1936, when Steinbeck and Collins first toured Central Valley fields, it was already an established fact of life in California.[9]

"Bindlestiffs," largely single, footloose men, made up most of the labor force of the great wheat farms of the 1870s and 1880s. But as the shift to fruits and vegetables increased the need for labor during the harvests and other intensive work periods, Chinese and other immigrants entered the farm labor market. Workers followed the varied crops up and down the state, creating the nation's first modern migrant agricultural labor force. When federal immigration restrictions beginning in 1882 affected the supply of Chinese labor, growers turned to Japan, southern Europe, and even India. When further restrictions in the early twentieth century affected these regions, attention shifted to Mexico and the Philippines.

Steinbeck and Collins believed that the Dust Bowl migration was fundamentally transforming rural California society by changing the ethnic composition of the agricultural labor force. By 1935 the great wave of Dust Bowl migration was displacing many, though by no means all, of the nonwhite immigrant laborers in California fields. "Farm labor in California," Steinbeck predicted, "will be white labor, it will be American labor, and it will insist on a standard of living much higher than that which was accorded the foreign 'cheap labor.' " In an editorial accompanying the series, the *News* agreed, arguing that the Dust Bowl migrants "are Americans of the old stock. . . . They cannot be handled as the Japanese, Mexicans, and Filipinos." Neither Steinbeck nor the *News* stooped to the crude racist vocabulary so common to the era, but both in effect contended that only white Americans could successfully resist conditions that had regularly been imposed on nonwhites and immigrants. As Steinbeck put it, the new arrivals "will refuse to accept the role of field peon, with attendant terrorism, squalor, and starvation."[10]

In fact, Okies proved less willing to organize and join unions than the Mexicans and Filipinos who had preceded them in California fields. The union-organizing drives of largely immigrant workers in 1933 and 1934, while ultimately failing, were far more successful than those of 1938 and 1939, when American-born Okies dominated the labor force. The Dust Bowl migrants still considered themselves independent farmers and found it difficult to give up their traditional rural individualism. When Tom Joad was urged to bring his family out on strike in *The Grapes of Wrath*, he replied, "Tonight we had meat. Not much but we had it. Think Pa's gonna give up his meat on account of other fellas?" Later in the novel, the death of his friend at the hands of anti-labor vigilantes moved Tom to become a union organizer. In the end, however, little came of the ambitious efforts to organize either white or nonwhite agricultural workers in California during the 1930s.

The most important opponent of unionization was the Associated Farmers, Inc., an organization of leading growers and their powerful corporate allies. The Associated Farmers also opposed the federal migrant camp program, fearing that the settlements would become centers of union-organizing activity. In addition, local townspeople often resisted the establishment of migrant camps in their areas, arguing that camp residents would place a burden on schools, relief programs, and other community institutions. Tom Collins and other Resettlement Administration officials were acutely aware that the towns also harbored substantial prejudice against the migrants; in one Central Valley community the local movie theater required "Negroes and Okies" to sit in the balcony. In spite of such feelings, the Resettlement Administration and its successor, the Farm Security Administration, eventually established fifteen California camps before the program was liquidated after World War II. But even at their height in the late 1930s, the settlements were still considered demonstration projects and served only a small fraction of the migrant population.

John Steinbeck and Tom Collins were dedicated New Deal liberals generally supportive of Franklin Roosevelt's welfare state response to the Great Depression's economic and social devastation. But the camps were the only New Deal program designed specifically to serve California farm laborers. Social Security, unemployment insurance, the minimum wage, and the National Labor Relations Act did not cover agricultural workers. The New Deal was primarily a political response to the depression and, unlike farm employers, the migrants had little political clout. While California growers obtained federal price supports for some products, legally enforced marketing orders for others, and massive government expenditures for irrigation projects, migrant laborers received a small, poorly funded camp program that never got beyond the demonstration stage.

Steinbeck recognized the migrants' political weakness and urged the establishment of a "militant and watchful organization" on their behalf. The group would be composed of "middle-class people, workers, teachers, craftsmen, and liberals," and it would fight for farm workers' rights against what Steinbeck called the "vigilanteeism" and "fascism" of the Associated Farmers and its allies."[11]

The Simon J. Lubin Society was exactly the kind of organization Steinbeck had in mind. Named for a Progressive reformer who had fought for farm workers' rights, the Lubin Society struggled mightily to assist the migrants' cause. In 1938, Steinbeck allowed the group to publish his *News* articles in pamphlet form, under the title *Their Blood Is Strong*. In the same year he uncharacteristically let his name be used by a similar group, the John Steinbeck Committee to Aid Agricultural Organization, formed by Hollywood actor (and future member of Congress) Helen Gahagan Douglas. But the Lubin Society and the John Steinbeck Committee were no match for the Associated Farmers, whose allies in the state legislature blocked agricultural labor reforms proposed by liberal governor Culbert Olson and his director of immigration and housing, Carey McWilliams.

Setbacks such as these did not daunt Tom Collins or, for that matter, John Steinbeck. In early 1938 the two men were on the road again in rural California, traveling in the "old pie wagon" and gathering material for a projected "big novel" on the Okie migration. They witnessed the devastating effects of that winter's floods on the Central Valley's Little Oklahomas. Collins later described how he and Steinbeck worked "for forty-eight hours, and without food or sleep," helping "sick and half-starved people whose camps had been destroyed by the floods." "We couldn't speak to one another because we were too tired," Collins remembered, "yet we worked together as cogs in an intricate piece of machinery."[12]

These and other experiences found their way into the letter and spirit of *The Grapes of Wrath*, published in the spring of 1939. The novel took the nation's reading public by storm, going through ten printings between March and November of that year. The story's public exposure was dramatically increased by Darryl Zanuck's movie version, starring Henry Fonda. At one point Steinbeck, worried that Hollywood would soften or dilute the novel's message, asked Zanuck if he believed the story. The moviemaker admitted that he had hired a detective agency to investigate whether the book had accurately depicted the migrants' plight. Zanuck told Steinbeck that "the conditions are much worse than you reported." At the author's suggestion, Zanuck hired Collins as a technical advisor for the film, and needless to say he argued for a realistic portrayal. Zanuck shot much of the movie in Collins's old stomping grounds, at the Weedpatch Camp and the countryside around Arvin. The film was released in early 1940, shortly before Steinbeck won the Pulitzer Prize.

Even the popularity of *The Grapes of Wrath*, however, did not produce significant public programs to assist the migrants. Foreign affairs and the coming U.S. involvement in World War II increasingly captured the nation's attention. By the end of 1940, reporter Ernie Pyle noted that the Okies no longer made headlines: "People sort of forgot them." A year later, the labor surplus of the depression had been transformed into an extraordinary wartime shortage of workers. Migrants who were not subject to military service found well-paying jobs in California's booming shipyards, aircraft factories, and other defense plants. The Joads and their fellow Okies ultimately found economic salvation, not in the small farms they dreamed of owning, but in urban industry fueled by billions of federal defense dollars.

California growers, desperate for labor, once again turned to Mexico. Hundreds of thousands of new workers crossed the border, many of them arriving under terms of the U.S. government's Bracero Program. With the farm labor force no longer dominated by white Americans, social conditions in rural California received little attention or sympathy. Not until the Delano Strike of 1965, in an era sensitized by the Civil Rights movement, did issues raised in *The Grapes of Wrath* return to broad public consciousness. And not until 1975 did the state legislature establish an Agricultural Labor Relations Board similar to the one Steinbeck advocated in 1936.

By this time, academic historians were beginning to question Steinbeck's portrayal of the Okies as a kind of heroic rural proletariat. Walter Stein's *California and the Dust Bowl Migration* (1973) emphasized the migrants' cultural and political conservatism, a point reinforced by James Gregory's landmark study, *American Exodus: The Dust Bowl Migration and Okie Culture in California* (1989). Gregory argued that the Okies were committed to a traditional view of "plain folk Americanism," including old-time religion, small farm ownership, self-reliant individualism, and conservative populist political values. According to Gregory, the migrants were active participants in a conservative process of maintaining their core values and creating a vibrant Okie subculture. Charles Schindo, in *Dust Bowl Migrants in the American Imagination* (1997), contended that Steinbeck and his fellow 1930s liberals were elitists who misinterpreted the Okie experience and then imposed that leftist misinterpretation on the American consciousness.[13]

While John Steinbeck undoubtedly made errors of fact and interpretation, contemporary scholars must be careful not to replace these inaccuracies with a series of equally invalid assumptions that are products of our own neoconservative age. Steinbeck's powerful narrative of the depression experience is more than simply a piece of American popular culture. It also contained much insight into California history. Okie families often resisted paternalistic measures advocated by reformers like Tom Collins, but the migrants could still appreciate the specific amenities and services supported by the reformers and offered in the government camps. Although the Okies were not as willing to engage in collective action as were Mexican or Filipino farmworkers, thousands of Dust Bowl migrants nevertheless went on strike in 1937 and 1938, as depicted in *The Grapes of Wrath*. While Steinbeck may have been wrong to portray the Okies *only* as helpless victims, that does not alter the fact that the migrants were indeed victimized by social and economic forces beyond their control.

Back in December 1939, after he had seen the movie version of the novel, John Steinbeck wrote to Tom Collins: "Saw the picture and it is swell. . . . You did a wonderful job."[14] Shortly thereafter, Collins dropped by Steinbeck's home in Los Gatos, only to find the house deserted. The novelist, recently separated from his wife, had moved on in his life and in his career, leaving the migrants and Tom Collins behind. The two men were never to meet again.

Steinbeck lived for most of the rest of his life on the East Coast, returning to California only for an occasional visit. But the best of his later novels, *Cannery Row* (1944) and *East of Eden* (1952), revisited the California of his youth, particularly Salinas, the upper Salinas Valley, and Monterey. In 1962 he was awarded the Nobel Prize for literature, but even this honor did not earn the approval of the eastern literary establishment. Indeed, some New York critics attacked the Nobel committee for its choice, arguing that Steinbeck was a sentimental moralist unworthy of literary distinction. John Steinbeck died in 1968; though a successful novelist, he was still very much the outsider he had been for most of his life.

Although *The Grapes of Wrath* was written over sixty years ago, Steinbeck's depiction of extreme poverty is not without relevance today. In his time, homelessness and despair existed within the larger context of the depression, and the general public was, for a while at least, genuinely touched by the suffering of migrants. In our time, prosperous Americans seem all too willing to accept the presence of homeless people on the streets and a desperate underclass in the ghettoes. The sense of shock and indignation with which Steinbeck wrote seems tragically absent in contemporary America. We can, then, still learn much from John Steinbeck and from the activist spirit of his silent collaborator, Tom Collins, "who lived it."

Notes

1. Jackson Benson, "Tom, Who Lived It: John Steinbeck and the Man from Weedpatch," *Journal of Modern Literature* (April 1976): 151–210.
2. On California during the Great Depression, see Kevin Starr, *Endangered Dreams: The Great Depression in California* (New York, 1996); Leonard Joseph Leader, *Los Angeles and the Great Depression* (New York, 1991); William Mullins, *The Depression and*

the *Urban West, 1929–1933: Los Angeles, San Francisco, Seattle, and Portland* (Bloomington, 1991); and Richard Lowitt, *The New Deal and the West* (Bloomington, 1984).

3. For biographical information on Steinbeck, see Jackson Benson, *The True Adventures of John Steinbeck* (New York, 1984).

4. For general histories of the Okies' story, see James N. Gregory, *American Exodus: The Dust Bowl Migration and Okie Culture in California* (New York, 1989); and Donald Worster, *Dust Bowl: The Southern Plains in the 1930s* (New York, 1979).

5. John Steinbeck, *The Grapes of Wrath* (New York, 1964), 270.

6. Benson, *The True Adventures of John Steinbeck*, 340.

7. Ibid., 347.

8. Steinbeck, *The Grapes of Wrath*, 317.

9. Carey McWilliams, *Factories in the Field: The Story of Migratory Farm Labor in California* (Boston, 1939).

10. Charles Wollenberg, ed., *The Harvest Gypsies: On the Road to the Grapes of Wrath* (Berkeley, 1988), 56–57.

11. Benson, *The True Adventures of John Steinbeck*, 410.

12. Ibid., 411.

13. Walter Stein, *California and the Dust Bowl Migration* (Westport, CT, 1973); James N. Gregory, *American Exodus: The Dust Bowl Migration and Okie Culture in California* (New York, 1989); Charles J. Shindo, *Dust Bowl Migrants in the American Imagination* (Lawrence, KS, 1997).

14. Benson, *The True Adventures of John Steinbeck*, 411.

Suggested Readings

Benson, Jackson. *The True Adventures of John Steinbeck*. New York: Viking, 1984.

———. "Tom, Who Lived It: John Steinbeck and the Man from Weedpatch," *Journal of Modern Literature* (April 1976): 151–210.

Gregory, James N. *American Exodus: The Dust Bowl Migration and Okie Culture in California*. New York: Oxford University Press, 1989.

McWilliams, Carey. *Factories in the Field: The Story of Migratory Farm Labor in California*. Boston: Little, Brown, 1939.

Parini, Jay. *John Steinbeck: A Biography*. New York: Henry Holt, 1995.

Schindo, Charles J. *Dust Bowl Migrants in the American Imagination*. Lawrence: University of Kansas Press, 1997.

St. Pierre, Brian. *John Steinbeck: The California Years*. San Francisco: Chronicle Books, 1983.

Stein, Walter. *California and the Dust Bowl Migration*. Westport, CT: Greenwood Press, 1973.

Steinbeck, John. *The Grapes of Wrath: Text and Criticism*. New York: Penguin Books, 1997.

Wollenberg, Charles, ed. *The Harvest Gypsies: On the Road to the Grapes of Wrath*. Berkeley: Heyday Books, 1988.

10

Four Migrant Stories
African American Women in Wartime California

Gretchen Lemke-Santangelo

California recovered from the Great Depression more rapidly than most regions of the country, largely because in the late 1930s the federal government began directing significant monies to Los Angeles and Bay Area—based defense industry plants. As the U.S. government prepared for the nation's likely involvement in the spreading conflicts in the Pacific and in Europe, it slowly started to develop a massive military-industrial complex, and California was the single most important beneficiary. The slow stream of federal dollars that would lift the state's economy in the late 1930s turned into a flood once the United States entered the war. Between 1941 and 1945, nearly $40 billion in military appropriations transformed California's economy into a massive industrial and high-tech machine.

World War II altered California's social and cultural fabric as much as its economy. The business boom produced a severe labor shortage, providing women and persons of color with access to jobs that they had previously been denied. Middle-class women flocked to defense plants, thousands of African Americans left dreary conditions in the South in hopes of cashing in on the boom of well-paying military jobs in California, and the state even started a Bracero program through which it recruited Mexicans to fill vacant agricultural labor posts.

In this essay, Gretchen Lemke-Santangelo, associate professor of history at St. Mary's College, takes us into the bustling World War II era by exploring the experiences of four African American women who journeyed from small southern towns to northern California in search of greater opportunities and better lives.

During World War II, four women—Cornelia James, Faith McAllister, Willa Henry, and Lacey Gray—embarked on life-altering journeys. Although their ages, birthplaces, and family histories varied, they shared a common dream of a better future. All were raised in towns and cities in the South during the age of Jim Crow. As African Americans, their lives were circumscribed by the economic hardship, emotional pain, and physical danger associated with racial segregation

Marshall
Law

147

and discrimination. They experienced firsthand what writer Pauli Murray described as "the pervasive irritant" of racism, "the chronic allergy, the vague apprehension which made one uncomfortable and jumpy." They were part of a generation that "knew the race problem was like a deadly snake coiled and ready to strike, and that one avoided its dangers only by never-ending watchfulness."[1]

The opportunity to escape these limits came for our four subjects in the early 1940s, as war industrialists with huge defense contracts transformed California into a potential Canaan for African American and women workers. Experiencing a mixture of fear, excitement, hope, and uncertainty, each summoned the individual will and courage to leave the South. However alone they may have felt in making this momentous decision, each became part of a vast migratory stream. As their personal journeys unfolded, countless other women and men were joining them in the same search for economic opportunity and greater social freedom.

Wartime California: The Historical Backdrop

What did these four women hope to find in wartime California? Between 1941 and 1945 the federal government invested over $70 billion in California's aircraft, shipbuilding, and other war-related industries. As wartime labor demands grew, gender and racial barriers to industrial employment fell, providing unprecedented economic opportunities for black and female workers. But black migrants were attracted by more than just jobs. Most of them also sought freedom from segregation and discrimination. Word of opportunity, spread by labor recruiters, newspapers, railroad workers, and the first wave of migrants, helped fuel the westward exodus. Before long, newcomers, mainly from Mississippi, Louisiana, Texas, Arkansas, and Oklahoma, transformed California's demographic landscape. The San Francisco East Bay Area, which became the nation's shipbuilding center during the war, witnessed some of the most dramatic changes. In Richmond, for example, the African American population grew from 270 in 1940 to 10,000 in 1945. During the same period, Oakland's black population increased from 8,462 to over 37,000.[2]

Most newcomers found better lives in California: access to the voting booth, a broader range of jobs, improved educational opportunities, and escape from the more brutal manifestations of Jim Crow. But California was not the Promised Land. With the exception of black business leaders and a small core of civil rights activists who recognized the economic and political advantages of the demographic shift, most established residents—white and black—regarded migrants as unwelcome competition for jobs, housing, and public space. Racial barriers, although firmly established before migrants arrived, actually proliferated during the war years. Restrictive covenants and discriminatory real estate and lending practices confined African American migrants to the least desirable sections of Bay Area cities, producing severe overcrowding and de facto school segregation. Even federally funded war housing, administered by local housing authorities, was allocated on a segregated and racially preferential basis. Employment discrimination and workplace racial harassment were widespread, even in industries that received federal defense contracts. And several labor unions, most notoriously the Boilermakers, steadfastly refused to admit black members or created second-class, Jim Crow auxiliaries. Finally, numerous hotel, restaurant, and bar owners refused to serve black patrons, posting signs that announced, "We Refuse Service to Negroes."[3]

Many established black residents, who were alarmed over rising racial tensions and restrictions, also viewed migrants with hostility. But while many black old-timers initially accepted negative stereotypes of migrants as uninhibited, dirty, lazy, and immoral, their opinions softened over time. As Virginia Cravanas, a prewar black resident, observed: "In California we didn't have anything. We just got the crumbs. . . . We resented the influx because we thought we were doing the right thing— changing things gradually. But we weren't doing a thing. We were really the bottom of the bucket, working as stock clerks and maids. Newcomers came in and called attention to what we were denied. When they came out here they felt this was the land of milk and honey, and they were going to get some because they never had anything anyway."[4]

Working-class migrants did indeed push for change, using their southern heritage of self-determination, mutual aid, and institution-building to dismantle some of the Bay Area's more tangible racial barriers and secure a visible role in local politics. Just as significantly, newcomers transformed the region's culture, forcing vastly outnumbered old-time black residents to adjust to their tastes and preferences. Indeed, just as established white and black residents generated hostile stereotypes to secure their positions within a rapidly changing society, black migrants used positive representations of their southern traditions to forge a common identity, maintain family stability, establish communities, and resist the discrimination that threatened to dislodge them.

Women, constituting roughly one-half of all newcomers, played a central role in the migration and community-building process. Most were born during the first quarter of the twentieth century, when white supremacy became firmly entrenched in the American South. Whether raised in urban or rural areas, church and family formed the center of migrant women's childhoods. Within these two institutions that helped shelter them from the brutality of segregation and discrimination, women learned that their survival was linked to reciprocal relationships and mutual aid networks that connected kin and neighbors.[5]

For the most part, migrant women were neither bitterly poor nor middle class. As the wartime boom transformed the Bay Area into a land of opportunity for black southerners, most had the resources to leave the South and little economic incentive to stay behind. Had they remained, few could have expected little more than a domestic service job paying two dollars or less per week.[6] Women usually made the decision to leave for California with other family members and often followed a pattern of chain migration. Husbands, brothers, and fathers often moved first, while women stayed behind to pack, sell livestock and household possessions, and prepare older family members and children for the journey. During the trip itself, by car or train, migrants often coped with loneliness, fear of the unknown, and the trials of caring for young children in cramped quarters. Those who traveled by train were confined to separate, poorly equipped Jim Crow cars for much of the journey, a final humiliation on the road to greater freedom.[7]

Upon arrival, women performed most of the orientation tasks associated with settling their families in a new location. Most initially lived in crowded, makeshift accommodations, often doubling up with friends, relatives, or new acquaintances. Many, however, eventually moved into wartime housing projects that offered more privacy, space, and modern amenities.[8] Greater residential stability, in turn, supported the establishment of community ties and permanent institutions. Once settled, women founded or joined churches, mutual aid associations, and social organizations. They also engaged in political and civic activism by joining the PTA, NAACP, National Council of Negro Women, and the Bay Area Council against Discrimination. Finally, they facilitated chain migration by offering temporary shelter and financial assistance to friends and relatives who followed in their footsteps.[9]

As they struggled to establish stable homes and build new institutions, most African American migrant women joined the paid labor force. In the past most had worked in domestic service, but during the war their employment options expanded to include a range of industrial and service sector jobs. However, even as the war produced greater economic opportunities for African American migrant women, their economic status in relationship to other workers remained the same. Defense industries hired white women first and trained them to fill better-paying, less dangerous jobs. By the time large numbers of black women were hired in 1943, war production had peaked and started to decline within a year.[10]

Migrant women also had to contend with hostility from white workers and supervisors, union discrimination, and lack of advancement and promotions. But however much discrimination they faced, many, like Faith McAllister, relished the fact that "we were at least getting paid to put up with it. In the South it had been nothing but hard work and bad treatment. Here I was making more in a day than I made back home in a month." Thus, although they filled the least desirable jobs in the defense economy, their employment represented a tremendous improvement over the jobs they had previously held.[11]

The story of African American women's migration becomes particularly dramatic and poignant when we view their lives through the memories of individuals such as Cornelia James, Faith McAllister, Willa Henry, and Lacey Gray. Respectively, a child, a young single mother, a college student, and a married woman on arriving in California, these four women and their stories illuminate both common features of the migrant experience and the individual variations embedded in historical events and processes.

Four Migrant Experiences

Cornelia James was born in Louisville, Arkansas, in 1933, the last of five children and the only daughter of hardworking, deeply religious parents. Her father, a traveling evangelist and part-time construction worker, kept his wife and youngest children at home with the help of his older sons. Together they managed to survive the hard economic times of the Great Depression and insulate their loved ones from the most brutal manifestations of Jim Crow. Cornelia's dominant memories, in fact, revolve around the security provided by a large extended family and church community. "When I was young," she recalled, "that's all there was—family and church. It knit us all together and helped us pull through. Church was more than it is today. Our school met there. We had meetings all during the week, and Sunday worship lasted all day and into the evening. The adults sometimes worked with white people, but other than that we had our own world."[12]

In 1941, Cornelia's father ventured out to California, intent on freeing his family from economic hardship and discrimination by establishing a ministry among newly arrived migrants from the South. Work in the Richmond shipyards, however, proved a quicker means of reaching his goal. The oldest son and his wife, accompanied by Cornelia, were the first to follow. "Then came my second and third brothers. Then about eighteen months later my mother and baby brother came out, because she had to sell all of the livestock and household things." This was a typical pattern followed by migrant families. Often, after immediate family had relocated, other relatives, friends, and even ministers would follow. Eventually, so many arrived from the same community that migrants established social organizations named for their hometowns, like the Vicksburg Club.[13]

For Cornelia, who had read stories in class about "sunny California," the trip with her brother and sister-in-law was high adventure. Departing Louisville in a truck "with a house on the back," they headed first to Shreveport for gas ration stamps and then on to California via Route 66. At night the family pulled off to the side of the road to rest, rather than risk the rejection that black travelers often experienced when seeking a bed at a white-owned establishment.[14]

Although "it was pouring down rain when we got to California," Cornelia quickly felt at home in her new surroundings. When her mother arrived the following year, the family moved into a Richmond warhousing project that, while segregated into black and white sections, provided amenities that other migrant households lacked. Many families, Corneila recalled, "lived in trailers and huts out in North Richmond. The housing shortage was so bad that if you had any kind of little shed, people were living in it." Better yet, her project had space for a garden. "Mother and the lady next door, a cousin from back home in Arkansas," planted familiar vegetables and shared their produce with their neighbors. In this manner the women built relationships that fostered a strong sense of community. "People could trust each other," Cornelia said; "[they] watched children for each other, and shared whatever they had."[15]

Church also remained a fixture of family life. Although Cornelia's father never established a ministry, her brother founded the second black Baptist congregation in Richmond. The church, she recalled, started out small but grew rapidly with the wartime influx of migrants. In time other churches, all replicating southern styles of worship, sprang up as well. The projects, however, offered a host of more worldly diversions that had not been available back home. "Each project had a recreation center where they had dances for kids, reading rooms, tennis courts, volleyball courts, a baseball field and card room. You had a place to go and meet people."[16]

In Richmond, Cornelia attended an integrated school. Initially she was one of only three black students in her class. With each passing week, however, more migrant children arrived and the school was forced to adopt double sessions to accommodate the influx. "But although we went only half a day, we learned more than kids do now because we got down to business." When Cornelia entered her teens, after the end of the war, more schools had been built to ease the overcrowding. But white flight out of Richmond, coupled with housing discrimination, contributed to de facto segregation in public education. By the time she graduated, her high school was well on the way to becoming almost all black.[17]

As whites fled to the surrounding suburbs, jobs left as well. The thriving community of Cornelia's childhood, a once-promising experiment in racial integration, became a postwar black ghetto. "[There] used to be a real downtown. We had department stores, movie theaters, restaurants all up and down the avenue. All that is gone now, but we still have our churches." The postwar demolition of war-housing projects created added disruption, uprooting and scattering migrant families throughout the city. But "church," Cornelia recalled, "held my family and all our friends and relatives together."[18]

Cornelia, who came to California as a child, made the transition with the support of her parents and older siblings. Other migrants, however, had already reached adulthood and assumed the responsibilities of parenthood. For single mothers such as Faith McAllister, migration was an act of courage. But even she could count on the support of relatives and friends. An only child, Faith was born in Utility, Louisiana, in 1917. Her mother, a single parent, worked as a domestic servant for white families. Like many black parents, she attempted to shelter her daughter from the white world. According to Faith, "Mother wanted something better for me, and wouldn't let me help out [with domestic work]. Tried to keep me in school and at home." But her elementary school, which met at Mt. Olive Baptist Church, terminated at the seventh grade.

Like many other southern towns, "Utility didn't provide much for black kids." When she was twelve, she and her mother joined relatives in St. Louis so Faith could go on to high school.[19]

The big city, however, pulled Faith in other directions. In Utility her tightly supervised world revolved around church, school, and home. St. Louis, in contrast, contained a large, bustling black community with a host of exciting diversions for "a green country girl." After three years of high school, Faith fell in love with a dashing, older musician and recalls that she "nearly broke my mother's heart" by marrying him. The relationship ended after a few years, and Faith, now with two young sons to raise, found a job as a waitress in a black-owned restaurant.[20]

The opportunity for migration came when "war broke out and they were hiring in the shipyards." An uncle moved to California first and then sent for Faith. After taking a training course, she became a welder at Richmond's Kaiser shipyards, "making more in a day than I made back home in a month." The work, however, was dangerous. "They were in such a hurry to build those ships, and that made things unsafe." Faith and other black workers also experienced racial hostility from white coworkers. The supervisors, she recalled, were mostly white. "I never saw a black leaderman in welding. I had a black woman friend who was a leaderman, but only over those black ladies who swept up." As historian Karen Anderson observed, "Whatever the hierarchy of preference, . . . black women could always be found at the bottom," both during and after the war. So although black women certainly made more money in California, they still made less for "putting up with it" than white workers made for dishing it out. [21]

Faith's mother soon joined her and life took on a more settled pattern. They pooled their savings and bought a house in West Oakland, found a church, and connected with other transplanted southerners. Sharing food, part of a larger cultural tradition of reciprocity, was central to their home and their community-building efforts. As Faith noted, "[We] always had company here and back home. Mother loved to cook . . . made good peach cobblers and apple pies. And we had a vegetable garden. . . which she and I cared for. And if there was something she couldn't find out here, like seasonings and pecans, relatives back home would send them. Those were good times gathered around the table with friends."[22]

Despite the demands of work and child care, Faith found time for community service. She joined the NAACP, the Federation of Colored Women's Clubs, the PTA, and the Order of the Eastern Star. "People from the South," she commented, "had more drive and determination to change things. We were tired of discrimination. It was just about as bad out here. The only thing they didn't have was lynch parties and things . . . and we were set on fighting it."[23] Indeed, her commitment to institution-building and civic activism, shared by many other migrants, added strength and momentum to earlier, more modest efforts to improve the Bay Area's racial climate.

As the war drew to a close, Faith received a layoff notice from the shipyards. But she never gave a thought to returning to the South, because "my sons could never have taken it back there." With a mortgage to pay, she found a job as a nurse's aide at a local hospital and worked there for the next thirty years. "Six days a week, including Sundays, so I had to quit going to church. I made sure that my sons went, though, and it kept them out of trouble."[24] Thus, Faith followed a pattern established by her mother: making personal sacrifices to shelter and protect her offspring.[25]

Many women such as Faith moved to California to create better lives for their children. Others, without the responsibilities of parenthood, simply sought personal freedom and opportunity. Willa Henry was born in Elmgrove, Texas, in 1922 to a family that valued education. "My father was a graduate of Texas College but couldn't support us on a teacher's salary, so he worked at a cotton gin. All of his four sisters were schoolteachers, too." From an early age, Willa was expected to follow in the family tradition, but Jim Crow presented some formidable barriers. To attend high school, Willa had to move to Jacksonville and board with a first cousin who owned a pharmacy. Once she graduated, in 1939, her grandfather and aunts pooled their resources so she could attend Prairie View College.[26]

While she was away at college, her father and uncles moved to California. "[Franklin Delano] Roosevelt had just passed anti–job discrimination legislation and word spread all over about work in the shipyards." In June 1942, Willa returned to Elmgrove for summer break just as an uncle "came back for his wife." She left with them for California and "never looked back." Willa roomed with an aunt and uncle in Oakland until her father sent for her mother and sisters. By then, "I was working at the shipyards and supporting myself. They were giving all kinds of classes for clerical training at the navy and army bases, but there was no money in that. [I] took welding classes instead and got paid to learn." After training in vertical, horizontal, and overhead welding, Willa went to work at the Kaiser shipyards on the night shift. "The hard part was having to drag that long cord around and wear the leather coveralls and heavy helmet. Then I got an easier job as a shipfitter and went on the day shift and did that until I was laid off in 1945."[27]

Like Faith, Willa remembered racial tensions in the workplace and surrounding community. "We all worked together, but you know how prejudiced white people can be. And even the native blacks had an antagonistic attitude toward us. [They] said we had come here and changed the whole system with our different culture. A black lady down the street from my parents even suggested to a white neighbor that maybe we'd all leave if no one sold us anything." Despite such antagonism, Willa took pride in the fact that black southerners had creatively adapted to segregation by building their own institutions. Black Californians, in contrast, "didn't even have their own businesses. In the South black people had to be self-supporting. That's why you see so many more professionals there. They had their own businesses and schools. The blacks in the South had learned to work for themselves."Although somewhat of an exaggeration, her observation accurately reflected migrants' pride in their long history of self-help and institution-building.[28]

After receiving her layoff notice from Kaiser, Willa never considered looking for another welding job. A male coworker "said that if he had my training he could get a job anywhere. But I just gave it up . . . [because I] knew they wouldn't be hiring women." Instead, she applied to Armstrong Business College for clerical training, but was "told that they didn't accept colored students. Gave the excuse that they couldn't because part of their policy was to guarantee their graduates jobs, and they had problems placing colored at that time." Soon after, she married a career military man, found a job at the post office, and started a family. Like Faith, she took an active role in her church and community.[29]

Yet another group of migrant women came to California as wives and mothers. Lacey Gray was born in 1916 into a large farming family in Longleaf, Louisiana. "Father worked at the sawmill and farmed his own land. He owned eighty acres and raised corn, cotton, livestock, and all kinds of vegetables. Mother helped out and minded us eleven children." By the age of nine, Lacey was helping with farm chores, "chopping cotton and hoeing corn." Church and school were her only diversions. Her school, financed and run by black parents, terminated at the seventh grade and was two and a half miles from her house. "When you finished that, you would have to go off to school—to Alexandria or Baton Rouge or someplace like that—but my mother wasn't able to send us off." A white high school was located a mile away, "but we couldn't go to that." The town of Longleaf was also segregated. "If you went into a cafe you had to come in through the back. And when I started working out—cleaning homes for people—you had to go in through the back."[30]

From the time she finished school until she married at twenty-one, Lacey worked for white families, earning $1.25 per week. Lacey soon moved back with her parents while her husband took on a better-paying job in a distant southern city, a survival strategy that was all too common among working-class black families in the discriminatory labor market of the South. In July 1943, Lacey's husband left for California after hearing about jobs in Richmond from relatives who had moved there earlier. Four months later he sent for her, and she made the trip by train. After boarding the Jim Crow car in Lake Charles, Louisiana, Lacey drank some contaminated water and became ill. Some black soldiers who shared her segregated compartment came to her assistance, helping her change trains and caring for her daughters while she slept. Relief came in El Paso, when, "praise the Lord, we could sit anywhere."[31]

After the long journey with small children, Lacey found little comfort in her new surroundings. "We moved to North Richmond and roomed there for a month. Just one room with the four of us in the same bed until we got into the projects." War housing was a vast improvement over their temporary accommodations. Rent was $35 per month for a 1-bedroom apartment, "and that included water, gas, lights, everything. Everybody was happy with the price, lots of children, and it was safe." Neighbors also connected them to a nearby church, the congregation founded by Cornelia James's brother.[32]

As they settled in, Lacey joined the NAACP, PTA, Order of the Eastern Star, a social club, and various auxiliaries within her church. Her husband "made enough working at the shipyard to support us, and free me up to do public work." After the war, he continued on as the family's sole breadwinner, working at a variety of jobs in Richmond and Oakland. The couple built their own home after searching unsuccessfully for existing housing in a "decent" neighborhood. "It was segregated residentially, you know. You could only buy in certain parts of town. And even when we found our lot, some white people lived nearby, but they moved out." Yet despite such problems, Lacey had few doubts that California was a better place to raise her daughters than Louisiana.[33]

African American Communities in Postwar California

Following the war, the economic vitality of migrant communities was undermined by white and capital flight, poorly planned redevelopment projects, and continuing residential and employment discrimination. Like Lacey, however, most migrants were determined to stay. Black workers, the first to lose their wartime jobs, were forced into jobs well below their skill levels, necessitating two wage earners in most families. Although some migrant women returned to domestic service, a majority worked in the low-wage manufacturing and service sectors. The more fortunate secured government employment, usually in custodial or clerical positions, that afforded higher wages and better job security. In any case, their economic contribution was vital to the survival of their families and neighborhoods during the postwar period.[34]

Simultaneously, women continued their tradition of public activism, building and maintaining institutions that helped their communities withstand and resist persisting barriers to equal housing and employment. Churches, which provided a variety of social services, continued to be an important outlet for activist women. Others, however, formed neighborhood associations, organized boycotts of local businesses that refused to hire black workers, registered voters, led school desegregation campaigns, created new chapters of the NAACP and National Council of Negro Women, and staffed community development projects funded in the 1960s during the War on Poverty.[35]

Despite their relocation to California during the war, most black women maintained close ties to the South. Few migrant women envisioned their move as a final separation from those who remained behind. Through letters, frequent return visits, and phone calls, women continued to draw on the advice and cultural traditions of family and friends back home. Lacey, for example, still thinks of herself as a southerner and returns to the family farm in Longleaf each November for extended visits with her two sisters. "Wasn't too many of our people who had their own land, and Daddy never wanted it sold. But my sisters are too old to farm now, and no young people want to stay." While the land and other tangible connections to the South may dissolve over time, migrants' speech patterns, food preferences, music, religious values, and personal histories are firmly embedded in their California offspring. Just as significantly, their southern folk heritage is now an integral and permanent part of California's rich and varied cultural landscape.[36]

Notes

1. Pauli Murray, *Song in a Weary Throat* (New York, 1987), 36.

2. Gerald Nash, *The American West Transformed: The Impact of the Second World War* (Bloomington, 1985), 26, 66, 67; Robert O. Brown, "Impact of War Worker Migration on the Public School System of Richmond, California, from 1940 to 1945" (Ph.D. diss., Stanford University, 1973), 109, 110; U.S. Congress, House Committee on Naval Affairs, *Investigation of Congested Areas*, 78th Cong., 1st sess., 1943, vol. 1, pt. 3, 855; Marilynn S. Johnson, *The Second Gold Rush: Oakland and the East Bay in World War II* (Berkeley, 1993), 51–55; Charles S. Johnson, *The Negro War Worker in San Francisco* (San Francisco, 1944), 4–6; William Sokol, "Richmond during World War II: Kaiser Comes to Town," typescript, University of California, Berkeley, 1971, 13–14.

3. Oakland Institute on Human Relations, *Seminar Report on What Tensions Exist between Groups in the Local Community* (Oakland, 1946), n.p.; Johnson, *Second Gold Rush*, 143–84; Katherine Archibald, *Wartime Shipyard: A Study in Social Disunity* (Berkeley, 1947), 56, 69–79; Wilson Record, *Minority Group and Intergroup Relations in the San Francisco Bay Area* (Berkeley, 1966); Harvey Kerns, *Study of the Social and Economic Conditions Affecting the Local Negro Population* (Oakland, 1945); Floyd Hunter, *Housing Discrimination in Oakland, California: A Study Prepared for the Mayor's Committee on Full Opportunity and the Council of Social Planning* (Berkeley, 1963).

4. Virginia Cravanas, interview by author, Oakland, California, February 4, 1991.

5. Aggregate Statistics from fifty oral interviews conducted by the author with former migrants between 1990 and 1991; Cy W. Record, *Characteristics of Some Unemployed Shipyard Workers in Richmond, California* (Berkeley, 1947), and Johnson, *The Negro War Worker in San Francisco*, also contain background information on black migrants; William E. Montgomery, *Under Their Own Vine and Fig Tree: The African American Church in the South, 1865–1900* (Baton Rouge, 1992).

6. Aggregate Statistics; Johnson, *The Negro War Worker in San Francisco*, 2–14.

7. Aggregate Statistics.

8. Ibid.

9. Ibid.

10. Ibid.; Karen Anderson, "Last Hired, First Fired: Black Women Workers during World War II," *Journal of American History* 69 (June 1982): 82–97; Gretchen Lemke-Santangelo, *Abiding Courage: African American Migrant Women and the East Bay Community* (Chapel Hill, 1996), 124–31.

11. Aggregate Statistics; Faith McAllister, interview by author, Emeryville, California, May 2, 1991.

12. Cornelia James, interview by author, Richmond, California, May 21, 1991.

13. Ibid.

14. Ibid.

15. Ibid.

16. Ibid.

17. Ibid.

18. Ibid.

19. Faith McAllister, interview.

20. Ibid.

21. Anderson, "Last Hired, First Fired," 84; Faith McAllister, interview.

22. Faith McAllister, interview.

23. Ibid.

24. Ibid.

25. Ibid.

26. Willa Henry, interview by author, Oakland, California, September 26, 1990.

27. Ibid.

28. Ibid.

29. Ibid.

30. Lacey Gray, interview by author, Richmond, California, May 21, 1991.

31. Ibid.

32. Ibid.

33. Ibid.

34. Aggregate Statistics; U.S. Department of Labor, *Women Workers in Ten Production Areas and Their Postwar Employment Plans*, U.S. Women's Bureau Bulletin #209; Earl R. Babbie and William Nichols III, *Oakland in Transition: A Summary of the 701 Household Survey* (Berkeley, 1969), 108–9; Lemke-Santangelo, *Abiding Courage*, 124–31.

35. Lemke-Santangelo, *Abiding Courage*, 155–77.

36. Aggregate Statistics; Lacey Gray, interview.

Suggested Readings

Broussard, Albert S. *Black San Francisco: The Struggle for Racial Equality in the West, 1900–1954.* Lawrence: University of Kansas Press, 1993.

Johnson, Marilynn S. *The Second Gold Rush: Oakland and the East Bay in World War II.* Berkeley: University of California Press, 1993.

Lemke-Santangelo, Gretchen. *Abiding Courage: African American Migrant Women and the East Bay Community.* Chapel Hill: University of North Carolina Press, 1996.

McBroome, Dolores Nason. *Parallel Communities: African Americans in California's East Bay Community, 1800–1963.* New York: Garland Publishing, 1993.

Moore, Shirley Ann Wilson. *To Place Our Deeds: The African American Community in Richmond, California, 1910–1963.* Berkeley: University of California Press, 2000.

Nash, Gerald. *The American West Transformed: The Impact of the Second World War.* Bloomington: Indiana University Press, 1985.

11

Edison Uno
The Experience and Legacy of
the Japanese American Internment

Alice Yang Murray

Often celebrated as a time of economic revival and growth in California, World War II also witnessed one of the state's most tragic moments. In February 1942, President Franklin Roosevelt issued Executive Order 9066, which required the incarceration of all Japanese Americans, citizens or not, living in the western half of the continental United States. Within several months, more than 100,000 Japanese Americans, the majority from California, had been placed in a series of isolated internment camps located throughout desolate deserts in the American West. Despite the fact that the Federal Bureau of Investigation (FBI) had only a year earlier released the Munson Report, which found no evidence of any likelihood of Japanese American sabotage, the U.S. government conflated race with national identity in suddenly arguing that all Japanese Americans represented a potential security threat.

Once in the camps, all internees were required to sign loyalty oaths to the United States. For those Japanese Americans born here and thus already full American citizens, this seemed an insulting redundancy. And for those who had emigrated from Japan and were thus ineligible for citizenship under race-based naturalization laws, this required renouncing their national citizenship without the right to obtain a new one. In other words, they became persons without a country.

Many Japanese Americans fought back in the courts, challenging the imprisonment's constitutionality, but in two different Supreme Court decisions, the nation's leading justices sanctioned the deprivation of rights as a legitimate wartime necessity. Some Japanese American men, determined to prove their loyalty to the United States, volunteered for military service and formed what became one of the most decorated army units in American history.

In this essay, Alice Yang Murray, associate professor of history at the University of California, Santa Cruz, explores the life of one internee, Edison Uno. Murray reveals how the injustice of the wartime imprisonment reverberated among Japanese Americans in the following years and would re-emerge as an issue in the nation's political consciousness.

It is history which no one can deny. It is a legacy
that will be etched in the annals of history, whether
we like it or not. Therefore, it seems to me that we
who have survived the experience have a responsibility to make certain our perspectives are documented in the many interpretations of this historic
event in our lives.[1]

In 1974, Edison Uno directed that exhortation at Japanese Americans
who had been uprooted from their homes on the West Coast and
confined in internment camps guarded by military police during World
War II. During the 1970s, Uno was part of a small group of former
internees who urged Japanese Americans to publicly discuss the anguish
that individuals, families, and the ethnic community had experienced
because of the wartime incarceration. By reminding the public that
120,000 Japanese Americans had been victimized by racism and hysteria during World War II, Uno insisted, former internees could help prevent a similar injustice from occurring in the future.

Uno's campaign to promote the history of internment initially received little support from the Japanese American community in the
1970s. Many former internees resisted his efforts to end three decades
of silence. They believed it was better to forget the past and feared discussions of internment would reopen old wounds. Some Japanese Americans repressed memories of the wartime camps because they could not
bear to remember the incarceration. Other former internees hoped that
remaining quiet would spare their children the pain they had endured
in the camps. Some even blamed themselves for being confined behind
barbed wire, and they refused to discuss the experience because they
were ashamed. Many Japanese Americans also worried that criticizing
the history of the camps might arouse a backlash and revive the anti-
Japanese hatred that had caused the mass incarceration.

Edison Uno, however, remained determined to revive the history of
internment. To encourage Japanese Americans to remember and de-
nounce the mass incarceration, Uno promoted new scholarly research
on the causes and consequences of internment. These studies documented the extensive anti-Asian and anti-Japanese prejudice that long
preceded the attack on Pearl Harbor, the racism of the government officials who decided to intern Japanese Americans, the violation of the
constitutional rights of 70,000 American citizens of Japanese descent,
and the misery of many internees within the camps. By publicizing this
history of racism and suffering, Uno and other activists helped Japanese

Americans resurrect long-buried memories of internment. They also successfully lobbied to repeal a law that allowed for the recreation of internment camps, established historical landmarks at internment camp sites, and initiated a movement for redress that eventually won a national apology and monetary compensation for former internees, in 1988.

Born in 1929, Edison Tomimaro Uno grew up at a time when people of Japanese ancestry were taunted by racial slurs and subjected to legal discrimination. Since the arrival of Chinese immigrants in the 1840s, nativist groups had portrayed people of Asian ancestry as a "yellow peril." Chinese laborers were depicted as heathen "coolies" who stole jobs from white Americans by working for subhuman wages and who spread immorality and disease. After successfully agitating to end Chinese immigration in 1882, the exclusionist forces focused their attention on the supposed threat from Japan. They denounced Japanese immigrants as cheap laborers, spies for Japan's emperor, and sexual predators. Japanese immigrant women were condemned for encouraging the formation of families and permanent settlement in America. While the children of Japanese immigrants were citizens by virtue of their birth on U.S. soil, they were not spared from these attacks and were made to attend segregated schools. No matter how long they had lived in the United States, the anti-Asian forces argued, any individual of Japanese ancestry was incapable of assimilating or becoming a "true" American.

Ironically, Edison's father, George Kumemaro Uno, came to the United States from Japan in 1905 at the age of nineteen because he had been educated by American missionaries and told that America was "the land of the free and the home of the brave."[2] Hired as a railroad foreman because of his English-language skills, George traveled throughout the country before moving to Oakland to join an uncle who developed an import-export business, canning fish and seafood. In 1912, George sent for and married his childhood sweetheart, Kita Riki, who had also been schooled by American missionaries. The couple moved to Salt Lake City, Utah, in 1916, where George became a florist and helped found the Japanese Church of Christ while Kita oversaw a rapidly expanding family that would eventually include ten children.

During the ten years that the Unos lived in Utah, anti-Japanese groups on the West Coast successfully lobbied for state and federal laws that codified the second-class status of Japanese Americans. In 1913, California had passed the Alien Land Law to prevent Japanese immigrants from owning land within the state. Other western states followed suit and forced many Japanese immigrants to circumvent these laws by purchasing land in the names of their citizen children. George and Kita's dreams of becoming citizens were shattered when the Supreme Court ruled in 1922 in *Ozawa vs. U.S.* that Japanese immigrants, regardless of their qualifications, could never become naturalized citizens. Exclusionist groups from California also tried to stem the flow of immigration from Japan. These anti-Japanese forces celebrated a great victory when the Immigration Act of 1924, aimed largely at restricting immigration from southern and eastern Europe, also terminated all immigration from Japan.

Well aware of the long history of anti-Japanese discrimination in California, the Uno family nevertheless returned to the state and settled in Los Angeles in 1926 because of the temperate weather. Advised by doctors to avoid cold and dampness, George left the floral industry and became a traveling salesman of custom-made men's suits. Kita continued raising their children and in 1929 gave birth to Edison, their ninth child.

Edison was only twelve years old when Japan attacked Pearl Harbor in December 1941. The outbreak of war revived suspicion and hatred of Japanese Americans, and FBI agents immediately began to arrest male immigrants throughout Hawaii and the West Coast. Most of these immigrants were interrogated because they were leaders of the ethnic community and had been under surveillance for at least a year. Many were Buddhist priests, Japanese language teachers, officials of the Japanese Association, and newspaper editors.

FBI agents came to the Uno house and tore apart floorboards, the fireplace, and even walls in a vain search for contraband. Edison's father was arrested by the FBI in February 1942 and classified as a "dangerous enemy alien" because Edison's brother, Buddy Uno, was living in Japan and working for the Japanese Army Press Bureau when the war started. George Uno and over 2,000 other male immigrants were separated from their families and interned, along with over 1,000 Germans and over 200 Italian "enemy aliens," in internment camps run by the Justice Department. Confined at Fort Lincoln, North Dakota, and Lordsburg and Santa Fe, New Mexico, George was not allowed to contact his family for a year and was separated from them until 1944. The Justice Department camps ultimately held 10 percent of all Japanese immigrants from the West Coast and over 2,000 Latin American citizens of Japanese descent, who were deported from their countries so the United States could exchange them for Americans held by Japan.

While Edison and the rest of the Uno family anxiously awaited news of George, their own future remained uncertain for a few months after the beginning of the war. A few individuals defended the rights of Japanese Americans. Walt Woodward, the publisher and editor of the *Bainbridge Island Review*, declared that Japanese Americans had not bombed anyone and deserved to be treated like any other group of Americans. Most of the public, however, refused to distinguish between imperial Japan and Americans of Japanese ancestry. Hostility toward both intensified as Americans listened to reports of a string of Japanese victories in the Pacific. News stories about Pearl Harbor inflamed anger about American losses on Wake Island and in the Philippines. The media presented the most outlandish rumors of Japanese treachery in Hawaii as verified facts. Headlines announced that an effective fifth column of Japanese spies on the island had helped the enemy launch a successful sneak attack. False accounts of Japanese pilots wearing Hawaiian high school and university rings proliferated. Newspapers even declared that Japanese plantation workers had cut sugarcane into arrows, directing enemy pilots to their targets. It did not matter that all of these reports were later proven untrue. Conditioned by decades of "yellow peril" propaganda, many people were quick to believe that anyone with Japanese blood could never be trusted.

Historian Roger Daniels has analyzed the role of racism and hysteria in the decision to intern Japanese Americans. Leading California politicians, including Congressman Leland Ford, Governor Culbert Olson, Attorney General Earl Warren, and Los Angeles mayor Fletcher Bowron, fanned the flames of anti-Japanese prejudice and demanded that military authorities remove all Japanese Americans from the Pacific Coast to prevent espionage and sabotage. The commander of the Western Defense Command, Lieutenant General John L. DeWitt, also feared that Japanese Americans might endanger the security of the West Coast. Worried about an invasion from Japan of California, DeWitt wanted to avoid being caught off guard like his counterpart at Pearl Harbor. California politicians and Provost Marshal Allen Gullion easily convinced the anxious and paranoid DeWitt that only the mass exclusion of all Japanese Americans would keep the West Coast safe.[3]

In February 1942, DeWitt sent a memo to Secretary of War Henry Stimson, calling for the removal of all Japanese Americans from the West Coast because "the Japanese race is an enemy race" and "racial affinities are not severed by migration." DeWitt proclaimed that second- and third-generation Japanese Americans also needed to be excluded because, while they might be citizens, "the racial strains are undiluted." The "very fact that no sabotage has taken place to date," DeWitt explained, was a "disturbing and confirming indication that such action will be taken." Of course, this was a no-win situation for Japanese Americans; nothing could counter assumptions that they were disloyal. In this climate, the fact that no one was arrested for spying or sabotage did not vindicate Japanese Americans. The "sneaky Japs," according to DeWitt, were simply attempting to lull Americans into a false sense of security before revealing their treacherous ways.[4]

Some members of the government and military recognized that DeWitt's logic was skewed. Curtis Munson, an intelligence specialist for Franklin Delano Roosevelt, issued a series of reports to the president, the War Department, and the Western Defense Command, denouncing proposals for mass exclusion. After consulting with the Honolulu FBI, Naval Intelligence in southern California, and British Intelligence in California, Munson concluded that Japanese Americans were no more likely to be "disloyal than any other racial group with whom we went to war." Munson urged the president or vice president to publicly defend the loyalty of Japanese Americans, to quell the rising hysteria on the West Coast.

FBI director J. Edgar Hoover agreed with Munson's view that the public hysteria against Japanese Americans was baseless and irrational. Hoover assured Attorney General Francis Biddle that any individual who might pose a threat to national security had been rounded up by his agents. Biddle and other members of the Justice Department argued against plans for mass removal in meetings with War Department officials and President Roosevelt. After the War Department and Roosevelt accepted DeWitt's recommendation, however, neither Hoover nor Biddle criticized the decision to remove all Japanese Americans from the West Coast.

There was, in fact, little public outcry when President Roosevelt signed Executive Order 9066 on February 19, 1942, authorizing the War Department to designate military areas from which "any and all persons may be excluded." The order never specifically named Japanese Americans, but everyone knew they would be the only group targeted for removal. Earlier, DeWitt had hoped to remove German and Italian "enemy aliens" as well but was overruled by officials who wanted to maintain the support of millions of German American and Italian American voters. Japanese Americans, however, wielded little political influence, because immigrants could not vote and most of the second generation had not yet reached voting age.

The 158,000 Japanese residents of Hawaii also lacked political clout but were spared mass exclusion because they provided a vital pool of labor. Japanese Americans on the West Coast made up less than 2 percent of the population, while Japanese residents in Hawaii constituted 35 percent of the entire population. Realizing that these residents played a critical role in the civilian and military economies, General Delos Emmons opposed plans to remove all Japanese residents from the islands. In stark contrast to his counterpart, General DeWitt, Emmons refused to comply with Washington's requests for the removal of Japanese residents from the islands. Japanese residents in Hawaii still endured discriminatory treatment under martial law and were subjected to travel and work limitations. Almost 1,500 individuals were arrested and interned by the Justice Department because of their prominent roles as ethnic community leaders. There was, however, no mass exclusion of Japanese residents in Hawaii.

Early proposals to force Japanese Americans to leave the southern portion of Arizona and the western sections of California, Oregon, and Washington were transformed into plans for mass incarceration. Public officials in the Mountain States complained that Wyoming and Idaho refused to become dumping grounds for the hated "Japs" from California. Governors of these states, with the exception of Colorado's Ralph Carr, vehemently opposed plans for a "voluntary evacuation" from the West Coast and called for the confinement of Japanese Americans in "concentration camps." By the end of March 1942, the government implemented a procedure to remove Japanese Americans from their homes on the West Coast and place them in camps surrounded by armed guards. The internees included 3,000 Japanese Americans who had been assured that moving from the western half of California to the eastern half would satisfy the authorities.

Most Japanese Americans had less than a week's notice before being forced to leave their communities. Many sold businesses, homes, and cherished belongings for a fraction of their value because they were allowed to bring with them only what they could carry. The Unos were shocked when former friends and neighbors offered a pittance for their stove, refrigerator, washing machine, and beds. Mrs. Uno, however, told her children that she would rather destroy her piano than sell it for a mere two dollars.

When the Unos appeared at the specified departure point in Los Angeles in April 1942, they and other Japanese Americans had no idea of their destination. After being tagged with numbered labels, they were sent to one of sixteen assembly centers located at racetracks and fairgrounds near their homes. The Unos went to the Santa Anita racetrack, where many internees had to live in whitewashed horse stalls that still reeked of manure. Assigned to a barrack in the parking area, the Unos said that the cots in their quarters were so crowded that you had to back out of the room to make a bed.[5] Family members endured repeated interrogations by FBI agents who wanted to collect incriminating evidence against George.

After a few weeks in an assembly center, most Japanese Americans were sent to one of ten relocation centers administered by the War Relocation Authority in remote and desolate areas. The Unos spent several months at Santa Anita before they were sent to the Granada Relocation Center in southeastern Colorado in November 1942. This arid and dusty camp, nicknamed Amache after the name of the daughter of a Cheyenne chief, was the smallest of the camps and held 8,000 Japanese Americans. Located approximately one mile south of the Arkansas Valley, the camp was bordered on the west by a sewer farm, dump pile, and cemetery and on the east by a prairie that extended into Kansas.

Amache and the other WRA camps were surrounded by barbed wire, watchtowers, and armed guards. Facilities at the ten camps varied but all were quite minimal. The average family of six shared a single room that measured twenty by twenty-five feet. Privacy was scarce because room dividers often fell short of the roof and some communal bathrooms lacked partitions. The WRA provided the Unos only with steel army cots, a stove, a broom, and a coal bucket. The Unos and other industrious internees made their own furniture from scrap lumber and planted gardens to supplement the unappealing and starchy camp food.

Initially, internees could not leave the center without being accompanied by someone not of Japanese ancestry. The Unos waited in long lines for the mess halls and the bathrooms, and fought a losing battle against the dust that perpetually seeped through the barrack planks. Some individuals held baseball games, dances, and English-language classes in the camps. Many others, however, complained about the discriminatory pay scale for camp jobs, the exclusion of immigrants from community government positions, the banning of the Japanese language at public meetings, inadequate medical care, and rampant rumors that camp personnel stole food. The biggest source of resentment was caused by the loss of freedom without trial or hearing.

In the 1970s, historians called for the recognition of protesters within the camps as heroic resisters. Attacking earlier depictions of disloyal or misguided dissidents, new studies by Gary Y. Okihiro, Arthur A. Hansen, and David A. Hacker expressed admiration for internees who criticized the cooperative and pro-assimilation stance of the Japanese American Citizens League (JACL) and participated in mass demonstrations against the WRA. Some angry internees had attacked Japanese Americans who they believed had collaborated with the government, and JACL leaders who were accused of informing against immigrant leaders to the FBI were beaten up at the Poston and Manzanar camps at the end of 1942. After two men were arrested for the attack at Poston, internees mounted a general strike that effectively shut down the camp until administrators agreed to negotiations. At Manzanar, a large group of internees protested for the release of an arrested suspect, but were confronted by military police who opened fire on the crowd, killing two people and wounding nine others.[6]

In February 1943 tensions skyrocketed at all of the camps when the WRA required all internees over the age of seventeen to answer a poorly designed "leave clearance" application. The WRA hoped this loyalty questionnaire would enable Japanese Americans to leave camp for military service or resettlement in the Midwest and the East, and never anticipated that two questions would provoke intense controversy. Question Twenty-seven asked internees if they were "willing to serve in the armed forces" of the United States wherever ordered, and Question Twenty-eight required internees to "swear unqualified allegiance" to the United States and "forswear any form of allegiance" to the Japanese emperor. Approximately 68,000 internees answered both questions with an unqualified "yes," but 5,300 answered "no" and 4,600 either refused to answer or qualified their responses.

The WRA did not consider the injustice of asking elderly immigrants to serve in the military or to forswear allegiance to Japan when they were denied American citizenship and feared deportation to Japan. Some internees were alienated by the racism they had endured and refused to risk their lives for a country that imprisoned them. Some citizens even thought that "forswearing" allegiance to Japan in answer to Question Twenty-eight might trap them into admitting an allegiance they never had. Others answered "no" to comply with parental wishes or to appease angry protesters who pressured and sometimes threatened Japanese Americans within the camps. Some elderly immigrants feared that answering the questionnaire would allow the government to push them out of camp into hostile white communities, without providing compensation for their lost businesses and property or allowing them to return to the West Coast.

The loyalty questionnaire tore apart families and friends. Those who answered "yes" to the two key questions left camp for military service or jobs and college programs in the interior and on the East Coast. "No" respondents who refused to change their answers were segregated at the Tule Lake camp in northern California. The army repressed a demonstration at Tule Lake and declared martial law over the camp until January 1944. Later that year, the WRA failed to restrain groups of pro-Japanese militants who coerced immigrants into requesting "repatriation" to Japan and citizens into renouncing their citizenship. Before the WRA regained control of the camp, seven out of every ten adult citizens applied to renounce their citizenship. Research by Donald E. Collins notes that while 12.5 percent of 70,000 internee citizens requested renunciation, most tried to nullify their applications by citing the atmosphere of terror at Tule Lake. After a 14-year legal battle, almost 5,000 were finally able to regain their citizenship rights.[7]

Scholars have also examined the intense conflict generated within the camps over the issue of military service. Leaders of the JACL had lobbied for military service rights because they believed demonstrations of patriotism would help Japanese Americans combat racism. Despite the fact that their families remained imprisoned behind barbed wire, 1,200 Japanese Americans volunteered to serve in segregated combat units. When Selective Service began drafting Japanese Americans at the beginning of 1944, however, more than 300 men refused to comply with draft procedures until their citizenship status was clarified. Many of these draft resisters suffered prison terms of two to four years but were pardoned in 1947 by President Harry Truman. Approximately 23,000 Japanese Americans, more than half of them from Hawaii, served in the Military Intelligence Service, the 100th Infantry Battalion, and the 442d Regimental Combat Team, and received over 18,000 individual citations. The 442d fought in seven major campaigns in Italy and France and became famous as the most decorated unit in American military history for its size and length of service.[8]

Family members and friends sometimes stopped speaking to each other because they took different positions on the loyalty questionnaire and on military service. The hostility between some of Edison's siblings was particularly extreme. His oldest brother, Kazumaro Buddy Uno, had been a pro-Japan supporter during the 1930s and served as a civilian journalist attached to the Japanese Army Press Bureau in Shanghai after 1940. A bitter critic of American racism, Kazumaro was accused of mistreating Allied POWs during the war, at the Bunka Camp in Tokyo. Edison, however, also had three brothers who served in the U.S. Army during the war. Howard and Stanley Uno were among the first Japanese Americans to volunteer for the Military Intelligence Service. In April 1944 a Japanese American newspaper published a letter by Stanley declaring that the three brothers considered Kazumaro a traitor and pledged his "destruction." The letter upset the youngest Uno brother, 16-year-old Robert, who had accompanied Edison, his sister Kay, and his mother in transferring from Granada to Crystal City, Texas, in February 1944, to be reunited with his father. Robert answered "no" to Question Twenty-seven in May 1945, but a few months later changed his answer to "yes" and declared that after being pressured by immigrants to answer negatively, letters from his brothers in the army had convinced him that they were fighting for his place in America.[9]

Other Japanese Americans who also wanted to stay in America were able to return to the West Coast at the end of 1944, when the Supreme Court decided in *Endo* that the government could not continue to detain "concededly loyal" citizens. The same Supreme Court also affirmed the constitutionality of the government's curfew, exclusion, and internment policies in the *Yasui*, *Hirabayashi*, and *Korematsu* decisions. After the *Endo* decision, two-thirds of the internee population chose to go back to the West Coast.[10] Edison, however, did not return to Los Angeles until the fall of 1946, more than a year after the war ended. He remained in Crystal City to stay with his father, who was still classified as a "dangerous" alien because of Kazumaro's wartime activities. In November 1945 the Justice Department decided to deport George Uno to Japan. He successfully appealed the order but was not released until September 1947. When Edison finally left after 1,647 days in camp, he was told he was the last American citizen to be released.

Unlike most former internees, Edison wanted to remember and discuss the injustice of internment. After graduating from a Los Angeles high school and attending law school before a heart attack cut short his ambition to be a lawyer, Edison became a community activist and a lecturer of Asian American Studies at colleges throughout the San Francisco area. In 1967 he initiated a virtual 1-man crusade to wrest an

apology from Supreme Court Chief Justice Earl Warren for his advocacy of internment as California's attorney general in 1942 and his opposition to the return of Japanese Americans to the West Coast in
1943. While Warren never publicly acknowledged any guilt for his wartime conduct, Uno's campaign may have contributed to a private expression of regret that Warren confided to another Japanese American
for his support of internment.

Edison's Evacuation and Relocation course at San Francisco State
University examined the racism that caused internment and benefited
from the work of scholars who, in the 1970s, were beginning to study
the issue. Linking internment of Japanese Americans with racism against
other people of color, Uno's classes, community speeches, and newspaper columns throughout the late 1960s and early 1970s urged Japanese
Americans to discuss the history of internment. While only a small number of internees responded to Uno's appeal to share their camp experiences with the public during the 1970s, those Japanese Americans helped
launch a crusade that would affect the entire ethnic community and the
nation in the next decade.

Together with young student activists, many of whom were the children of silent internees, this small band of protesters argued that former
internees had a duty both to recount the pain they had suffered because
of racial discrimination and to defend other groups targeted because of
their skin color. Many of these activists were dismayed at the way newspapers and magazines praised quiet former internees for supposedly proving that racism could be overcome without demonstrations against the
government. Throughout the late 1960s and the 1970, most media accounts depicted Japanese Americans as "model minorities" who won
economic success in America without militant protests. While other
minorities complained about racism, these articles declared, former internees recovered from the losses they experienced during World War II
because they valued hard work, education, and a respect for authority.
The articles invariably concluded that other racial groups, especially
African Americans, could take a lesson from Japanese Americans who
had pulled themselves up by their own bootstraps.

Condemning media portrayals of prosperous and contented former
internees, Edison Uno tried to publicize a history of Japanese Americans still traumatized by the wartime incarceration. In newspaper articles and speeches, Uno declared that the silence of former internees
was evidence not of recovery but of how much individuals and the community had suffered during the war. Many internees would not speak

Institu
Racism

about the camps, Uno explained, because they could not face their memories of life behind barbed wire or were afraid that sharing this history would lead to more attacks against Japanese Americans. In other words, Uno stated, silent Japanese Americans were still being victimized by racism.

In 1969, Uno joined student activists in a pilgrimage to Manzanar to clean and restore the camp's remains and to encourage discussion of how internment affected Japanese Americans. He became part of the Manzanar Committee that organized future pilgrimages, publicized the history of internment in news and television coverage, and convinced the state of California to designate historical landmarks at Manzanar in 1973 and Tule Lake in 1977. Uno and the other Manzanar Committee members fought the Historical Landmarks Advisory Committee over the wording of the landmark plaques. The Advisory Committee wanted to depict Manzanar as a "relocation center" and a "self-contained city" created "as a result of the hysteria of the early days of World War II." The Manzanar Committee, after battling for a year and a half and enlisting the support of state representatives, made sure that the plaque described Manzanar as a "concentration camp" that was produced by "hysteria, racism, and economic greed." After another round of negotiations and contentious public hearings, the Tule Lake plaque also declared that "racism, economic and political exploitation, and expediency" had created "American concentration camps."[11]

Edison also served as head of a grassroots committee that lobbied the federal government to repeal Title II, a law allowing the attorney general to "detain" suspected threats to "national security." In the late 1960s, Uno and cochair Raymond Okamura feared that the government might use Title II, a 1950 Cold War law permitting "mass imprisonment" during an "internal security emergency," against civil rights activists, antiwar protesters, ghetto rioters, and Chinese Americans suspected of being Communists. Between 1967 and 1969, Uno, Okamura, and a group of community activists launched a public education and publicity drive that reminded politicians, the media, and the general public about the injustice of internment and the danger of future mass incarcerations. After gaining the assistance of influential JACL lobbyists and Japanese American politicians, this crusade helped secure the repeal of Title II in 1971.[12]

When Edison Uno died of a heart attack at the age of forty-seven in December 1976, he was mourned as the father of the modern redress movement. He had called for reparations for former internees throughout the early 1970s, even though few Japanese Americans supported the cause. On the contrary, Uno was harshly criticized for rocking the boat by demanding redress. By the 1980s, however, the redress campaign he initiated received the widespread support of Japanese Americans. During commission hearings that were held throughout the country in 1981, more than 500 Japanese Americans expressed publicly—many for the first time—the pain and anger caused by internment. By speaking about their experiences at community events, participating in letter-writing and petition campaigns, and lobbying politicians, Japanese Americans won support for redress. This display of communal solidarity and grassroots activism that Edison Uno helped inspire contributed to the passage of the Civil Liberties Act of 1988, which authorized a national apology and payments of $20,000 to each former internee. The success of the redress movement was Edison's final and most important legacy.[13]

Notes

1. Edison Uno, " '42 Hysteria Led to Concentration Camps," *Pacific Citizen*, December 20–27, 1974.

2. Arthur A. Hansen, "Interview with Amy Uno Ishii," in *Japanese American World War II Evacuation Oral History Project, Part I: Internees*, ed. Arthur A. Hansen (Westport, CT, 1991), 41.

3. Roger Daniels, *Concentration Camps, U.S.A.: Japanese Americans and World War II* (New York, 1972).

4. U.S. Department of War, *Final Report: Japanese Evacuation from the West Coast, 1942* (Washington, DC: U.S. Government Printing Office, 1943), 33–34.

5. "Interview with Amy Uno Ishii," 65.

6. Gary Y. Okihiro, "Japanese Resistance in America's Concentration Camps: A Re-evaluation," *Amerasia Journal* 2, no. 1 (1973): 20–34; Arthur A. Hansen and David A. Hacker, "The Manzanar Riot: An Ethnic Perspective," *Amerasia Journal* 2 (Fall 1974): 112–57. For a critical analysis of early scholarship on internment, see Lane Ryo Hirabayashi, *The Politics of Fieldwork: Research in an American Concentration Camp* (Tucson, 1999). Paul R. Spickard critically evaluates JACL cooperation in "The Nisei Assume Power: The Japanese Citizens League, 1941–1942," *Pacific Historical Review* 52 (May 1983): 147–74. The Poston strike is described in Lane Ryo Hirabayashi, ed., *Inside an American Concentration Camp: Japanese American Resistance at Poston* (Tucson, 1995). For contrasting internee views of the Manzanar riot, see Sue Kunitomi et al., eds., *Manzanar Martyr: An Interview with Harry A. Ueno* (Fullerton, CA, 1986); and Karl G. Yoneda, *Ganbatte! The Sixty-Year Struggle of a Kibei Worker* (Los Angeles, 1983).

7. Donald E. Collins, *Native American Aliens: Disloyalty and the Renunciation of Citizenship by Japanese Americans during World War II* (Westport, CT, 1985).

8. Masayo Umezawa Duus, *Unlikely Liberators: The Men of the 100th and the 442nd* (Honolulu, 1987); Thelma Chang, *"I Can Never Forget": Men of the 100th/442nd* (Honolulu, 1991). Douglas W. Nelson analyzes draft resistance in *Heart Mountain: The History of an American Concentration Camp* (Madison, 1976).

9. Yuji Ichioka, "The Meaning of Loyalty: The Case of Kazumaro Buddy Uno," *Amerasia Journal* 23 (1997–98): 70, footnote 54.

10. Peter Irons reveals how the Justice Department concealed evidence from the Supreme Court to bolster the government's position in *Justice at War: The Story of the Japanese American Internment Cases* (New York, 1983). For accounts of resettlement experiences, see Valerie Matsumoto, "Japanese American Women during World War II," *Frontiers* 8 (1984): 6–14; and Gary Y. Okihiro, *Storied Lives: Japanese American Students and World War II* (Seattle, 1999).

11. Letter from John H. Michael to Warren T. Furutani, April 7, 1972, Manzanar Relocation Center Files No. 850, Office of Historic Preservation, California Department of Parks and Recreation, Sacramento, California; Tule Lake State Historical Landmark, March 16, 1977, Tule Lake Center Files No. 850-2, Office of Historic Preservation, California Department of Parks and Recreation, Sacramento, California. For more examples of nisei and sansei activism, see Jere Takahashi, *Nisei/Sansei: Shifting Japanese American Identities and Politics* (Philadelphia, 1997).

12. Raymond Okamura, "Background and History of the Repeal Campaign," *Amerasia Journal* 2 (Fall 1974): 73–94.

13. For accounts of Japanese American redress, see William Minoru Hohri, *Repairing America: An Account of the Movement for Japanese American Redress* (Pullman, WA, 1984); Roger Daniels et al., eds., *Japanese Americans: From Relocation to Redress* (Salt Lake City, 1986); Leslie T. Hatamiya, *Righting a Wrong: Japanese Americans and the Passage of the Civil Liberties Act of 1988* (Stanford, 1993); Yasuko Takezawa, *Breaking the Silence: Redress and Japanese American Ethnicity* (Ithaca, 1995); and Mitchell T. Maki et al., *Achieving the Impossible Dream: How Japanese Americans Obtained Redress* (Urbana and Chicago, 1999).

Suggested Readings

Chang, Gordon. *Morning Glory, Evening Shadow: Yamato Ichihashi and His Internment Writings, 1942–1945.* Stanford: Stanford University Press, 1997.

Daniels, Roger. *Prisoners without Trial: Japanese Americans in World War II.* New York: Hill and Wang, 1993.

Hansen, Arthur A., and Betty E. Mitson, eds. *Voices Long Silent: An Oral Inquiry into the Japanese-American Evacuation.* Fullerton: Japanese American History Project of the Oral History Program at California State University, Fullerton, 1974.

Hayashi, Brian. *"For the Sake of Our Japanese Brethren": Assimilation, Nationalism, and Protestantism among the Japanese of Los Angeles, 1895–1942.* Stanford: Stanford University Press, 1995.

Matsumoto, Valerie. *Farming the Home Place: A Japanese American Community in California, 1919–1982.* Ithaca, NY: Cornell University Press, 1993.

Murray, Alice Yang. *What Did the Internment of Japanese Americans Mean?* Boston: Bedford/St. Martin's Press, 2000.

Spickard, Paul R. *Japanese Americans: The Formation and Transformations of an Ethnic Group.* New York: Twayne Publishers, 1996.

Tateishi, John. *And Justice for All: An Oral History of the Japanese American Detention Camps.* New York: Random House, 1984.

Weglyn, Michi. *Years of Infamy: The Untold Story of America's Concentration Camps.* New York: William Morrow and Company, 1976.

Yoo, David. *Growing up Nisei: Race, Generation, and Culture among Japanese Americans of California, 1924–1949.* Urbana: University of Illinois Press, 2000.

12

Joy Neugebauer
Purchasing the California Dream in Postwar Suburbia

Elisabeth Orr

The end of World War II marked a period of massive suburbanization in California that has continued to the present day. Sprawling suburbs, characterized by endless tracts of single-family homes and vast shopping malls, have steadily extended outward from all of the state's metropolitan centers.

The desire to relocate by thousands of veterans who had passed through California during the war, the passage of the GI Bill that offered veterans low-interest home loans, and the limitless acres of cheap, undeveloped land combined to create the postwar suburban boom. In subsequent years, the terms of the Interstate Highway Act created the infrastructure for further suburban growth, and the establishment of hundreds of high-tech firms funded by Cold War military budgets lured hundreds of thousands to California for high-paying jobs. From southern San Diego to Santa Rosa, millions of families have settled in suburban neighborhoods and commuted miles away for work and leisure. While the city of Los Angeles proper is home to 3.5 million people, for instance, more than 15 million people live in the suburban sprawl that extends outward from Los Angeles into five counties.

For many families, the ability to buy large, inexpensive homes in attractive and friendly neighborhoods made the American dream a reality. But suburban sprawl also increasingly came to mean environmental blight, long commutes, and the economic decline of inner cities. And all too often, people of color were unwelcome in these neighborhoods. In this essay, Elisabeth Orr, assistant professor of history at Long Beach City College, examines the experience of the Neugebauer family, who moved from Long Beach to the new Orange County suburb of Westminster in the 1950s. There they raised their children, along with thousands of other new suburbanites, against the backdrop of tremendous national social, political, and economic changes.

In 1956, Joy Neugebauer and her husband, Don, moved to their new suburban home in Orange County, California, just south of Los Angeles. With its agricultural past and sparse population, few would have predicted Orange County's future as one of the fastest-growing areas in the country. Joy Neugebauer did not imagine that she was taking part in history, nor could she have known how dramatically her life would change from wife and mother to community activist and eventually mayor of her suburban city. But her story is about more than one person or one family. It is about the efforts of one generation to achieve the American dream in suburbia, with its safe streets, good schools, and family-centered life-style. By moving to the suburbs in the 1950s and 1960s, white middle-class Americans transformed cultural expectations about the ideal place to live and attempted to pass on to their children the values and traditions that they deemed important.

In the years following World War II, Americans moved from cities to suburbs in record numbers. They sought the suburban "good life," which southern California epitomized with its temperate climate, plentiful sunshine, and access to beaches, mountains, and deserts. These migrants were lured by the suburban ideal as it was promoted by local boosters, developers, popular culture, and the California-based entertainment industry. California, one propagandist told Americans, "symbolizes a way of life or a state of mind if not a geographical area to most people."[1]

By the 1950s most middle-class Americans looked to suburbia as an idyllic setting in which to raise their children. Purchasing a suburban home allowed them to create a measure of financial security that they had lacked growing up during the Great Depression. Suburbia was also a refuge from increasingly overcrowded cities after an unprecedented number of Americans had moved from their small towns and rural areas during the war for defense-related jobs. Suburbs seemed to combine the best of urban and rural life by being within commuting distance of suburban job centers and yet set in a semirural area with yards and parks in abundance. Perhaps the most important reason of all for the growth of suburbia was the baby boom, which resulted in the largest single generation in American history. Parents with young children sought spacious houses, big yards, and safe communities in which to raise their new families. It seemed that after years of deprivation during the depression and World War II, Americans believed that more and bigger were better: more babies, bigger cars, more household appliances, more television sets, and their own large homes.

The Neugebauer family was just one of millions of families in the 1950s to take part in this national trend. Don and Joy Neugebauer, with their four (eventually seven) children, found their suburban tract filled with "people about in the same age group that we were, that just had young children or were just starting a family."[2] With age and parenthood in common, suburbanites like the Neugebauers worked together toward common goals in their communities. They participated in PTA, Little League, and local government, and supported a variety of civic groups including the Elks, Kiwanis, and Soroptimist Clubs. They threw parties with their neighbors and built friendships that lasted for decades. By examining the Neugebauer family's suburban experience, we can better understand how suburbia came to epitomize white, middle-class life in the 1950s and 1960s, what kinds of communities suburbanites created, and finally, postwar suburbia's impact on California.

The Lure of the California Suburban Dream

Originally from the Midwest, Don and Joy Neugebauer moved to southern California in 1956 so that Don could open his own industrial supply company catering to the aerospace industry. They already had several children and felt it was time to be out on their own. The Neugebauers hoped that with a bit of luck and a lot of hard work they could be successful. They had good reason for their optimism. Don had several years of experience managing a similar kind of industrial business in the Chicago area, and with the federal government spending millions of dollars on defense during the Cold War, aerospace companies throughout California thrived. World War II had already transformed the state's economy into an industrial powerhouse, creating labor shortages in San Francisco's shipbuilding industry as well as in Los Angeles's and San Diego's aircraft industries. With plenty of good middle-class and working-class jobs available, many Americans continued the trend of moving from less industrialized areas to those such as southern California, which were profiting from government defense contracts after the war.

The Neugebauers were not alone in coming to California for a new life in the 1940s and 1950s. In fact, by the mid-1950s, California had become the symbol of relaxed, outdoor living that made it number one among Americans as the "best state" and the "ideal place to live," according to a Gallup poll conducted at the time. The Los Angeles area ranked second in climate, beauty of setting, and nightlife.[3] Americans flocked to southern California; in the early postwar years, migrants formed nearly 70 percent of its population.[4]

Southern California's earliest suburban residents in the 1950s found housing in short supply since the market was already overcrowded—too few houses for too many people. Young couples doubled or tripled up in one- and two-bedroom apartments. The cause of the problem was simple: more Americans moved to California in the 1950s and 1960s than anywhere else, and by 1963 the state was growing three times faster than the rest of the country.[5]

Fortunately, southern California, and Orange County in particular, had lots of available land since much of the area had been used for agricultural production prior to and during the war. Postwar real estate developers knew an opportunity when they saw one: by buying up relatively inexpensive farmland, they could build suburban developments to house the burgeoning population. Orange County, the present-day site of Disneyland, strip malls, and tract homes, quickly became the center of the building frenzy. Cheap land and affordable houses combined with close proximity to Long Beach and Los Angeles to create a package that attracted thousands of young married couples.[6]

It was to Orange County that the Neugebauers moved their family from nearby Long Beach. Although the family business remained in Long Beach, a city founded in the late nineteenth century, the Neugebauers decided to look elsewhere to buy a home. They wanted an area with better schools and more spacious and affordable houses. Each weekend they explored neighboring communities looking for just the right place. One of the largest planned suburban communities anywhere, Lakewood, California, was located next to Long Beach, but for a family of six, the typical Lakewood 2-bedroom, 1-bath house was too small. To the south, Orange County towns like Westminster and Garden Grove were rapidly being transformed. Fields of celery, beans, and strawberries along with miles of orange groves were being plowed under to make way for new suburban developments that made sleepy little towns into suburban cities almost overnight. Billboards along local highways shouted, "Veterans, Look! No Down Payment. New 2-Bedroom Homes in the Heart of the Orange Groves, in Garden Grove." Veterans were offered monthly payments of $56, which put home ownership within the reach of most working-class and middle-class families.[7] Mortgage rates were so low at this time that it was cheaper to buy a house than to rent one. A key factor in the shift toward higher rates of home ownership was the Federal Housing Administration (FHA), which insured mortgages, making it possible to buy a house with little to no down payment. As a result, building in northern Orange County, and elsewhere around the country, continued at a frenetic pace from the mid-1950s through the 1960s.

When the Neugebauers first began looking for a new home in 1956, they saw many empty lots since the area was still largely rural. Real estate agents showed prospective buyers model homes sitting at the edge of the proposed development. Model homes helped potential buyers to more easily envision themselves and their furnishings in the new setting. The Neugebauers' first experience in looking for a house in Westminster gave them little reason to plan their future home there. Joy Neugebauer recalled that it was raining as they drove around with their four young sons, looking at new developments. That day the land for the proposed suburb was little more than a muddy field in an unincorporated area, not yet called Westminster. "There was an old, wooden paint-peeling sign that said 'Barber City,' " she remembered. "[It] was leaning over on a tilt because of the rain. We really laughed the first time we drove through the area and thought, 'Who'd want to live there?' But then we came back a few months later and went through the models. [We bought the house] because of the proximity to the school, and the floor plans, and the cost to purchase the home."[8]

The Neugebauers' purchase was representative of a larger trend. Compared to their parents' generation, the Neugebauers and their generation had a much higher rate of home ownership. For example, in 1934 in the midst of the Great Depression, 44 percent of Americans owned their own homes. By 1972, 63 percent were homeowners. At the same time, eighteen of the nation's twenty-five largest cities lost population as residents eagerly embraced suburbia as affordable, safe, and within commuting range of jobs. In addition, the ranks of the middle class grew tremendously during this period, further fueling the growth of suburbia. *Fortune* magazine estimated that the economy was growing so rapidly during the mid-1950s that the number of families moving into the middle class increased by 1.1 million per year. By 1956 there were approximately 16.6 million middle-class families in the United States, more and more of whom lived in suburbia. Further evidence of this trend lies in the fact that of 13 million new homes built in the 1950s, 85 percent were in suburbia.[9]

Communities in Orange County that went from small town to suburban city also experienced a shift in life-style that was part of a national trend. Joy Neugebauer recalled that when she moved there in 1956, Westminster had one grocery store called You Tell 'Em. There was no supermarket at all at that time, and she remembered there being only one little place to get gas for the car.[10] The small-town feeling soon faded, however, as the population of the county rose from 130,800 to a little over 1 million by the late 1950s, a 750 percent increase.[11] Small mom-and-pop stores whose Main Street locations lacked sufficient parking and whose prices were higher than those of the supermarket and department store chains were bypassed for newer, closer, and cheaper shopping centers.[12]

Transportation within newly suburbanized areas like northern Orange County contributed to the transformation. Country roads were no longer sufficient to carry the increasingly heavy traffic as suburbanites clogged local roads on their daily commutes. Soon, freeways were built to carry thousands of cars from Orange County to Long Beach and Los Angeles and back again. Seventh Street, which for decades had connected Long Beach to the Orange County communities of Westminster, Garden Grove, Santa Ana, and Orange, now became the 22 Freeway. Other freeways including the 5, the 91, and the 405 also cut across the Orange County region and linked newly built suburban areas to nearby cities where residents worked and shopped. Old downtowns declined further as the new freeways made it easier to get to upscale shopping centers. Freeways accelerated the rate of suburban development because they made it possible for residents to commute from farther and farther away. Southern California soon became known for traffic snarls and long commutes.

By the late 1950s cultural stereotypes had come to define white, middle-class families as suburban. Television shows like *Leave It to Beaver*, *Father Knows Best*, *Ozzie and Harriet*, and *The Donna Reed Show* were all set in suburbia and featured white middle-class families in which traditional gender roles prevailed. These series replaced earlier shows from the late 1940s and early 1950s that had depicted greater diversity in American life. *The Goldbergs*, for example, featured an urban, Jewish extended family and, although initially popular, the show was canceled by 1955, having become too ethnic for the times. The only show to successfully combine ethnic diversity and urban living was *I Love Lucy*, with its young urban couple, Lucy and Ricky Ricardo (a Cuban immigrant). Still, the show's setting changed from New York City to suburban Westport, Connecticut, in the 1950s, when its ratings began to slip. The move was a successful one and the show remained on the air. People of color were virtually absent in popular representations of middle-class life. The few urban critics who decried suburban conformity and viewed suburbia as a cultural wasteland were largely ignored by the enthusiastic young homeowners who embraced their new homogeneous communities.

Suburban Communities

Once the Neugebauers moved to Westminster, their lives reflected the values of other suburbanites in their generation. New suburban communities such as Westminster were child-centered and signaled a return to traditional gender roles that had briefly been overturned during the war years. The Neugebauers also followed this trend, with Don working in his business and Joy working in hers, the home. In addition, postwar suburban life ushered in a period of what *McCall's* magazine termed "togetherness," a renewed focus on family life and marriage that, according to historian Elaine Tyler May, offered comfort and stability after years of separation and loss during World War II. This renewed emphasis on family brought a sense of security in the early Cold War years, when fear of communism and the atomic bomb were never far away.

As a result, suburbanites created order in a time of crisis by organizing civic clubs, block parties, and coffee klatches. They built fences together, raised money for the PTA, and looked out for each other's children. Because their houses were all within the same price range, many of them even held similar kinds of jobs, or at least had similar income levels. The Neugebauers found their new neighbors came from backgrounds much like their own and included two teachers, a vice principal, a career military officer, and a telephone company executive. In the late 1950s they were all white with the exception of the military officer's wife, Mary, who was Japanese. She and Joy became good friends over the years and, despite earlier discrimination in California against Japanese Americans, Mary was warmly accepted by other neighbors.

Soon after moving to Westminster, the Neugebauers began to be involved in their community. They found it was easy to get to know people since "we were all busy putting in our lawns, [and] doing all the things that you do to a new home." The Neugebauers focused on raising their children, like most residents in suburban neighborhoods. Child rearing was made easier by the fact that nearly all of their new neighbors had young children, too. Joy Neugebauer remembered: "My son Dwayne had been born in March, just before we moved here, but when we looked across the street, four of my neighbors that we lived directly across from each had children by that October. So my son Dwayne had

Nanette, Steve, Arnold, and Theresa [who] were born the same year he was. So, as I say, we had very much in common. We each had new babies, and some of us [also] had children that were a few years older."[13]

This focus on children carried over into holiday celebrations. "On the Fourth of July we'd all share—fireworks were legal—we'd all do our displays on the street and have a lot of fun. We'd watch over our children together."[14] They had parties at Christmastime and birthday parties throughout the year. Because most of the mothers stayed home, the women of the neighborhood coordinated many of the activities and celebrations.

The Neugebauer boys were involved in numerous activities, as was typical of many suburban youth. They played Little League baseball, Junior American football, and basketball. They joined the Cub Scouts and later the Boy Scouts. They also joined neighborhood friends in spontaneous games at the nearby school playground.

While Don Neugebauer ran the family business, Joy was active in supporting whatever their sons were doing. "Wherever my children were involved, I was involved. My philosophy was when they went out the door the first day of school, I went with them because I was concerned about the environment they would find away from home, and I tried to shape it, worked to shape it in a way I felt would benefit them."[15]

Although there were only three elementary schools in the school district at the time, the number soon grew to nineteen elementary schools plus middle schools and high schools as the population of school-age children continued to grow throughout the 1960s. From Joy Neugebauer's perspective, "It was really the schools and the PTAs that . . . drew people together to form friendships and to work for the positive changes, [and] projects that needed to be done within the new community."[16] By working together, residents created a recreational sports program that included Little League baseball; they also organized their first Cub Scout packs and Boy Scout troops. Like other children of the baby boom generation, the Neugebauer boys were more involved in organized activities than any generation before them, a reflection of their parents' determination that their kids would have all the advantages they had missed themselves.

Suburban parents were determined to pass on their values to their children. A perfect example of this was the Neugebauer tradition of family dinners. "In the years when we had six or seven sons [at home], our dinner meal was at five. And all of our sons were at the table for that meal and we sat down to the table [together]. You didn't eat separately.

You ate together as a family," Joy recalled. "Every Friday night was considered family night because it wasn't a school night."[17] Such traditions not only created a sense of togetherness among family members, but they also provided a regular time for parents and children to communicate and to reaffirm the importance of certain values and beliefs.

Joy Neugebauer believed one result of growing up during the depression was that she and her husband had a "very strong work ethic." Coming from a family of eleven, with a father who worked in an Ohio paper mill to support them, Joy began working at the age of fourteen. "I bought all of my own clothes. I wasn't really expected to, it was just a matter of if I wanted them. If I wanted them, I would [work] and by that age I wanted to wear my own clothes, and not some that had belonged to somebody else." Despite their financial difficulties, or perhaps because of them, Joy's parents emphasized that education and personal responsibility were keys to improving their children's lives: "All of our sons had jobs when they came home from school. . . . First, they took off their school clothes and put on their play clothes. Each of them had a chore but the chore didn't last long. We had usually six [children] that were the age to have a chore, so none of them had too much to do but empty all the wastebaskets . . . , dust the furniture, . . . wash the two bathroom sinks. And this was something that would happen every day." Ultimately, the Neugebauer boys knew that "it was Dad's responsibility to go to work, and it was Mom's responsibility to take care of the house and cook, and it was their responsibility to go to school and to learn as much as they could and to apply themselves. That was much the same as with my childhood."[18]

Popular television shows reinforced the traditional gender roles in suburban culture. When a show like *Father Knows Best* (the title says it all) addressed a problem, not only was it able to be solved within the show's half-hour format, but the solution generally emphasized respect for authority, especially male authority. Such shows were tremendously popular in part because they portrayed American family life as cheery and relatively uncomplicated. Although suburban life was rarely so easy and sanitized as television portrayed, Orange County suburbanites still often remember their towns as "the ideal American community."[19]

This picture of the ideal was not a diverse one, and, in fact, racial and class homogeneity was key to the suburban vision. Working-class people and persons of color were often ignored in the suburban stereotype. When television shows portrayed suburbia and suburbanites as entirely white, they were not far off the mark. Suburban communities across the country *were* often completely white. Orange County suburbs were no exception. Although the county had previously been fairly diverse, with Japanese American farmers and Mexican American farmworkers in addition to Anglo farmers, relatively few nonwhites moved to these suburbs in the immediate postwar era. Restrictive covenants made it illegal for residents to sell their homes to nonwhites and to Jews prior to the 1948 landmark U.S. Supreme Court case *Shelley vs. Kramer,* which declared that restrictive covenants were unconstitutional. But even after that, informal gentlemen's agreements pressured residents in all white neighborhoods to sell only to other whites and Christians. In addition, real estate agents used racist "steering" practices to keep nonwhites out of white neighborhoods. In the new suburbs of northern Orange County, the nonwhite population was dwarfed by the incoming flood of white suburbanites. As a result, from 1950 to 1970 the nonwhite population of Westminster and nearby suburban communities such as Garden Grove was never much over 2 percent.[20]

Not all suburbanites were racist, of course, and families of color with adequate class standing could sometimes gain acceptance. When a black family, the Smiths, moved onto the Neugebauers' street in the early 1970s, Joy made sure they felt welcome and invited the wife, Marian, to her annual Christmas party along with all the other women on the street. She recalled that one neighbor had a negative response, saying, "If you invite Marian to your Christmas party, I won't be there." Joy invited Marian Smith anyway and the other woman showed up, evidently having rethought her position. Joy recalled, "The [Smith] family became very accepted on our street. He was a doctor and they became too affluent for our street and moved." The neighbors became so fond of them that "when the Smiths moved, the concern on the street was that the more affluent area that they moved into would not be as accepting of the children, and there was concern about the children being hurt."[21] As long as the population of nonwhites, especially blacks, remained low, suburbanites in California tended to be tolerant of individual families. This did not produce large-scale integration, however. It was not until the 1980s and 1990s that greater suburban integration was achieved, particularly among Asians and Latinos and to a lesser degree among blacks.

In terms of community involvement, Joy Neugebauer continued her work in a variety of community groups throughout the 1960s. Such organizations included Mother's March, which held fund-raisers each January to collect donations to help find a cure or a vaccine for polio, a devastating disease that often left its victims, young and old, paralyzed. Joy also served as president of the local PTAs at her sons' elementary schools, intermediate schools, and high schools—although not at the same time. When the boys were in Cub Scouts, she was the den mother, and when they were old enough to play Little League baseball, she was the team mother. At various times she also served as chairwoman for multiple sclerosis, muscular dystrophy, and heart disease fund-raising drives. "It seems like I was always organizing groups of people to go door to door to generate money to find answers to some of the health concerns, especially as they related to children," Joy recalled.[22] Her values as suburban housewife and mother were clear: children came first.

As her community involvement increased and she became more acquainted with the workings of the city, Joy Neugebauer began to believe that the local government was ineffective. She thought that Westminster's city council "did not serve the interests of the community. I felt the people I had met working as a volunteer deserved better representation than they were receiving." When news of a scandal broke, four of the city's council members were tried and went to prison on charges of accepting bribes for illegal zoning changes. Joy Neugebauer recalls feeling relieved, but she and other residents saw little change on the council. So, although busy with family and community responsibilities already, she pondered running for a council seat. When her husband suggested it, she responded, "Well, I'll think about it, Don, but remember when you're home babysitting and I'm on city council that it was your idea."[23]

In 1968, Joy Neugebauer ran for Westminster's city council. She spent only $72 on her entire campaign. She designed her own flyers, printed them up on white paper, and she and her children handed them out in the community. "It was really just something I felt I could do better than any of the men that were there. Not because they were men, but because they were the ones that were there. So I ran." Not only was Joy the first woman to run, she was also the first to be elected. Moreover, at the first council meeting she attended, she was elected mayor pro tem. In 1972 and 1976 she ran again, and each time was reelected. Sadly, Don was diagnosed with cancer in late 1974 and by January of 1975 he had died. Despite this personal tragedy and her new status as a single parent and head of the family business, Joy continued her involvement in politics. Although she had lost a bid for the U.S. House of Representatives in the Republican primary in June of 1974, she remained active in city government throughout most of the 1980s. In the 1990s she ran for a seat on the Orange County Board of Supervisors, but was again defeated. She remained undaunted, however. "My philosophy is that it doesn't matter if you win. If you challenge someone, force them into a runoff, a person that is so deeply entrenched, it forces them to reevaluate and do a better job, work for more people. So, as I say, I've never really mourned any of my losses."[24] As an active member of the Republican Party, Joy Neugebauer's political views were in line with those of many white, middle-class suburbanites of her era who believed in low taxes, smaller government, and more local control of schools and social services. Although today Orange County residents hold diverse political views, in the 1950s and 1960s the county established its reputation for political conservatism in stark contrast to more liberal Los Angeles County.

Just as Joy Neugebauer began to take on the public and previously male role of city council member, the women's movement was taking hold throughout the country. Though she was not a member of the movement herself and would probably not consider herself a feminist, in many ways she again mirrored national changes by working full-time to support her family and becoming involved in the previously male world of local and national politics. Joy Neugebauer finished raising her youngest sons by herself after her husband's death at a time when many women found themselves in a similar position due largely to a rising divorce rate, rather than to death. Fortunately, she was able to make the transition more gracefully than many women because of assistance from her sons and because she was able to step into the family business. In that position she negotiated multimillion-dollar contracts, a role she would never have been given at the time in corporate America. In recent years, Joy Neugebauer has become active in Westminster's historical society, and in the late 1990s she was reelected to another term on the city council. As a member of the historical society, she has taken on the task of teaching children, many of whom are immigrants, about the history of Westminster. She hopes they will take pride in it as she has and that they will carry on the values of those who came before.

The city of Westminster continued to evolve as a postwar suburb in the 1970s and 1980s when it became home to Little Saigon, an ethnic enclave of Vietnamese refugees. Orange County has become overwhelmingly suburban, with freeways that shuttle commuters north to Los

Angeles, east toward Riverside and San Bernardino Counties, and south toward San Diego County. The entire region of southern California, including many of Orange County's suburbs, has become racially diverse as Asian and Latino immigrants have moved in. The white population in the region has declined to a degree as some whites have moved out, relocating to northern California and out of state. The black population has remained small in Orange County, though it, too, is growing as African Americans also move to suburbia for a piece of the California dream.

Conclusion

Joy Neugebauer's story illustrates California's postwar suburban experience. By marrying, having a large family, moving to the suburbs, becoming homeowners, and getting involved in community organizations, she and her husband typified the lives led by many white, middle-class women and men. One result of this new American suburban culture—centered on child rearing and community—was that white and middle-class came to be defined as suburban. By working in child-oriented organizations such as the PTA and Little League and on children's health issues such as polio, Joy Neugebauer and other suburban women created communities that reflected their values. Suburban men, like Don Neugebauer, also worked on their own piece of the dream, largely that of financial security and home ownership. For suburbanites of Don and Joy Neugebauer's generation, the communities they created were a dream come true, "the ideal place to live." Although there were many people who were left out of the postwar suburban dream, those outside, such as African Americans and to a lesser degree Asians and Latinos, were increasingly able to achieve suburban home ownership in the 1970s, 1980s, and 1990s. Divorced women and their children often found themselves shut out, however, by the high prices of suburban houses that skyrocketed in Orange County and California in general in the 1970s and 1980s. In recent years important issues in California and the nation—sprawl, the environment, immigration, higher energy costs, and education—have all been related in one way or another to suburbia. The suburban way of life in California is often taken for granted today because it has become the norm for so many in the state, whether in aging postwar suburbs or in newer suburban developments. The postwar vision of suburbia as a good place to live and an ideal place to raise one's children persists to this day. The postwar suburban California dream has, in many ways, come to define the American dream.

Notes

1. James L. Parsons, "The Uniqueness of California," *American Quarterly* 1 (1949): 44.

2. Joy Neugebauer, interview by author, August 2 and September 14, 1995.

3. Roland Marchand, "Visions of Classlessness, Quests for Dominion: American Popular Culture, 1945–1960," in *Reshaping America: Society and Institutions, 1945–1960*, ed. Robert Bremner and Gary Reichard (Columbus, OH, 1982), 167.

4. "The California Way of Life: Climate and the Automobile Create a New Pattern of Indoor-Outdoor Living," *Life* (October 22, 1945): 105.

5. Eugene Burdick, "From Gold Rush to Sun Rush," *New York Times Magazine*, April 14, 1963.

6. Gerald D. Nash, *The American West Transformed: The Impact of the Second World War* (Bloomington, IN, 1985), 14.

7. Tyler Park advertisement, *Santa Ana Register*, January 8, 1950.

8. Neugebauer interview.

9. Kenneth T. Jackson, *Crabgrass Frontier: The Suburbanization of the United States* (New York, 1985), 216; Mark Baldassare, *Trouble in Paradise: The Suburban Transformation of America* (New York, 1986), 1; David Halberstam, *The Fifties* (New York, 1993), 142, 587; *Fortune* magazine figures found in Halberstam. *Fortune* considered anyone earning $5,000 per year or more to be middle class.

10. Neugebauer interview.

11. Leroy Doig, *The Town of Garden Grove* (Santa Ana, CA, 1966), 232; William Gayk, "The Changing Demography of Orange County," *Journal of Orange County Studies* 3/4 (Fall 1989/Spring 1990): 16.

12. Neugebauer interview.

13. Ibid.

14. Ibid.

15. Ibid.

16. Ibid.

17. Ibid.

18. Ibid.

19. Charmayne Bohman, interview by author, tape recording, Seal Beach, California, February 15, 1995.

20. U.S. Department of Commerce, *County and City Data Book: A Statistical Abstract* (Washington, DC, 1962), 476, 486, and *Census of Population and Housing* (Washington, DC, 1970). In Orange County as a whole, the white population remained the overwhelming majority until the 1990s, by which time Asian and Latino populations had grown substantially. The 2000 census revealed that many cities in the region had no majority population, including Westminster and Garden Grove.

21. Neugebauer interview.

22. Ibid.

23. Ibid.

24. Ibid.

Suggested Readings

Fong, Timothy. *The First Suburban Chinatown: The Remaking of Monterey Park, California.* Philadelphia: Temple University Press, 1994.

Jackson, Kenneth T. *Crabgrass Frontier: The Suburbanization of the United States.* New York: Oxford University Press, 1985.

Kelly, Barbara M. *Expanding the American Dream: Building and Rebuilding Levittown.* New York: State University of New York Press, 1993.

Kling, Rob, et al., eds. *Postsuburban California: The Transformation of Orange County since World War II.* Berkeley: University of California Press, 1991.

May, Elaine Tyler. *Homeward Bound: American Families in the Cold War Era.* New York: Basic Books, 1988.

Orr, Elisabeth. "Living along the Faultline: Community, Suburbia, and Multiethnicity in Westminster and Garden Grove, California, 1900–1995." Ph.D. diss., Indiana University, 1999.

Spigel, Lynn. *Make Room for TV: Television and the Family Ideal in Postwar America.* Chicago: University of Chicago Press, 1992.

Waldie, D. J. *Holy Land: A Suburban Memoir.* New York: St. Martin's Press, 1996.

13

S. I. Hayakawa
Asian American Radicalism and the Dilemma of American Liberalism

Daryl Maeda

Given California's vast and diverse population, it is not surprising that the state's political culture in the 1960s saw much agitation and support from almost every side of the political spectrum. Countercultural and progressive political movements, mostly centered in the Bay Area, attracted considerable national attention. The Black Panther movement that started in Oakland, the University of California at Berkeley's Free Speech Movement and massive antiwar protests, San Francisco's fledgling gay rights movement, and the emerging United Farm Workers' efforts in central and southern California were just some of the major pieces in the state's leftist political culture during the 1960s.

However, for all the attention radical movements and politics received, mostly conservative, white, middle-class suburban communities, such as those that sprang up throughout Orange County, exerted tremendous political power in local and state elections. In 1964, California voters not only sent conservative actor George Murphy to the U.S. Senate, but they passed Proposition 14, which overturned the state's Fair Housing Act, enacted only the year before. In 1966 voters sent another conservative actor, Ronald Reagan, to the statehouse as governor.

In this essay, Daryl Maeda, assistant professor of history at Oberlin College, explores how radical and conservative politics clashed in California through the career of S. I. Hayakawa, college president and U.S. senator. Hayakawa's liberal conceptions of racial politics were challenged by radical student groups at San Francisco State College in 1968, pushing him and many other California liberals to the political right.

On December 2, 1968, at San Francisco State College, a 62-year-old Japanese American man wearing a tam-o'-shanter hat pushed his way through a crowd of jeering college students and clambered aboard a parked truck. As the students heckled, acting college president Samuel Ichiyé (S. I.) Hayakawa unceremoniously unplugged an amplifier used to broadcast protest leaders' voices across campus. The students were participating in the Third World Liberation Front's strike for the establishment of a school of ethnic studies. Hayakawa's bold act would turn out to be one of the key moments in the history of 1960s student activism, catapulting him into the national consciousness as a hard-liner cracking down on campus radicals. The image of the feisty president

From the *Los Angeles Examiner,* Hearst Newspaper Collection, Department of Special Collections, University of Southern California Library. *Courtesy of the University of Southern California on behalf of the University of Southern California Specialized Libraries and Archival Collections*

was broadcast across the nation and published in numerous newspapers, and the *San Francisco Chronicle* went so far as to call his actions a "bravura performance."[1] Hayakawa later parlayed his status as a conservative hero into a seat in the U.S. Senate, where he represented California from 1977 to 1982.

The year 1968 was a critical turning point in California and U.S. history. The southern-based civil rights movement of the earlier part of the decade had focused on integration of public facilities, voting rights, and interracial understanding and cooperation. However, the mid- to late 1960s brought new attention to the problem of race in urban settings in the North and West. New social movements by blacks, Chicanos, Asian Americans, and American Indians using terms such as "power" and "self-determination" insisted that communities of racially oppressed people should be the ones to define their own needs and control the means of meeting those needs.[2] California in general and the San Francisco Bay Area in particular were hotbeds of radicalism during the late 1960s and early 1970s. The Bay Area witnessed massive anti–Vietnam War protests, the formation of the Black Panther Party in Oakland, the Native American occupation of Alcatraz Island, the rise of the counterculture, and the beginnings of the women's movement.

With the rise of these new social movements, mainstream American liberals such as Hayakawa who supported civil rights reforms (even if only tepidly) found themselves caught between radicals on the left and reactionaries (including explicit segregationists) on the right. The confrontation at San Francisco State between student radicals and Hayakawa illustrates the dilemma of American liberalism: like most liberals, Hayakawa opposed outright discrimination but remained committed to a shared American political identity and hence could not accept demands that oppressed groups should be able to control their own communities.

Although Hayakawa ended his career as a conservative, he did not begin it so. Throughout the 1940s he was a quintessentially liberal public intellectual who consistently advocated racial equality. But by the late 1960s the political ground had shifted beneath his feet, and he found himself opposed to radical students committed to gaining racial justice via black, brown, red, and yellow power. Tracing Hayakawa's journey from liberal to conservative illuminates a larger movement in American politics in which the liberal consensus of the 1930s through the 1950s splintered in the late 1960s, due in no small part to the increased emphasis on race brought about by the various power movements.[3] Nowhere did the splintering occur more graphically than in California.

S. I. Hayakawa was born on July 18, 1906, in Vancouver, British Columbia, to working-class parents who had emigrated to Canada from Japan. He in turn migrated to the United States in 1929, where he earned a Ph.D. from the University of Wisconsin and taught English at the Illinois Institute of Technology and the University of Chicago. Throughout the 1940s he acted as both an academic and a public intellectual, publishing a popular semantics textbook, *Language in Action* (1941), and a weekly column from 1942 to 1947 in the *Chicago Defender*, a leading black newspaper of the time.[4]

Hayakawa's work as a semanticist and his opinions printed in the *Defender* both exhibited a strong belief in American liberalism. Throughout his tenure as a *Defender* columnist, Hayakawa expressed his faith in the democratic system, insisted on the value of interracial cooperation and coolheaded communication, and emphasized the intrinsic irrationality of racism. Hayakawa's position on race mirrored that of Gunnar Myrdal, whose highly influential 1944 opus, *An American Dilemma*, represents the quintessential expression of mid-century American racial liberalism.[5] Demonstrating his faith in what Myrdal termed the "American Creed" of equality for all, Hayakawa argued that people of all races could claim the rights of American citizenship in spite of the fact that individual whites might be prejudiced.[6] The key to ending racism, according to Hayakawa, was to promote interracial understanding. Once white people were made aware of their own unexamined prejudices, they would naturally and inevitably work toward eliminating discrimination.

In one *Defender* column, Hayakawa praised liberal whites for writing essays on "If I Were a Negro," because he believed, "The trouble with most whites is not cruelty or viciousness, but simply thoughtlessness." Whites permitted discrimination to continue "out of ignorance" of its pervasiveness and consequences. If "only a few thousand" whites in Chicago would thoughtfully write such essays, Hayakawa opined, "an enormous step forward will have been taken in this whole matter of race relations."[7] Hayakawa's position was typically liberal, since he believed that the problem of racism was not systemic but an aberration from American ideals.

Hayakawa's liberalism also infused his academic work, in which he offered general semantics (his specialty) as a solution to the problem of prejudice.[8] He portrayed general semantics as "an attempt to blast from their very roots the old habits of mind, the old stupidities, the old prejudices, the old nonsense, that make otherwise civilized human beings behave like savages." Rather than being "harmless idiosyncrasies," prejudices were "case[s] of serious mental deficiency. A 'prejudice' is a point at which your brains stop working."[9] Hayakawa's explication of semantics clarified his other pronouncements on race. According to his diagnosis, rational thought is a necessary and sufficient antidote to racism. Showing whites the errors of their ways—that is, the irrationality of their biases—constitutes the only and best strategy to combat racism. Once attention is brought to their fallacious patterns of thought, whites will logically and inevitably begin to eradicate racism. His faith in the transformative power of general semantics led Hayakawa to optimistically predict that within two decades humans could overcome the outdated moral system that allowed such irrational social systems.

Ironically, it would be just over two decades later when Hayakawa would confront head-on a different type of racial thinking at San Francisco State. Hayakawa's theory of general semantics ignored questions of power, such as who gets to define terms and to whom they are applied. Perhaps more important, it was bereft of any analysis of interests and therefore ignored the extent to which economic exploitation and social oppression convey benefits to some at the expense of others. This theoretical blind spot, which Hayakawa shared with most American liberals at mid-century and retained throughout the remainder of his life, would inevitably lead him into conflict with 1960s radicals who based their analyses precisely upon considerations of power and interests.[10]

Hayakawa vaulted into the national spotlight in late 1968 as a result of having been named acting president of San Francisco State College, a campus in profound turmoil. From November 6, 1968, to March 21, 1969, students at San Francisco State mounted the longest student strike in U.S. history. Led by the multiracial coalition of black, Latino, Native American, and Asian American students calling themselves the Third World Liberation Front (TWLF), strikers demanded the establishment of an autonomous school of ethnic studies, in which Third World people would control faculty hiring and curricula, and there would be open admissions for people of color.[11]

At the height of the strike, thousands of students participated actively. They typically gathered in the morning to march, picket, and urge other students not to attend classes. After marching around campus chanting slogans, they gathered in the central area of the campus, usually around noon. Speakers addressed massive rallies, their voices booming out through amplifiers. After the rally the crowd would disperse, some going to classrooms to inform students and faculty that classes were, as of that moment, dismissed. Hayakawa called in the San

Francisco Police Department, putatively to restore order. The Tactical Squad became an occupying force on campus, regularly beating and clubbing strikers and bystanders while breaking up rallies. Over the course of the strike, police arrested some 700 students.[12] By dint of their energy and organization, the TWLF strikers succeeded in effectively shutting down the campus at times.[13]

While TWLF participants in general disdained Hayakawa and his antistrike tactics, for Asian American strikers, Hayakawa, as a Japanese American, constituted a particularly vexing problem. The conflict between Asian American radicals and Hayakawa revealed deep variances between their respective understandings of race and how to ameliorate racism. Whereas Hayakawa—drawing upon his liberal past—believed that racism was merely a problem of ignorance and therefore could best be fought through educating whites, the strikers saw racism as an institutional and societal problem of oppression and exploitation that could only be solved by addressing systematic inequalities. In other words, Hayakawa sought to abolish racial distinctions, while the strikers sought to even out socioeconomic inequity between races.

Asian Americans actively participated in the Third World Liberation Front strike as equal partners. Indeed, three of the six TWLF member organizations were composed of Asian Americans: Intercollegiate Chinese for Social Action (ICSA), Pilipino American Collegiate Endeavor (PACE), and Asian American Political Alliance (AAPA). ICSA focused on connecting students with social problems in San Francisco's Chinatown; members volunteered at various social service agencies, taught English to immigrant youth, and ran a youth center.[14] PACE was also concerned with the link between campus and community; its members recruited and tutored Filipino American college applicants. PACE leader Ron Quidachay served as TWLF chairman the year before the strike, an indication of the deep involvement of Asian Americans in the coalition.[15] Although the San Francisco State branch of AAPA was composed primarily of Japanese Americans, AAPA stressed the connections between the histories of various Asian ethnic groups and the need for multiethnic Asian American unity.[16] For all of these groups, the TWLF coalition was a way to connect to other Third World people in seeking their goal of making the college serve the needs of their respective communities more effectively, particularly in terms of providing opportunities and a relevant education to nonwhite students. The fact that Hayakawa, as a Japanese American, refused to acknowledge the legitimacy of Asian American demands particularly irked these Asian American organizations.[17]

Upon being named acting president, Hayakawa moved decisively to end the strike. At the first press conference after his appointment, he announced that as of 8:00 A.M. on December 2, the college would reopen. He ordered the faculty to report to class on that date and effectively threatened to fire those who did not. He threatened students who did not "conduct themselves with propriety and dignity" or who engaged in "creating disturbances interfering with the work and study of others" with suspension, expulsion, or other discipline. Finally, he promised a police presence on campus, "to the fullest extent necessary to maintain and restore peace."[18]

Along with reopening the college, Hayakawa declared a state of emergency, the rules of which prohibited students, faculty, staff, and the public from carrying firearms on campus, but pointedly allowed police officers to do so. More important, it suspended use of the Speakers Platform and amplification equipment (except with approval of the administration) and prohibited "interference with classes or administrative processes." It promised violators immediate suspension.[19] The ban on amplifiers in particular was aimed at preventing the large-scale rallies that had galvanized strikers and their supporters, and it was this dictum that provided Hayakawa with the stage for his most noteworthy public performance—the unplugging of the sound truck.

Hayakawa's status as an Asian American figured prominently in his role at San Francisco State in two major ways. First, he was held up as an example of a nonmilitant, nonwhite person as a way to delegitimate the strikers' demands. The conservative journal *Seminar* clearly viewed Hayakawa as a problem for militant blacks. A telling cartoon published in *Seminar* shows two black radicals wearing sunglasses and leather jackets, one with an ammunition belt slung over his shoulder, standing before a seated Hayakawa at the president's desk at San Francisco State College. The two men look puzzled and the caption asks, "How Does One Handle Nonmilitant Minorities?" In the lower right-hand corner, a tiny head cries "Banzai!"[20] The cartoon makes anti-strike arguments using Hayakawa's race in two ways. First, it highlights him as a nonwhite person who opposes the strike, thus undermining the strikers' claims by asserting that "reasonable" minority members like Hayakawa do not support them. Second, the shout of "Banzai!" positions Hayakawa specifically as Asian. This reference tapped into a popular discourse that claimed that Asian Americans—in contrast to blacks and other vocal minorities—had overcome discrimination by working hard rather than resorting to protesting.[21]

Similarly, the *San Francisco Chronicle* published a political cartoon featuring a samurai suit of armor and a caption reading, "Complete suit of Japanese armor is what S. I. Hayakawa should find next to his Christmas tree."[22] Because the *Chronicle* consistently lauded Hayakawa's get-tough policies at San Francisco State, the cartoon constituted an endorsement of Hayakawa in racial terms. It suggested that Hayakawa should sheath himself in his status as a nonwhite person—specifically, as an Asian American, given the Japanese imagery—when attacked by campus militants, and that being a minority should shield him from charges of racism.

Furthermore, his reputation as a nonmilitant Asian American appears to have been a critical factor in Hayakawa's being named acting president. In 1968, amid rising tensions on campus, President John Summerskill resigned, and as Chancellor Glenn Dumke embarked on a search for a successor, he announced that four or five "Negroes" were among the candidates being considered.[23] The chancellor's attempt to find a black president apparently failed, however, as Summerskill's successor turned out to be the conspicuously white Robert Smith. When Smith in turn resigned in November, Dumke immediately tapped Hayakawa. According to Smith, Hayakawa's appointment came as "a bolt from the blue," shocking both faculty and administrators. Prior to being named acting president, Hayakawa had not taught frequently on campus, had never served on important university committees, and had not held an administrative post. His unfamiliarity with the San Francisco State bureaucracy became clear at the first meeting after his appointment, when he had to be introduced to many of the key people in the room.[24]

Yet despite his prior noninvolvement in campus affairs, as the crisis at San Francisco State escalated, Hayakawa had made his politics abundantly clear by his participation as a prominent member of an antistrike group called the Faculty Renaissance.[25] Furthermore, he had "agonized" about disorder on college campuses in a memo to Dumke.[26] The chancellor's choice of an antistrike Asian American to lead the campus could hardly have been accidental. By tapping a nonwhite person who was a vocal opponent of the strike, Dumke sought to quash the strike with an administrator whose race would immunize him from charges of racism.

Dumke's strategy backfired, as strikers refused to accept Hayakawa as a representative of Third World people and instead challenged his racial authenticity. To strikers, Hayakawa was an "Oriental 'white racist' " and a "Tojo Tom," both terms that implied his politics were in contradiction with his skin.[27] Similarly, a "Wanted" poster portrayed a photograph of Hayakawa against a backdrop of the San Francisco Police Department's Tactical Squad in riot gear and listed his aliases as "Paper Puppet, Bootlicker, Ruling Class Lackey." The poster insisted that though Hayakawa might be a Third World person, he served the interests of the "racist corporate policies of the Board of Trustees of San Francisco State College."[28] Thus, the poster highlighted the distinction between identity based solely on racial characteristics and identity as an expression of political commitments. By calling Hayakawa a puppet and lackey of racists, the poster asserted that though he might be a member of the Third World in strictly racial terms, his political beliefs betrayed the interests of Third World people.

In a similar vein, the San Francisco State Strike Committee—composed of white supporters of the TWLF—deemed Hayakawa's appointment a diversionary move. They alleged that by selecting Hayakawa, "a member of the Third World," the trustees intended "to take any legitimacy away from the demands [of the TWLF] and counter the charge of racism." Comparing Hayakawa to nonwhite U.S.-backed rightwing dictators such as Vietnam's Nguyen Cao Ky and Nguyen Van Thieu and Haiti's François Duvalier, the Strike Committee condemned the trustees for "slickly and snakily" using him in a desperate attempt to "break the struggle against racism on this campus."[29]

The second way in which Hayakawa's race figured in his role at San Francisco State was in the way that he positioned himself as a racial middleman. He claimed to be able to adjudicate campus tensions impartially because as an Asian American, he was neither black nor white. At his first press conference after being named acting president, he offered his services as a mediator: "In a profound sense I stand in the middle. I'm not white and I'm not black. I'm appealing to my Oriental friends that I might be a channel to bring black and white together."[30] Beyond offering himself as a nonblack, nonwhite individual, Hayakawa also positioned Asian Americans—as a group—between black and white, with his reference to his "Oriental friends." Hayakawa's racial middleman quote became part of the discourse around the strike, even appearing in a *Time* magazine profile of the acting president and the unrest at

San Francisco State.[31] Hayakawa styled himself an expert on race relations, in part because of his tenure as a columnist at the *Defender*, and at times exhibited a genuine sympathy with blacks. He professed support for a department of black studies in principle, but lamented that the rational demands of black radicals were unfortunately mixed up with the notion that force and intimidation were appropriate tactics to attain their goals.[32]

Although he accepted the legitimacy of black demands, Hayakawa's understanding of the motivations of Japanese American supporters of the strike was critically flawed. Hayakawa proclaimed sympathy with blacks, saying, "We [Japanese Americans] are a colored race of non-whites—we've been through the same thing but we've been able to come through it better than the Negroes have." He asserted that the black studies department was more important than other ethnic studies departments because the "Negro needs this more than any of us."[33] Hayakawa reasoned that blacks needed ethnic studies more acutely than Asian Americans because Japanese and Chinese Americans, like white ethnics, possessed intact cultures and awareness of their histories, while slavery had completely erased black culture and historical memory.[34] Only by assuming that Asian Americans held no stake in the confrontation at San Francisco State could Hayakawa claim to be a racial middleman. Asian American supporters of the strike participated not only to support blacks and other Third World people but also because they believed Asian Americans suffered from racism and would benefit from a multiracial insurgent movement. In other words, Asian American strikers believed that Asian Americans were not racially between black and white, but were more properly placed with other nonwhite people in the United States.

While a portion of San Francisco's Japanese American community supported Hayakawa in his actions against the strikers, a significant segment vehemently opposed his policies. Hayakawa's Japanese American detractors sought to dispel the notion that Japanese Americans as a group opposed the strike. They worried that Hayakawa's actions would be seen "not as acts of an individual but of [the] whole . . . Japanese Community." Strike supporters feared that Hayakawa, as a Japanese American, was performing the dirty work for whites. As one commentator asked rhetorically, "Isn't Hayakawa doing exactly what a certain segment of the White Establishment always wished they could do except that a White person could never have gotten away with it?"[35] Several students staging a prostrike demonstration emphasized their ethnic, and thereby racial, basis for striking. Wearing kimonos and carrying signs reading "Japanese Americans support this strike!" three female members of the AAPA conspicuously displayed their Japanese ethnicity and clearly sought to distance the Japanese American community from Hayakawa.[36] Furthermore, a Japanese American group wrote letters to several local newspapers supporting the TWLF and pointing out that Hayakawa was not a proper representative of the Japanese American community.[37]

Raymond Okamura, an important older supporter of the student activists at both San Francisco State and Berkeley, used the language of identity in urging his fellow Japanese Americans to support the students. He wrote, "Our generation, the Nisei, has succumbed to the pressures of assimilation. The new generation, the Sansei, want to regain a lost ethnic identity, and are seriously challenging the blind acceptance of white middle-class values."[38] Okamura rejected assimilation as a means to gain racial equality and favored creating Japanese American, or more widely, Asian American identity as a basis for fighting against racism.

The TWLF strike forced Hayakawa to confront head-on the issue of abolishing racial distinctions versus building upon them to challenge racism. The TWLF demand for a school of ethnic studies was founded on the idea that only racially oppressed people had the experiences to understand the unique needs and interests of their own communities and cultures. This stance directly contradicted Hayakawa's commitment to achieving interracial understanding. Whereas Asian American strikers sought to build Asian American studies as an autonomous field of inquiry, Hayakawa preferred to ignore racial distinctions.

After five months of protracted struggle, the strike ended in March 1969. The administration agreed to establish a school within which black studies and other ethnic studies would be taught. However, the school received far fewer than the fifty full-time professors students had demanded; students were not granted full autonomy over faculty hiring and curricula; and while the administration agreed to increase admissions for students of color, it did not grant the open admissions. Nevertheless, the settlement marked a major achievement for the TWLF student radicals.

S. I. Hayakawa remained true to his assimilationist politics after the end of the strike. Later, cashing in on his fame won during the strike, he ran for the U.S. Senate as a conservative Republican and was elected, serving a single term from 1977 through 1982. In the Senate he opposed redress and reparations for Japanese Americans imprisoned during World War II, claiming that the incarceration was "neither a mistake nor an injustice," because the "immigrant generation" were "enemy aliens," most of whom "spoke poor English or none at all."[39] Instead of recognizing that Japanese immigrants remained aliens because they were denied naturalization rights, Hayakawa painted them as only ambiguously American because they were not fully assimilated. He also attributed prewar anti-Japanese prejudice to the "yellow peril"-mongering press, coupled with the fact that most whites lacked firsthand knowledge of Japanese Americans. Ignorance, not economic gain, motivated white racism, he argued. Senator Hayakawa clearly retained the faith in rationality that he had exhibited in his prior incarnation as a general semanticist. Furthermore, when he admonished "Japanese Americans . . . Black Americans and Mexican Americans and all other ethnic political groups" to "stop playing ethnic politics" and instead to "continue to think of America as 'One Nation, Under God, Indivisible,' " Hayakawa echoed the assimilationism of his earlier career.[40] However, in opposing redress and reparations, Hayakawa found himself at odds with nearly the entire segment of Japanese American political organizations.

Most tellingly, Hayakawa introduced a constitutional amendment to make English the official language of the United States. Hayakawa's logic in backing the English-only movement remained remarkably consistent with his prior positions: he believed that bilingualism threatened the nation's ability to maintain a public sphere shared by all citizens. Without a "common language," the nation risked hopeless fragmentation.[41] Thus, to the end of his career Hayakawa retained his commitment to the ideal of resolving the claims of vying interest groups within a shared democratic system, while ignoring issues of unequal access to the system.[42]

Hayakawa did not seek reelection after completing his term as U.S. senator, but instead in 1983 founded an organization, U.S. English, that sought to promote English as the official language of the nation. He also served as special advisor to the secretary of state on East Asia and the Pacific Islands from 1983 until 1990. By the time Hayakawa died in California on February 27, 1992, his importance as a public figure had diminished considerably, though his obituary ran in newspapers across the country.

S. I. Hayakawa was a key figure in California history as an exemplar of the changing nature of racial liberalism during the late 1960s and early 1970s. As the confrontation at San Francisco State College showed, this era saw less emphasis among people of color on the need to educate and cooperate with liberal whites, and more demands for self-determination. This shifting of political style had abundant importance in California, which beginning with the immigration reforms of 1965 has become an increasingly multiracial state. (According to the 2000 census, no single racial or ethnic group can now claim a majority of the population of California.) Hayakawa represented the last gasp of a brand of liberalism that Asian American radical students and their allies deemed untenable. The TWLF strike resulted in the establishment of the first school of ethnic studies, an academic discipline that is now taught at hundreds of colleges and universities. Although Hayakawa opposed ethnic studies as divisive, since the late 1960s many Americans have come to understand the histories and cultures of people of color as core to the nation's identity. For the Asian American radicals at San Francisco State, confronting Hayakawa enabled them to clarify their opposition to his assimilationism and their understanding of Asian Americans as a racialized group. Hayakawa's inability to recognize the logic of the demands of Asian American students and their TWLF allies demonstrated the incompatibility of his liberalism with analyses of race and power, and hence exemplified the dilemma of American liberalism.

Notes

1. *San Francisco Chronicle*, December 3, 1968.

2. On these social movements, see William Van Deburg, *New Day in Babylon: The Black Power Movement and American Culture, 1965–1975* (Chicago, 1992); William Wei, *The Asian American Movement* (Philadelphia, 1992); Paul Chaat Smith and Robert Allen, *Warrior, Like a Hurricane: The Indian Movement from Alcatraz to Wounded Knee* (New York, 1996); Andrés Torres and José E. Velázquez, eds., *The Puerto Rican Movement: Voices from the Diaspora* (Philadelphia, 1998).

3. Maurice Isserman and Michael Kazin make an argument similar to this one in their essay, "The Failure and Success of the New Radicalism," in Steven Fraser and Gary Gerstle, eds., *The Rise and Fall of the New Deal Order, 1930–1980* (Princeton, 1989).

4. *New York Times*, February 28, 1992.

5. Gunnar Myrdal, *An American Dilemma: The Negro Problem and Modern Democracy* (New York, 1944).

6. S. I. Hayakawa, "Second Thoughts," *Chicago Defender*, November 6, 1943.

7. Ibid., May 22, 1943.

8. S. I. Hayakawa, *Language in Action: A Guide to Accurate Reading and Writing* (New York, 1941), 27.

9. S. I. Hayakawa, "Second Thoughts," *Chicago Defender*, July 3, 1943.

10. For a succinct and contemporaneous definition of "black power," see Stokely Carmichael and Charles V. Hamilton, *Black Power: The Politics of Liberation in America* (New York, 1967).

11. Third World Liberation Front, "School of Third World Studies" (San Francisco, 1968), 4, quoted in Kuregiy Hekymara, "The Third World Movement and Its History in the San Francisco State College Strike of 1968–1969," Ph.D. diss., University of California, Berkeley, 1972, 127; "Ten Demands of the Black Student Union" and "Five Demands of the Third World Liberation Front," reprinted in William H. Orrick Jr., *Shut It Down! A College in Crisis: San Francisco State College, October 1968– April 1969. A Report to the National Commission on the Causes and Prevention of Violence* (Washington, DC, 1969), 151.

12. William Barlow and Peter Shapiro, *An End to Silence: The San Francisco State Student Movement in the 60s* (New York, 1971), 260–61, 314.

13. However central the strike at San Francisco State might have been in the national consciousness in 1968, its visibility has diminished significantly in the decades hence. In many historical accounts, Berkeley stands in for campus activism in general. (Indeed, Berkeley also had a TWLF strike for ethnic studies, though its strike started later and was shorter than the one at San Francisco State.) The failure of historians to properly evaluate the significance of the strike at San Francisco State and other less prestigious institutions of higher learning speaks to an implicit elitism that continues to color campus activism as white and middle-class.

14. Wei, *Asian American Movement*, 17–18.

15. Ibid., 18–19.

16. Ibid., 19–20.

17. Karen Umemoto provides the best account of Asian American participation in the strike in "On Strike! Shut It Down!" *Amerasia Journal* 13 (1989): 3–41.

18. "Public Statement by President S. I. Hayakawa," November 30, 1968, in San Francisco State University, Hayakawa Folder #1 (81).

19. "Declaration of Emergency," December 2, 1968, in San Francisco State University, Hayakawa Folder #1 (81).

20. *Seminar: A Quarterly Review for Newspapermen* 12 (June 1969): 7, reprinted from the *Denver Post*, November 29, 1968.

21. For a debunking of the Model Minority Myth, see Ronald Takaki, *Strangers from a Different Shore: A History of Asian Americans* (New York, 1989), 474–84.

22. *San Francisco Chronicle*, December 10, 1968.

23. Ibid., April 11, 1968.

24. Robert Smith et al., *By Any Means Necessary: The Revolutionary Struggle at San Francisco State* (San Francisco, 1970), 205–6. This is an insiders' account—Smith served as president and Pentony as deputy president of San Francisco State—and exhibits all of the proadministration biases one might expect.

25. President Smith strongly implies that Hayakawa orchestrated a coup d'état and positioned himself as the next president; see Smith et al., *By Any Means Necessary*, 193–94, 206–7.

26. S. I. Hayakawa, "Education in Ferment," in James McEvoy and Abraham Miller, eds., *Black Power and Student Rebellion* (Belmont, CA, 1969), 199.

27. James McEvoy and Abraham Miller, "On Strike . . . Shut It Down," in McEvoy and Miller, *Black Power and Student Rebellion*, 29.

28. San Francisco Historical Center, San Francisco Public Library, Folder "SFSU Strike. Flyers."

29. San Francisco Strike Committee, "On Strike: Shut It Down," n.p., quoted in William H. Orrick Jr., *Shut It Down! A College in Crisis*, 60.

30. *San Francisco Chronicle*, November 27, 1968.

31. *Time* (December 6, 1968): 83.

32. *San Francisco Chronicle*, February 22, 1969; *San Francisco Examiner*, February 22, 1969.

33. *San Francisco Examiner*, February 22, 1969.

34. Hayakawa, "Education in Ferment," 207.

35. Jeff Matsui, "Sounding Board," *Pacific Citizen*, January 10, 1969.

36. *San Francisco Chronicle*, January 11, 1969.

37. San Francisco State University, AAPA Folder.

38. *Pacific Citizen*, April 18, 1969.

39. S. I. Hayakawa, personal letter to Senator Larry Pressler, May 17, 1988, quoted in *Congressional Record*, 100th Cong., 2d sess., 1998, 134:118:11257.

40. S. I. Hayakawa, *Congressional Record*, 97th Cong., 2d sess., 1982, 128:21:29213.

41. S. I. Hayakawa, *English Language Amendment, Congressional Record*, 98th Cong., 2d sess., 1984, 12–18.

42. The story of Hayakawa's seeming rightward drift mirrors, in interesting ways, that of the Jewish neoconservatives such as Irving Howe, Irving Kristol, and others associated with journals such as *Commentary* and *Dissent*; see Alan Wald, *The New York Intellectuals: The Rise and Decline of the Anti-Stalinist Left from the 1930s to the 1980s* (Chapel Hill, 1987).

Suggested Readings

Barlow, William, and Peter Shapiro. *An End to Silence: The San Francisco State Student Movement in the 60s*. New York: Pegasus, 1971.

Brinkley, Alan. *Liberalism and Its Discontents*. Cambridge, MA: Harvard University Press, 1998.

Ho, Fred, et al., eds. *Legacy to Liberation: Politics and Culture of Radical Asian Pacific America*. New York: Big Red Media, 2000.

Takahashi, Jere. *Nisei/Sansei: Shifting Japanese American Identities and Politics*. Philadelphia: Temple University Press, 1997.

Umemoto, Karen. "On Strike! Shut It Down!" *Amerasia Journal* 13 (1989): 3–41.

Wei, William. *The Asian American Movement*. Philadelphia: Temple University Press, 1992.

Zia, Helen. *Asian American Dreams: The Emergence of an American People*. New York: Farrar, Straus, and Giroux, 2000.

14

César Chávez
The Serpent and the Dove

Frank Bardacke

From the use of Indians under the mission system to the widespread use of undocumented migrants today, California agribusiness has always profited from the ability to attract inexpensive and often disempowered laborers. More often than not, farmworkers have been poor migrants and persons of color. The work is exhausting and backbreaking, entailing long hours under difficult conditions with little pay.

Throughout the long history of California agriculture, farmworkers have continually agitated and struggled for better wages and conditions. In the 1930s, for instance, Japanese American and Filipino American labor unions won strikes resulting in improved circumstances. But such victories have been few and far between.

California farmworkers' greatest era of political success came in the 1960s under the leadership of César Chávez, who grew up in Imperial Valley labor camps and in the early 1960s helped to form the United Farm Workers (UFW). The UFW engaged in numerous strikes and political protests, including a 300-mile march to Sacramento, ultimately winning a minimum wage of $1.70 per hour for farmworkers in 1970. Chávez's passionate determination won him the loyalty of thousands of farmworkers, but his efforts were not without critics or controversy. According to California author Frank Bardacke, a teacher at the Watsonville Adult School, Chávez's real achievement lay in the way he was able to nurture and provide energy for the fledgling Chicano Rights movement of the 1960s and 1970s. Bardacke criticizes Chávez's contributions to the farmworkers' movement, arguing that by focusing on the tactics of boycotts rather than on strikes, he did more to nurture white liberal support than to galvanize and mobilize farmworkers themselves.

> Behold I send you forth as sheep in the midst of wolves; be ye, therefore, wise as serpents and harmless as doves. MATTHEW 10:16

The politics are transparent; the historical significance is opaque. The law that made March 31, the birthday of Mexican American labor leader César Chávez, a mandated holiday for state employees and an optional "day of service" for California public school students included no benefits for California farmworkers. No political mystery here: at the end of the twentieth century, Sacramento politicians found a way to please Latino voters while not taking any money out of the pockets of agribusiness. But what is the historical meaning of this conveniently structured holiday? At the very least, it suggests an irony: César triumphed in California while farmworkers continued to lose.

Nor does this contrast between the honoring of César Chávez and the dishonoring of farmworkers stand alone. The same legislators and governor who created César Chávez Day rejected a bill that would have held California growers jointly responsible for their labor contractors' labor code violations. They thereby continued the legal fiction that growers do not employ the farmworkers who make them rich. And here the irony deepens: labor contractors replaced Chávez's defeated United Farm Workers (UFW) in the early 1980s, and were the major instrument through which growers attacked farmworker wages and working conditions. That attack was not entirely successful. Workmen's compensation, unemployment insurance, and a favorable farm labor law—all won during the height of the UFW's power in the late 1960s and 1970s—remain intact. But the grower offensive was powerful enough. By the time of César's death in 1993, farmworker wages had fallen at least 25 percent from their highs in the 1970s, and conditions in the fields were nearly as bad as when César first entered farmworker politics in 1962.[1]

So the question remains, how are we to understand the contradictory juxtaposition of César's symbolic victory and the farmworkers' material defeat? My answer depends on a distinction between César's unofficial position as "first president of the Chicano Nation" and his official position as president of the United Farm Workers. Once those two roles are considered separately, some of the César Chávez Day irony disappears. Chávez can be celebrated, without reservation, as a Mexican American leader, an inspiration to the short-lived Chicano Nation, and an example of the possibilities of Latino political power. But the celebratory mood ends when we turn to César's record as a union leader. His relationship to the farmworker movement is so fraught with contradiction and difficulty, so filled with betrayal and tragedy, that a proper historical account evokes emotions that dwarf these common ironies.

César as First President of the Chicano Nation

In the summer of 1966, after scores of striking farmworkers and hundreds, even thousands, of supporters walked the length of California's

San Joaquin Valley, a triumphant Luis Váldez, cofounder of Teatro Campesino, predicted the future, using the past tense: "Under the name of *huelga* [labor activism], we had created a Mexican American *patria* [nation], and César Chávez was our first *presidente*." Both tenses proved true. César Chávez became a combination hero and godfather to what came to be called the Chicano Nation. But the past tense was equally accurate: Chávez's position as Mexican American president was rooted in his farmworker union leadership, which first gained national attention with this dramatic pilgrimage through the San Joaquin Valley.

The Mexican American college students who created the Chicano Nation in the late 1960s and early 1970s needed the farmworker movement as much as (and probably more than) that movement needed them. Consider Jorge García, a Fresno State College senior in 1966, one of only sixty-five Spanish-surnamed students in that school of 14,000. His parents were farmworkers in Dinuba. He had spent a good part of his own youth in the fields. Getting to college had required hard work. In order to do well in school, he had focused so intently on his English (with the help and support of his parents but the disapproval of his grandparents) that he began to lose his Spanish. After high school he went to a seminary in Fresno, then to a community college, and finally to Fresno State. Once there, he could say good-bye to the fields. He was on his way to becoming a teacher, a successful Mexican American, when the pilgrimage came through town. "I went to the rally and it changed my life," García recalled. "It was like looking in the mirror and seeing the rest of myself, the part that I had left behind in my struggle to get out of the fields. I thought college was a ticket to paradise. I realized then that I couldn't be in paradise unless I could be there as a whole person. And that meant helping farmworkers."[2]

Jorge García and thousands of Mexican American students like him from rural and urban communities entered politics as supporters of César Chávez and the UFW. They set up student organizations whose first order of business was to help the farmworkers whom they had either literally or figuratively left behind. They visited Delano, the union's birthplace, bringing money, clothes, and food; they picketed grocery stores that handled "scab" grapes; they demanded that their schools begin to teach farmworker history. To create a new identity, they needed to reconstruct their connection to their real or imagined past. Through acts of solidarity with struggling farmworkers, they could reject the professional world they were about to enter and declare themselves part of the working-class *raza* they were about to leave. They proudly took as their new name a derisory word that had meant a low-caste Mexican north of the border. They were no longer aspiring Mexican Americans; they were now Chicanos.

Never abandoning farmworker solidarity, the members of the new Chicano movement sought to make a place for themselves and their own history in their colleges and universities. They fought for Chicano studies or, together with others, for Third World studies. They pressured campus administrators to admit more persons of color and provide them financial support. They tried to build ties to various barrio groups and organizations so they could use their education to serve their old communities. Many opposed the Vietnam War, and through the antiwar movement came to identify with the national and international left. They fought in defense of undocumented workers and called for open borders. And some rejected the American two-party electoral system and made various attempts to set up independent political parties.

César Chávez remained a hero to these students, but he was not one of them. He was older, born twenty miles north of Yuma, Arizona, in 1927, a child of the depression and a veteran of World War II, the two great events that shaped the previous Mexican American generation. Moreover, he had sharp differences with many of the political positions of the new Chicano generation he had inspired. He was not a Chicano nationalist; he was dubious about the celebration of Aztlán, opposed open borders, and did not like all the *raza* (race) talk. The mature César did not need militant nationalism. He was not anxious about his own identity; he could appreciate other cultures and ways of life. But some of his rejection of Chicano nationalism was politically convenient, even necessary. In the late 1960s, amid the fledgling Chicano movement, César was building a diverse coalition of grape boycotters, of which Chicano students were but one part. Chávez could not afford to be a separatist if he wanted to hold together a coalition that included unions, churches, and antipesticide consumers.

César was especially critical of any attempt at independent political action, and risked isolating himself from his most fervent Chicano support by openly opposing the La Raza Unida Party. Again, the requirements of the boycott coalition were primary. The Democratic Party, chief losers if La Raza Unida were to be successful, actively supported the boycott. But César's defense of the Democrats went far beyond this particular tit for tat. He worked in tandem with the Democratic Party throughout his entire political career. His first political act, in 1952, was registering Mexican Americans to vote in San Jose, a campaign that was clearly in the interest of Democrats and could not have been successful without Democratic Party assistance. Throughout the 1950s, César—along with Fred Ross, Gilbert Padilla, and Dolores Huerta—built the Community Service Organization into the country's most powerful Mexican American group by registering 300,000 new and mostly Democratic voters, mobilizing them to go to the polls, and then pressuring politicians to respond to their agenda. In 1958, César was such an important player in California Democratic Party politics that he could get Governor Pat Brown on the phone. In the mid-1960s he extended his influence to the Kennedy wing of the National Democratic Party; and his long-term cooperation with Pat Brown's son Jerry contributed to the UFW's greatest political triumph, the 1976 California Farm Labor Law. This commitment to Democratic Party politics even survived César's death, as the UFW's greatest political asset today is its ability to register and mobilize Latino voters and to win concessions from Democratic Party politicians. Even César Chávez Day is, to a certain extent, one of those concessions.

But if César Chávez opposed the Chicano movement's separatist impulse, withdrew himself from many of their struggles, and opposed their most important political initiatives, how did he simultaneously remain their hero? To a certain extent, Jorge García's experience has already answered that question: the farmworker movement was a precondition for the new Chicano identity and the politics that followed. Throughout the 1960s and 1970s, Chávez and the UFW continued to inspire even those activist Chicanos with whom he seriously differed.[3] But César's seminal role in the Chicano movement does not completely explain his remarkable staying power. After all, César remained a hero even after the Chicano movement stalled and disintegrated in the mid-1970s, after the Democrats lost the California governorship and Chávez lost much of his political access in the early 1980s, and after the UFW was defeated in the fields in the mid-1980s. What sustained his reputation despite this string of political defeats?

The answer is that César Chávez was not and is not a hero just to Mexican Americans and other Latinos. During the mid- and late 1960s he became an exemplary hope of American liberals. At the time of the 1966 farmworker pilgrimage, the liberal/radical cooperation of the early civil rights movement was over, and white liberals could find no home in the new movement for Black Power. They were horrified by the northern ghetto riots. Moreover, liberal president Lyndon Johnson, soon after defeating conservative Barry Goldwater, escalated the war in

Vietnam—and initially, most liberals stuck by his side. There was war at home and war abroad. Many people who had been so hopeful at the beginning of the 1960s now watched the twin terrors of the nightly news: black rioters burning American cities, white radicals burning American flags.

Enter César Chávez and the grape boycott. César provided a constructive, nonviolent political alternative to those horrified by the rioters and radicals. "Boycott, Baby, Boycott," UFW picketers chanted to make sure everyone got the point. The simple, peaceful act of not eating grapes would help grateful farmworkers win a union contract. The simplicity and hopefulness of the appeal attracted millions. In the midst of the campaign, in the cataclysmic year of 1968, César fasted. He did so, he said, to remind his own followers to be nonviolent. He appeared on the cover of *Time*. Many other major magazines and newspapers wrote feature stories about him, warning that if his movement did not prevail, a more violent alternative would take its place. The press championed César as the new Chicano leader, and attacked or ignored the two possible alternatives—Corky Gonzalez and Reis Tijerina—who were almost as important to the early Chicano movement as César but could not receive an official seal of approval because they denounced the two-party political system and advocated self-defense. With this wide support, the grape boycott became the most successful consumer boycott in American history. Thousands worked in the boycott campaign, and polls reported that one-third of all adult Americans had committed themselves to not eating grapes. The contract was won, and although the victory did not belong to liberals alone, it was one of their few achievements of the late 1960s and early 1970s. Is it any wonder that César won a permanent place in liberal hearts? Or that thirty years later, after the larger hopes of the Chicano left had come to grief, his triumphant grape boycott would still be remembered and honored?

But César cannot be dismissed as the Latino most favored by white liberals. Yes, he became a liberal hero, but he was also the leader of the farmworker movement and a chief inspiration to the new Chicano youth before most liberals ever heard about him. The liberal media did not make him; he was picked up by them. He is often called the Mexican American Martin Luther King, and he deserves the title, although King was more troublesome to larger numbers of people in his time and widely celebrated only after he was assassinated. César was celebrated during his lifetime and was bothersome to a narrower, albeit powerful, sector: California agribusiness. César was also similar to Jackie Robinson: he was the first Mexican American to play in the political big leagues, and just like Robinson he refused to alter his style once he got there. César was not a nationalist and certainly not a separatist, but he was not an accommodating assimilationist either. He did not win power by ingratiating himself to liberal, white America. He did not remake himself in order to be accepted. He was proud of his Mexican heritage, his farmworker roots, and his bilingual intelligence. And he was proud of the collective struggle that had propelled him into prominence. When we honor him, we can honor all of that. There need be no irony.

César as Defeated Farmworker Leader

The rise and fall of the Chicano movement, unmistakable in its broad sweep, cannot be precisely located in time. It began in the mid-to late 1960s and ended about a decade later. The trajectory of the UFW, however, is much easier to chart chronologically, its fortunes bouncing between dramatic highs and lows. Starting with nothing in 1962, the union won a few labor contracts in the mid-1960s, and then, after the successful boycott in1970, had almost the entire California table grape industry under contract, covering tens of thousands of workers. In 1973, however, the growers refused to re-sign with the UFW, and since then the union has never been able to reestablish itself in the table grape industry. But the union bounced back in 1975 when Governor Jerry Brown and the California legislature passed the Agricultural Labor Relations Act, which provided for state-supervised elections in the fields. The UFW won a majority of those elections, and contracts covering half of the vegetable industry. Then, in 1979, the union won a major vegetable strike—pushing wages up significantly—and some sectors of agribusiness publicly declared that they now accepted the union's continued presence in the fields. But within the next few years, the union lost almost all of its vegetable contracts, was reduced to a couple of thousand workers under contract, and retreated from active organizing in the fields. That retreat lasted nearly a decade, as it was not until after César's death in 1993 that the union tried to reenter the fields, with mixed results.

What happened? To a certain extent, the union was simply overwhelmed by the power of agribusiness, its friends in high places (especially Republican George Deukmejian, who became governor in 1982), and a conservative, antiunion ethic that swept the country in the mid-1980s. But that is not even half of the story. Quite unexpectedly, after

the 1979 strike victory, the UFW tore itself apart. Many of its top organizers left or were forced out, and a virulent internal faction fight ripped
the union asunder, leaving it incapable of countering the 1980s grower
offensive. No full answer to the question of how the growers defeated
the union can ignore the prior question of how and why the union
wrecked itself. And here we reach a sad, even tragic, conclusion. César
Chávez, so responsible for the union's victories, was also deeply impli-
cated in its demise—not just he personally, of course, but the strategic
policies, leadership style, and religious commitment that he impressed
upon the union.

This story begins with the contradictions inherent in the boycott
victory. The triumphant table grape boycott transformed the UFW into
a peculiar twin-souled institution: a cross between a culturally diverse
farmworker advocacy group, highly skilled at boycott activities, and a
mostly Mexican and Mexican American, Catholic farmworker union.
Under the skillful guidance of Chávez, these two souls reinforced each
other, especially in the early years when boycotts and threats of boycotts
so directly and obviously led to fundamental improvements in
farmworkers' lives. But even at the beginning, the two souls occasionally lived in contradiction. Sending farmworkers to work in the boycott
offices of U.S. cities, for example, was a major factor in making the
boycott so successful, as the workers themselves became the best advo-
cates for the boycott and the UFW. But placing workers in boycott cities also meant that the most dedicated and articulate strikers did their
political organizing work among boycotters, not among farmworkers.
This tactic was part of a strategy that reduced the importance of
farmworker organizing and focused on supporters instead. As such, it
was neither wrong (the UFW needed outside support to win) nor impossible to reverse, but it turned out to be the first intimation of a coming disaster.

Similarly, and even more perniciously, in the later stages of the boycott—when all hope of winning the grape contracts in the fields had
been abandoned—the UFW often mobilized farmworkers into staged
events whose purpose was neither to educate the workers nor to directly
improve their lives, but rather to mobilize the support of distant boycotters. What UFW strategists called "legitimacy strikes," sometimes
involving hundreds of workers, were not meant to win, but rather to
legitimize later boycotts.[4] Such strikes may have helped the boycotts,
but they often embittered the farmworker participants against the UFW.
Later, this technique degenerated into "publicity strikes," whose sole pur-

pose was to produce anti-grower and anti-Teamster publicity but whose defeats only added to the list of farmworkers suspicious of the UFW.[5]

What began as an intimation, a small contradiction within a successful strategy, ended in a major internal conflict. In 1979, in the midst of the most successful strike in UFW history, in a period when boycotts had become less effective and farmworkers—their dues and their strikes—had become a larger part of the UFW's power, a debilitating internal struggle broke out over the relationship between the two souls of the union. This was an open struggle, with most of the union staff on one side and the rank-and-file leaders of the Mexican farmworker membership on the other. It broke into public view at the 1979 Salinas UFW convention, when farmworkers on the floor of the convention began chanting, "*Huelga, huelga, huelga*," while members of the executive board and other officials sitting on the stage answered with a competing chant of "Boycott, boycott, boycott."[6] In this internal struggle, César Chávez led those who upheld the boycott as the essence of the UFW, and then subsequently (in 1981) purged from the union the leading farmworkers (and the few union staffers) who had opposed him.[7]

César's role was no great surprise. By the time this internal UFW debate burst into full bloom, César had grown much more comfortable at organizing boycotters than at organizing farmworkers, and had already told many admiring newsmen and biographers that the boycott, which he described as "the most nearly perfect instrument of nonviolent change," was his greatest contribution to the farmworker movement.[8] He had no patience with those—in his own union!—who questioned its effectiveness. Furthermore, by the time these questions were raised, César had become accustomed to forcing out those on the union staff who he suspected might oppose him. On this question the opponents were right out in the open. The earlier staff purges had harmed the UFW, but not mortally. This time, however, César fired the leaders of the farmworker movement, demoralizing them and their followers and alienating them from the union. The successful grower offensive soon followed.[9]

The issue of religion in the UFW repeats and reinforces this dynamic in a minor key. Once again, that which propelled the UFW to victory eventually contributed to its defeat, and César was right in the middle of both the rise and the fall. César was a serious Catholic whose religious beliefs were rooted in the folk piety of his mother and the religious instruction of his convent-trained grandmother. As a child he had taken to that training so well that a Yuma priest waived the requirement that he submit to further Church-directed religious instruction before receiving his first Holy Communion. Later he became an altar boy, an adult who regularly attended Mass, and a committed *cursillista*—a member of a Church-directed movement for lay Catholic renewal. He was first recruited to politics by a Catholic priest who introduced him to Catholic Social Action, and he self-consciously constructed the early UFW on the principles of Catholic worker associations spelled out in 1891 by Pope Leo XIII in *Rerum Novarum.* Periodically, when the UFW found itself in a particularly difficult political predicament, Chávez responded with a dramatic act of personal penitence, fully within the traditions of the Catholic Church and Mexican folk piety.

Although his religion was not essentially a political device, César's faith turned out to be extremely useful. The UFW used religious symbols to help organize the overwhelmingly Catholic farmworkers and elicit sympathy from supporters. César's piety—especially his dramatic 1968 fast—helped pull the union together and situated the boycott as the exemplary nonviolent alternative to those turbulent times. But César's religious intentions also contributed to the UFW's fall, as the internal life of the organization came to resemble a religious order rather than a labor union. One of the people who lived in the union headquarters at La Paz—an isolated, former TB sanitarium in the Tehachapi Mountains—and who witnessed firsthand César's attempt to mesh trade unionism and religious commitment, put it this way: "César never wanted to be just a trade union leader, he wanted to be Mother Teresa."[10]

La Paz was not only supposed to be the union's chief administrative and political headquarters; César also tried to make it into a kind of ashram, an intentional beloved community. But a beloved community has a unity of belief and purpose, a suspicion of difference and dissent that is inimical to a trade union representing tens of thousands of workers. It was at La Paz, in César's efforts to build a religious community around him, that the first large purges began. And while the union's center at La Paz was going through the travails of forced unanimity, the union staff began to mimic the Catholic Church's hierarchical politics, whereby the pope commands and cardinals, bishops, and priests, in turn, announce and obey his orders. In the union, as in the Church, those who refused were transferred to other assignments or were excommunicated. And when people left the union they left quietly, unwilling to share their criticisms with people outside the faith.

The UFW, however, needed a democratic ethic—not a hierarchical, Catholic one—in order to thrive. UFW members were a diverse group;

they worked at different jobs, under different contracts, in widely scattered areas. They did not share the common commitment that is assumed in a religious community. They had different interests that required open political discourse to resolve. They also had differences over what they wanted from their union and what they thought the best union strategy might be. But there was little space in the UFW for the expression of such differences. People were expected to follow César's directions, which came to be beyond question. When a group of ordinary farmworkers wanted to see him about a grievance that they could not resolve locally, they did not make an appointment, a *cita*. They had to get an *audiencia*, an audience, as if they were going to see the pope.

The union's hierarchical Catholic ethos was reinforced by a thoroughly antidemocratic structure. Until 1980 no farmworker could be elected to a full-time UFW staff position. People were appointed to the staff and owed their positions to those who appointed them, rather than to the rank and file from which they came. Nor were there any locals in the union—it has remained one body since its inception. Also, until 1980, the only structural loci of democratic control in the union were the local ranch committees and the biannual national convention. But ranch committee members continued to work in the fields and were not on the staff. Usually they ended up with much less power than the local "field office," where people appointed by La Paz worked as full-time union officers. Eventually, most ranch committees became nothing but transmission belts for union policy, and only occasionally sounding boards for disagreement from the ranks. Similarly, the national conventions were primarily staged affairs, marked by near unanimity, as the assembled delegates endorsed the proposals of the unopposed executive board candidates.

This kind of rigid, antidemocratic structure could not survive serious internal disputes, and the union fragmented in the wake of the 1979 strike. It was during that 9-month strike—one of the most powerful strikes in California agricultural history—that the dispute between boycotters and strikers first surfaced. César ordered the strike called off and replaced by a boycott. But the strike leadership, elected by their fellow strikers and supported by a few staff members, refused to obey the order. After this defiance the strike won an amazing victory, which included as a new provision in the contracts the election by the rank and file of full-time representatives ("paid reps") who would become part of the union staff and would be paid as if they continued to work in the fields. This meant that for the first time people came onto the staff who owed their positions not to other staffers (and ultimately to César) but rather to the rank and file that had elected them. And those elected were largely the victorious strike's leaders, the very people who had defied César's wishes and then won their own victory.

The final calamity unfolded quickly. The new staffers fought for their own power inside the union; César interpreted their fight as an attempt to take the union away from him and blocked their every initiative. The newly elected leaders then sought to run their own partial slate of candidates for the executive board against César's handpicked candidates. César controlled the convention and through a series of maneuvers denied the opposition the right even to vote for their own candidates. The opposition walked out of the convention and took their complaints to the press. César responded by firing them from their jobs as paid reps. Workers in the fields, the ones who had elected the representatives to begin with and whose issues the paid reps were championing when they initially locked horns with César, were mostly confused by the fight between their immediate leadership and their, by then, famous president. Those who were not demoralized divided into two opposing factions. Feuding workers sat in different sections of the buses that took them to the fields, refusing to talk to one another. The growers, emboldened by the division, moved against the union. The workers could not get themselves together to respond and César, defeated, stopped organizing in the fields and withdrew to his beloved community.

Over the next ten years, César presided as the UFW became less a union and more a cross between a farmworker advocacy group and a small family business. During another long fast in 1988, Chávez successfully focused public attention on pesticides in the fields and unsuccessfully tried to renew a table grape boycott. In 1993, César Chávez died in his sleep, not far from the Arizona homestead where he had been born. His good friend and colleague, Leroy Chatfield, who had seen him shortly before, said that although César was only sixty-six, he seemed more like 122, as he had compressed so much living into one overloaded lifetime.

An Interethnic Complication and a Conclusion

My easy distinction between César, the Latino icon, and César, the farmworker leader, is useful for this essay, but it obscures several complications. I will mention just one. César Chávez was thoroughly Mexican American. His paternal grandfather voted in Texas elections and homesteaded a 100-acre Arizona farm a few years before Arizona even became a state. César grew up on that farm, in what he remembered as an idyllic childhood filled with games and chores. In the late 1930s, César's father lost both the homestead and his own adjacent farm to falling agricultural prices, a flash flood that destroyed a homemade irrigation system, and a scheming Anglo lawyer. At the age of eleven, César was thrust with his family into the migrant stream, where the youngster's life became a calamity. A short-handled hoe replaced his childhood toys; cheating contractors humiliated his proud father, a master horseman; the family's 1930 Studebaker became their home. Like so many other Mexican American farmworkers who returned from World War II, César did not go back to the hated fields. He was working in a San Jose lumberyard when Father Donald McDonnell started him on his organizing career by introducing him to the ideas of Catholic Social Action.

When César first started organizing farm workers in 1962, he began in an area and a crop where many Mexican American families lived and worked. Their life stories were somewhat different from his—they did not typically come from failed homesteads elsewhere in the United States—but they shared his Mexican American roots, and many of their parents or grandparents had come to the United States in the 1920s. These folks, these grape workers, were César's first constituency. But after the end of the Bracero Program in 1965 (when as a matter of semi-official policy the Mexican border was thrown open to illegal immigration), the character of California farmworkers changed. Mexican immigrants became the overwhelming majority of farmworkers by the mid-1970s, replacing Mexican Americans, Filipinos, Anglos, and others who had dominated the labor force since the 1920s.

Mexican Americans who continued to work in the fields often viewed the new immigrants with suspicion, believing them to be a threat to their jobs and union. César Chávez shared and encouraged this view. Angered by the use of undocumented workers against UFW strikes, he campaigned vigorously against illegal aliens. He not only blamed them for lost strikes but had some of them removed from union jobs. In 1974 he initiated a national campaign against "illegals," testified in Congress for increased activity by the Immigration Service, and ordered UFW staffers to finger illegals to the Border Patrol.[11] Ultimately, this policy rebounded sharply against the UFW in the fields, where the growing majority of workers had friends and relatives who were undocumented.

The union's reputation of being against illegals hurt it immensely and was partly responsible for its many defeats in table grape elections after the passage of the Agricultural Labor Relations Act.

The final internal battle that so debilitated the union shared this same interethnic dimension. In the fight between the old union staff, led by César, and the rank-and-file union leadership, the union staff were primarily Mexican Americans—or, as they still called themselves at the time, Chicanos—while the rank-and-file leadership and membership were overwhelmingly Mexican immigrants. The dispute was not only about boycotts versus strikes and staff power versus rank-and-file power; it was also a struggle between Chicanos and Mexicans. That battle covered a world of differences: language, relationship to Mexico, and, most important, the place of agricultural work in peoples' lives. For many Mexican immigrants the California fields are not a disaster, as they had been for César. Rather, they are a step up in the world. Wages in the United States are, and have been over time, about ten times higher than wages in Mexico, and a job in the California fields can mean either the well-being of a family back home in Mexico or the possibility of successful family emigration to the United States. Certainly, the work is hard and people do not want their U.S.-born children to do it, but many immigrant farmworkers are quite successful on their own terms.

This was especially true for the paid reps who battled César Chávez for some power within the UFW. They were all Mexicans as opposed to Chicanos. Many were well-paid skilled farmworkers for whom the fields had been a success story. They were confident in their own abilities and had just led a great strike victory. They were not deeply religious people; many of them came from the anticlerical tradition inside the Mexican left. They were not comfortable with the UFW's pious style. They did not want to wear old work clothes when they went to news conferences—as was standard UFW practice—nor appeal for support on the basis of their downtrodden condition. They sought solidarity, not charity. The cultural difference between their worldview and the dominant worldview within the union staff was enormous. In some sense, César was right. Such people could not be granted significant power within the union without changing the whole nature of the enterprise.

So we come upon a final irony. César, the Latino icon, was partly undone by contradictions within the Latino community. But history is filled with ironies, as action is always rife with unintended consequences. In the case of César Chávez, Latino politicians and liberal admirers have been so anxious to establish him as a hero that they have bowdlerized the ironies from his story. They need not. Irony does not automatically degenerate into cynicism. It does not drive out hope—it leavens it. When César Chávez's tale is reduced to hagiography, it loses most of its historical and political value. And those who can celebrate César's life and triumphs only by exorcising that which is uncomfortable, or by blurring the contradictions and betrayals, mask the tragedy of his political trajectory, make him banal, and rob his story of its anguish and its grandeur.

Notes

1. *San Jose Mercury News*, December 23, 1990; *Sacramento Bee*, December 8–11, 1991; John C. Hammerback, *The Rhetorical Career of César Chávez* (College Station, TX, 1998).
2. Jorge García, interview by author, December 11, 2000.
3. Carlos Muñoz Jr., *Youth, Identity, Power: The Chicano Movement* (New York, 1989), 7.
4. Larry Itliong, interview by Jacques Levy, in possession of author, April 4, 1969.
5. Robert García, interview by author, October 20, 1994.
6. Hermilio Mojica, interview by author, October 3, 1994; Jerry Cohen, interview by author, June 25, 2001.
7. *Los Angeles Times*, September 6, October 25, 1981; *New York Times*, December 6, 1981; *Village Voice*, August 14, 1984.
8. Dick Meister and Anne Loftis, *A Long Time Coming: The Struggle to Unionize America's Farm Workers* (New York, 1977), 144.
9. The list of staff purged or forced out is long. Among the most prominent were executive board members Philip Vera Cruz, Gilbert Padilla, Jessica Govea, and Marshall Ganz, and top aides Eliseo Medina, Jerry Cohen, and Nick Jones. The best-known rank-and-file leaders fired by Chávez were Mario Bustamonte, Hermilio Mojica, Aristeo Zambrano, Rigoberto Pérez, Sabino López, and Berta Batres.
10. Gretchen Lamb, interview by author, March 12, 1995.
11. Agenda, Monthly Newsletter of the National Council of La Raza, November 1974; *Riverside Daily Enterprise*, July 11, 1973; "Illegals Project 1974," Folder 4, Box 7, United Farm Workers Archives, Wayne State University Library, Detroit, Michigan; Gilbert Padilla, interview by author, December 20, 1997.

Suggested Readings

Coplon, Jeff. "César Chávez's Fall from Grace." *Village Voice*, August 14 and 21, 1984.
Daniel, Cletus E. "César Chávez and the Unionization of California Farm Workers." In Melvyn Dubofsky and Warren Van Tine, eds., *Labor Leaders in America*. Urbana and Chicago: University of Illinois Press, 1987.
Dunne, John Gregory. *Delano*. New York: Farrar, Straus and Giroux, 1967.

Jenkins, Craig J. *The Politics of Insurgency: The Farm Worker Movement in the 1960s.* New York: Columbia University Press, 1985.

Levy, Jacques E. *César Chávez.* New York: W. W. Norton and Co., 1975.

London, Joan, and Henry Anderson. *So Shall Ye Reap.* New York: Thomas Crowell Co., 1970.

Majka, Linda C., and Theo J. Majka. *Farm Workers, Agribusiness, and the State.* Philadelphia: Temple University Press, 1982.

Matthiessen, Peter. *Sal Si Puedes: César Chávez and the New American Revolution.* New York: Dell Publishing Co., 1969.

Muñoz, Carlos, Jr. *Youth, Identity, Power: The Chicano Movement.* New York: Verso Books, 1989.

Taylor, Ronald B. *Chávez and the Farm Workers.* Boston: Beacon Press, 1975.

15

New Immigrants to Silicon Valley, 1970–2000

Glenna Matthews

In the waning years of the twentieth century, economists began to speak of a "new economy" comprised of high-tech computer industries as the next step in the evolution of global capitalism. No state benefited more from this new economy than California, which has steadily drawn many of the nation's finest scientists, engineers, and programmers to its many bustling and very lucrative high-tech firms.

Thanks to federal military spending, California has for decades led the nation's high-tech economy. By 1962, 40 percent of the country's contracts for military testing and research went to California. By 1970 the state's rich community of scientists and engineers were helping to launch the microcomputer revolution, which became centered in Santa Clara County, known better today as Silicon Valley. Between 1960 and 1980 hundreds of thousands of high-tech jobs were created in this region. By the time Apple Computers opened its doors in 1977, Silicon Valley had become the nation's center for computer production, software development, and microelectronics research.

Silicon Valley's high-tech economy has provided considerable wealth for hundreds of thousands of Bay Area residents, as evidenced in part by the region's notoriously high housing prices. But in a manner reminiscent of earlier phases of economic growth in California history, wealth for some has been built in part upon the exploitation of others. In this essay, Glenna Matthews, a visiting scholar at the Institute of Urban and Regional Development, University of California, Berkeley, explores an often ignored sector of Silicon Valley's population—the thousands of recent immigrants who provide cheap manufacturing labor and domestic service for the region's booming firms.

Caleb left Oaxaca, Mexico, in 1997. He explained that in his region of Mexico there was so much desperation owing to unemployment and poverty that people would resort to violence to put food on the table. Though he wanted to complete high school, circumstances were too grim for that to be a realistic possibility. He decided to come north in search of better wages and more opportunity, arriving first in Los

Banos in the Central Valley. There he worked in the fields, but met no English-speakers. He decided to move to the Santa Clara Valley to improve his situation, especially by learning English, and Caleb found a job in a restaurant preparing salads. As for housing, that was tough. Lacking papers, he could not sign a lease himself and had to rely on someone who had been in the United States long enough to legally make the arrangements. Many men then had to share the apartment to make the rent. Yes, there are risks, he says, but those risks start the minute a person decides to cross the border, so it is just part of the price you pay. He sends his parents money regularly, because they are old and he does not want them to work so hard in the fields. For recreation, he plays soccer or basketball with his friends.[1]

Also from Oaxaca, José left behind a wife and two children to try to improve his family's fortunes in the United States. In Mexico he was a barber, but he cannot obtain a barber's license in California because he is undocumented. Therefore, he works as a gardener. Like Caleb, he sends money home, but as a married man he has greater obligations, including not only his immediate family but also his parents and a sister who is a student. He would like his children to grow up here, but he does not know how that would be possible. He originally planned to stay three years, but now anticipates staying only two—he is very homesick—with the goal of returning to Mexico not merely with savings but with new skills at gardening. When nostalgia and loneliness threaten to overwhelm him, he plays his guitar for solace.[2]

Lien Phan has been in the United States longer than either Caleb or José, and she and her family are well established. She was born in Hue, Vietnam, in 1949, one of the fourteen children of a policeman and a retail saleswoman. All of the children attended high school, and Lien went on to college in Saigon, became a middle-school teacher, and was on the verge of obtaining her degree when Saigon fell to the North Vietnamese forces, thus terminating the U.S.-supported regime in South Vietnam. Necessarily, her education ended for the time being. April 30, 1975, was a memorable day for her, not only because the South Vietnamese regime collapsed but also because she wed a man who had been an officer in the South Vietnamese army. After the arrival of two children and much hardship under the new Communist rule, the family escaped in a small boat to Hong Kong in 1979. In March 1980 they left for Minneapolis, Minnesota, and a new life. They arrived with few resources and little English, but they came as a united family, with both husband and wife possessing skills and education.

Lien Phan in her San Jose backyard in 2001. From the private collection of Lien Phan.

Looking back, Lien credits many different sources of help in adjusting to life in America. The family received federal government support for three months. Her husband got a government grant to study electronics. Most important to her, however, was the personal tutoring in English that she received from her sponsor, who came once a week to help her develop adequate fluency. All her subsequent success, she believes, stems from this hands-on learning experience. In 1983 her husband graduated, and the couple decided to relocate in order to get away from the snow. Having relatives in San Jose, they chose Silicon Valley.

Lien's story is a mix of both good fortune—the educational background, the kind sponsor—and a truly impressive work ethic. Once in the Valley, the family lived in a 19-unit apartment complex in downtown San Jose, which the owner asked her to manage when he observed how organized and careful she was. The extra income from this arrangement enabled the family to save for the house they now own. With three children by this time, Lien obtained a job as a waitress at a small,

American-food restaurant in Santa Clara, an option made possible by her English skills. She also enrolled in an electronics school, where she learned to identify components, solder, and wire. After six months of training she got an assembly job. Within a few years and with more training, she had graduated to supervising others. By 1998 she was a manager, her two oldest children were university students, and the family was living in a 2-story house in San Jose.[3]

What should we make of these different immigrant experiences and the current status of immigrant workers in Silicon Valley? This was precisely the question addressed in San Jose on December 6, 2000, at the Summit on Immigrant Needs and Contributions sponsored by the Santa Clara County Board of Supervisors. As the 500 people in attendance listened to the results of an ambitious yearlong study, it became clear that, despite the riches generated by the high-tech industries in Silicon Valley, there is terrible privation for those who arrive without resources. It also became clear that the sheer number of immigrants has altogether changed the area's demographic profile. In 1970, San Jose's population was 7.6 percent foreign-born; in 1990 it was 26.5 percent foreign-born. No one knew in late 2000 precisely what the 2000 census would disclose, but the estimate presented at the meeting suggested that about 60 percent of the county's population consisted of immigrants and their children, with about 33 percent being the foreign-born themselves, a stunning transformation in the space of a few decades. Moreover, this transformation has coincided with and helped produce immense growth for San Jose: the city has gone from 95,000 people in 1950 to nearly one million in 2000. Its landmass has expanded from about seventeen square miles in 1950 to 171 square miles in 2000.[4]

To achieve the most accurate and useful knowledge about newcomers such as Caleb, José, and Lien, the county gathered several different types of information from several different groups. The five largest groups —Mexicans, Vietnamese, Chinese, Filipinos, and Indians—received the most careful scrutiny, consisting of a random sample drawn according to statistically sound principles and in conjunction with a study of a control group of native-born Americans. But there were also focus groups for several other immigrant constituencies as well as additional data-gathering about people on public assistance.[5] The resulting report illuminates much about the lives and experiences of these thousands of recent immigrants who have settled in the Valley from all over the world.

In the first place, the immigrants constitute a strongly bifurcated population, with some of the Asians, in particular the Indians and to a lesser extent the Chinese, doing very well—better than the general population, in fact. Lien represents this component of the population. On the other hand, the vulnerability of many newcomers such as Caleb and José leaves them wide open to exploitation: they are far likelier than the native-born to be paid under the table, for example, or to be required to take work home without being paid overtime.[6] For the largest group, those from Mexico, the "rate of negative working conditions is 47 percent higher than the rate for all immigrant groups, and 84 percent higher than for the U.S.-born."[7]

As to why they come to the Santa Clara Valley, one man from India, here on an H-1B visa (granting temporary entry on the basis of professional skills), had this to say: "I go back to India two or three times a year because of my work and there are parts of India where you take a train and go over there and they don't even have a rickshaw or a cab to take you to your destination. You have to walk. But everybody in the small town knows exactly what the job situation is in Silicon Valley. They know the H-1B quota level, when it is filled, when it is open again. They know exactly what kind of skills are required not just in California, but in Silicon Valley."[8]

Along with such ports of entry as New York, San Francisco, and Los Angeles, in other words, the Santa Clara Valley is one of the nation's regions most affected by the changes in national policy wrought by the Immigration Act of 1965. Together with succeeding laws that elaborated on some of its provisions, the 1965 act inaugurated a vast transformation in American immigration policy. The 1965 law, enacted in a Congress as liberal as any since the days of the New Deal in the 1930s, did not eliminate the quotas based on national origin that had been a keystone of the immigration restriction enacted in the 1920s, but it established much less discriminatory grounds for entrance than had previously been the case.[9]

With the plethora of jobs being created in high tech, the San Jose region became a mecca for people from all over the world, many of whom have arrived in a state of considerable neediness. Yet Silicon Valley itself—and its high-tech *wunderkinder*—have received so much media attention that this has tended to drown out the news that there are thousands of Valley dwellers who are, to use Franklin Delano Roosevelt's words from his Second Inaugural Address, "ill-housed, ill-clad, and ill-nourished." As has happened so many times before in California history, immigrant labor has helped to create wealth from which the workers themselves do not adequately benefit.

Where Do They Come From?

The counterparts to Caleb, José, and Lien a century ago would likely have been named Giuseppe or Rafaella, because Santa Clara County was then a major receiver of Italian immigrants. Among the other most important sending countries were Portugal, China, Japan, and Mexico, but the Immigration Act of 1924, which set up a system of quotas that discriminated against southern Europeans and Asians, slowed down the inflow from all but Mexico. As of 1970, shortly before the burgeoning semiconductor industry led to the Santa Clara Valley receiving the nickname of Silicon Valley, the county's residents included only 43,000 people of Asian American descent and 186,525 Latinos in a county with 1,065,313 residents. Fewer than 5 percent of the residents were African American, and thus the vast majority of the population were native-born Americans of European descent.

The Immigration Act of 1965, in conjunction with a war in Southeast Asia and violent turmoil in Latin America, transformed the Valley's population. As we have seen, the law did not eliminate quotas per se, but it established much less discriminatory grounds for admission to the United States than had previously been mandated. Significantly, it gave great weight to family reunification as a reason for permitting entry, though job skills were also part of the evaluation process. (In 1990, Congress passed a revised immigration statute that nearly tripled the number of H-1B visas, a number that was revised upward again in 2000.) Just as immigration laws were being eased, new electronics firms began creating tens of thousands of jobs in the Valley. Taken together, a new legal order, an overwhelming number of refugees, the creation of family networks that could lead to chain migration, and a pleasant climate led to the Asian American population growing sixfold between 1970 and 1990 and the Latino population doubling. Indeed, as of 2000, both the city of San Jose and the county had "majority minority" populations:

> Santa Clara County is a majority minority county with more Asian or Latino immigrants than any other Bay Area county. Approximately 49 percent [of the population] are white, 25 percent Latino, 23 percent Asian, and 3 percent Black. Similarly, the City of San Jose, the eleventh largest city in the United States with a population of 925,000, is a majority minority city and has more Vietnamese than any city outside of Vietnam. [By contrast] the white population was more than 80 percent of the county's population for most of the twentieth century, including as recently as 1970.[10]

The immigrants come from many different countries, for many different reasons, and with widely varying backgrounds. Those from China,

Taiwan, and India often have more education than the American norm, for example, while those from poor regions of Mexico frequently arrive with only an eighth-grade education, if that. Tens of thousands in the Valley have arrived without papers and are thus especially vulnerable. Nor can they easily return to their homelands for visits to family members left behind. Others, here legally, cannot return because of turbulence at home or because they would be subject to arrest. Some people —refugees from Cambodia, for example—have arrived so traumatized by their experiences that they can barely function at first. And then there are the thousands who are here temporarily on H-1B visas, in addition to their (usually female) spouses who cannot legally work at all. Finally, another group of immigrant men, primarily Taiwanese, fly back and forth to their homeland—and to other centers of high-tech production—so often that their compatriots refer to them as "astronauts."[11]

Occupational Niches for the Newcomers

The arrival of so many poor and often desperate immigrants from so many countries at the dawn of the local electronics industry offered high-tech employers an extraordinary opportunity to fill their production jobs with people unfamiliar with American labor laws, anxious not to make waves, and thus unlikely candidates for union organization. As a consequence, the Valley's production workforce in high tech, an estimated 40,000 to 50,000 hourly workers at the start of the twenty-first century, is completely nonunion and is overwhelmingly composed of immigrant women—90 percent, according to the estimate given at the Summit on Immigrant Needs.

In general, those who arrive in Silicon Valley gravitate toward preordained occupational slots thought to be appropriate for people from their country of origin, a pattern scholars refer to as "a segmented labor market," though there are, of course, exceptions to this pattern. Indeed, there is a pan-immigrant trajectory for those who arrive with poor English skills and few resources: they begin with low-skilled restaurant work such as cutting up lettuce for salads—the work that Caleb is doing—progress to hotel work as they learn more English, and eventually move into hospital work, which requires the most English of the three.[12]

Historically, Mexicans such as Caleb and José had been able to find jobs in food-processing plants, at one time more abundant in the Santa Clara Valley than in any other region in the country. Indeed, at the peak of the local fruit industry in the middle decades of the twentieth century, there were 100,000 acres planted in fruit trees and dozens of canneries and dried fruit-packing plants to process the bounty. People from a peasant background could find work in these plants, work that afforded, after the labor militancy of the 1930s, a union wage. One problem for Latinos had been that because Italians had dominated the cannery workforce before World War II, they controlled the union offices and manipulated job categorizations to their benefit for decades, even after the workforce became preponderantly Mexican American during the war. In the 1970s, however, a dissident group of Latinos and Latinas (working closely with the United Farm Workers, then at the height of their national prominence) filed suit against both their own union and the processors' organization under Title VII of the 1964 Civil Rights Act. Winning, they achieved not only better access to union offices but also more opportunity in the cannery jobs themselves. As a consequence, these jobs had the capacity to become vehicles for movement into such middle-class attributes as home ownership and college education for the next generation.[13]

Beginning in the late 1960s, however, the Santa Clara Valley's transformation created economic distress among Mexican immigrants. The orchards and canneries where they so often found employment all but vanished in the wake of the postwar growth and accompanying sprawl in the Valley, to say nothing of high-tech development and heightened costs for processors owing to increased environmental oversight beginning in the 1970s. In late 1999 the last cannery of any size, Del Monte Plant number 3 in San Jose, closed its doors and moved to Modesto in the Central Valley, leaving its nearly 1,500 employees with the choice of either moving inland or finding new jobs—jobs that rarely offered the same pay and benefits as the unionized work they had lost.

Dora Pérez's story is indicative of the way the fruit industry functioned to integrate Mexican immigrants into life in the Santa Clara Valley. In 1972, Pérez arrived from Mexico as an undocumented worker; she was seventeen years old and had only a sixth-grade education. She was able to get employment at Del Monte immediately because her father and her uncles had jobs there. Starting as a sorter, she worked her way up the ladder: she moved to a position greasing the machines and next to performing the work of a light mechanic. With this background, she then taught herself how to operate a forklift and was able to move into year-round work in a warehouse, a job paying $42,000 per year at the time the plant closed. The mother of four children, she proudly explained that she and her husband (through whom she achieved U.S. citizenship) have been able to send their two oldest children to college and to subsidize multiple sports activities as well as to own a home. In the fall of 2000, many years after Pérez left school, she was back in the classroom, though she acknowledged that the computer training that is being offered to displaced cannery workers was unlikely to result in a job that paid as well as the one she left.[14]

In fact, Mexican immigrants are underrepresented in all phases of the electronics industry, from production work to professional jobs to entrepreneurial activities, though Latinas did comprise a goodly proportion of the assembly workers in the early days of the industry. It is impossible to determine conclusively the reasons for this situation. Obviously, the lack of education that afflicts so many immigrants from poor regions explains why they do not have access to professional employment, but it does not explain their absence from production work. One possible reason is as follows: to a person, the consensus of those who have tried to organize various (unsuccessful) unions among electronics workers is that high-tech human resources (HR) departments have both skill and determination in evaluating the propensity to respond to organizers among prospective employees. From the 1970s on, the Mexican American barrio in East San Jose has seen social movement activism, led by the United Farm Workers, by cannery workers attempting to reform their union, and by other groups. It seems likely that the milieu produced by the activism in East San Jose would have been deemed undesirable by high-tech employers. While this is speculative, what is certain is that the number of Mexican workers employed in high tech began to dwindle at more or less the same time that activism heated up in the barrio.[15] The net result has been the situation documented at the Summit on Immigrant Needs, whereby Mexican immigrants such as Caleb and José are typically found in the most precarious, least remunerative employment.

The next largest group of immigrants, those from Vietnam such as Lien, began to arrive after the fall of Saigon in 1975 (coincidentally, just as the barrio activism was peaking) and they had many characteristics that made them attractive to HR departments in Valley industries. In particular, they were fleeing from a Communist regime and tended, especially at first, to have Republican affinities; they likely had no prior exposure to organized labor; and they were deemed to be hardworking and compliant.[16] Along with Filipinos, the Vietnamese soon comprised the group most sought after for production work.

Newcomers from Southeast Asia have encountered profoundly mixed circumstances. Though most arrived with few material resources, they have had, on average, a greater level of education than has been typical for immigrants from Mexico. Furthermore, as political refugees, they have received special assistance and special access to a number of programs, as the story of Lien Phan and her family demonstrates. On the other hand, as displaced people, they have had to struggle to reconstitute family lives in a very different environment from their home countries. One scholar has referred to their circumstances as "a high-demand, low-control situation that fully tests the refugee's emotional resilience and coping resources and produces severe psychological distress even among the best prepared and even under the most receptive of circumstances."[17] Some have succumbed to the pressure and, in contradistinction to popular myths about Asian American immunity from social dislocation, the Valley has seen Vietnamese gangs and Vietnamese on welfare.[18]

These hardships notwithstanding, by the mid-1980s there were beginning to be success stories among San Jose's Vietnamese: twenty-six medical doctors, seventeen dentists, five lawyers, fifteen full-time real estate agents, sixteen accountants, twenty-four insurance agents, over 200 engineers, and nearly 300 restaurants and small businesses. So dense were the entrepreneurial activities on the periphery of downtown by 1980 that Vietnamese immigrants have been widely credited with making a material contribution to the rebirth of San Jose's central business district.[19]

As of 2000 many Vietnamese immigrants also owned shops that they ran out of homes in East San Jose, a strategy that enhances the possibility of entrepreneurial activity for them and for other immigrants.[20] (Zoning regulations that are more relaxed than in other parts of the city permit this to take place.) Finally, by the late twentieth century, there had been enough truly substantial successes within this community that there was the capital required to launch high-tech enterprises (located in networks of so-called angel investors prepared to invest smaller amounts than the typical venture capitalist).[21]

The third largest group of Silicon Valley immigrants, those of Chinese descent, have the greatest disparities among them: 38.7 percent of the sample drawn for the Summit on Immigrant Needs had annual household incomes of $50,000 or less, while 31.7 percent had household incomes in excess of $130,000.[22] In the latter case, a significant proportion arrived with advanced degrees and, hence, the skills to command good salaries in the high-tech job market. (As of the early twenty-first century, in fact, an estimated one-third of Valley engineers are foreign-born, with those of Chinese and Indian descent predominating.) In addition, those of Chinese descent have launched a truly impressive number of high-tech firms, some 2,000 between 1980 and 1998.[23] But for those who arrive without either educational or material resources, the problems echo those of other impoverished immigrants to the Valley: a variety of negative working conditions that include under-the-table pay, disproportionate risks in terms of occupational safety and health, unstable employment, and low-wage jobs.

Like the Latinos and the Chinese, the Filipinos represent a group with a long history in the Valley and have likewise soared in numbers. As of 1970 there were 6,314 Filipino Americans in the county, of whom about half were foreign-born. In 1990 there were 61,518. Like Vietnamese women, Filipinas have been favored employees in electronics assembly, where they have been especially prominent in the workforces of National Semiconductor and Advanced Micro Devices. Indeed, along with the Vietnamese, they have been viewed as particularly desirable, a group qualified because they were "small, foreign, and female." One administrator brashly proclaimed: "Asian women are more subservient than American females: if I refer to them as 'girls' it's because to me they act like girls: they only speak when they are spoken to, do exactly as they are told, and so forth. So I play into it—I treat them firmly, like a father figure."[24] Another manager stated, "The blacks had their Black Power and the Mexicans with the Chávez thing. The Asians just work hard and don't rock the boat or go against the business or government or anything."[25] This manager confirms the idea that United Farm Workers activism made Mexican immigrants relatively less desirable to employers.

The Valley's Indian population also grew in size and consequence during the 1990s because highly educated Indian men have been the group most strongly recruited under the H-1B visa program. As a result of this pattern, their salaries have been much better than salaries among other immigrants. Despite the multiple disadvantages that have attached to the H-1B status (spouses cannot hold gainful employment and changing jobs might have imperiled one's green card status until legal reforms of 2000), enough Indians have stuck it out that they have begun to be notable players in the Valley. Two of the best known, for example, are Sabeer Bhatia, cofounder of Hotmail, and Vani Kola, founder and CEO of Right Works Software, who in March 2000 sold half of her company for $657 million.[26] Because they have tended to arrive with extensive educational backgrounds, Indian immigrants constitute the Valley's least exploited group of recent arrivals. On the other hand, because their immigration status has circumscribed their professional mobility, they have not fared as well as other professionals in terms of their ability to negotiate lucrative salaries for themselves.

Thus, the fate of all immigrants, even Latinos indirectly, has been intimately tied to the health of the local high-tech industry, which has been affected by the ebbs and flows of global capitalism. The flush times of the late 1990s made it possible to disregard the fierce competition with Japan that erupted within the semiconductor industry in the 1980s. That competition, however, profoundly shaped subsequent develop- ments. Though Valley firms such as Intel survived and ultimately pros- pered anew, the lessons from the 1980s have not been lost on the industry leaders. Prominent among those lessons has been the need to keep down labor costs both by outsourcing abroad where possible and by subcon- tracting at home.

The costs and benefits to Valley residents of the global economy can be briefly summarized. Though tens of thousands of production jobs have vanished as companies built assembly plants or wafer fabrica- tion facilities (for the manufacture of chips) elsewhere, so many new products have been developed in the Valley that employment levels have remained high. In short, it is not that the process of globalization has shrunk the volume of employment. Rather, it is that the blue-collar work that is left (particularly after the disappearance of the fruit indus- try) often lacks the type of stability and access to a full array of benefits that became hallmarks of blue-collar jobs in the postwar era. Thus, new immigrants who arrive with poor educational backgrounds must con- front a high-tech job market that is deteriorating in terms of employ- ment opportunities.

There are two types of high-tech enterprises that employ workers who may receive less than the full range of employee benefits. First, there are large contract manufacturing firms that produce nothing on which they affix their own brand name, such as Solectron. With head- quarters in Milpitas and founded in 1977 to develop products using solar energy, Solectron evolved into performing assembly work for such giants as IBM and Hewlett-Packard. By 1984 the firm had annual rev- enues of $54 million. Until 1992 it confined its operations to Silicon

Valley. That year it acquired facilities in Charlotte, North Carolina, from IBM and then began a global expansion. As of late 2000, it had upward of 35,000 employees and revenue for fiscal 2000 in the amount of $14.1 billion in U.S. currency.[27] It would be a mistake to equate working for Solectron with the sweatshop conditions found by immigrants who work, for example, in the garment industry. On the other hand, Solectron employees enjoy fewer benefits than do those with unionized work in other industries.

Second to the large firms is a plethora of "assembly houses"—many of which are immigrant-run—that put together components for other firms. According to an article in the *San Jose Mercury News*, "In the past, Asian immigrants looking to start a business might have opened a restaurant. Today, they'd rather own an assembly house. It's the new American dream."[28] These undertakings subcontract for larger companies such as Solectron and draw upon networks within immigrant communities, especially the Vietnamese, for the efficiency of their operations. Undercapitalized and lightly regulated, assembly houses often engage in practices that fly in the face of American law governing wages and hours, health and safety, and child labor, thus contributing to the vulnerability of the immigrant workforce.

From the time of the Franciscan missionaries and later the Fortyniners, California has received an immense influx of immigrants from around the world, though the influx has ebbed and flowed according to the dictates of national immigration policy. All too often these newcomers have been consigned to performing the least desirable jobs, beginning with nineteenth-century Chinese immigrants who were usually relegated to the dirtiest, most dangerous jobs upon their arrival, through the field labor of Mexican immigrants, to the garment sweatshop work that is still being done by immigrant workers in California in the early twenty-first century. This is the world in which Caleb and José are enmeshed. Yet despite such very real exploitation, there has been a counter story—one of immigrant success in small business or in stable bluecollar employment, even if the newcomers have arrived without much education. The story of Dora Pérez bears testimony to such possibilities, as the story of Lien Phan demonstrates that even those who come with few material resources have been able to succeed when they are equipped with an education. The point of this essay is that, ironically and tragically, such opportunity has actually declined in Silicon Valley, given the withering of good blue-collar employment.

Notes

1. Caleb, interview by author, October 26, 1999, Centro Obrero, Los Altos. A volunteer from the Centro translated for us.

2. José, interview by author, October 26, 1999, Centro Obrero, Los Altos.

3. Lien Phan, interview by author, January 17, 1998, San Jose. I was able to locate this remarkable woman through her daughter Rebecca, who was my student at San Francisco State University.

4. Glenna Matthews, " 'The Los Angeles of the North': San Jose's Transition from Fruit Capital to High-Tech Metropolis," *Journal of Urban History* 25 (May 1999): 459–56.

5. The focus groups were conducted among people from Bosnia, Russia, Ethiopia, South Korea, Taiwan, Somalia, and Iran as well as the five largest constituencies.

6. On June 27 and June 28, 1999, the *San Jose Mercury News* ran a series of hard-hitting articles about the incidence of piecework performed at home, working conditions that evoke terrible memories of the sweatshops of 100 years ago. The featured workers were all immigrants, principally Vietnamese.

7. "Bridging Borders in Silicon Valley," Report for the Summit on Immigrant Needs and Contributions, Office of Human Relations, County of Santa Clara, December 2000, 127.

8. "Bridging Borders," Transcript of global context focus group, 12.

9. Reed Ueda, *Postwar Immigrant America: A Social History* (New York, 1994), chap. 2.

10. "Bridging Borders," 22.

11. Bernard Wong, talk given to the California Studies Seminar, University of California at Berkeley, November 17, 1999.

12. Warren Mar, interview by author, September 24, 1988, Oakland. Mar, a bilingual Chinese American, delineated this trajectory by way of explaining why his work as an organizer for the Hotel and Restaurant Workers' Union has been so intertwined with the experiences of new immigrants.

13. I deal with these events in my forthcoming *Silicon Valley and the California Dream: Gender, Class, and Opportunity in Twentieth-Century San Jose*. My sources included Patricia Zavella, *Women's Work and Chicano Families: Cannery Workers of the Santa Clara Valley* (Ithaca, 1987), 64–69; accounts in the *San Jose Mercury News*, September 30, 1975, and the *San Francisco Chronicle*, June 25, 1976; and the *Alaniz* decision in the Sam Kagel Collection, Labor Archives and Research Center, San Francisco State University. I cannot specify the box number because I was allowed to go through the collection before it had been catalogued.

14. Dora Pérez, interview by author, September 28, 2000, San Jose.

15. Dr. Joseph LaDou, interview by author, September 21, 1998, Menlo Park. Dr. LaDou ran an industrial medicine clinic in Sunnyvale during these years and was well placed to observe the change from Latina to Asian workers.

16. On Republican affinities, see the *San Jose Mercury News*, August 28, 1999. On employers' stereotypes, see Karen J. Hossfeld, "Divisions of Labor, Divisions of Lives: Immigrant Women Workers in Silicon Valley" (Ph.D. diss., University of California, Santa Cruz, 1988). Professor Hossfeld is working on a book to be titled *Small, Foreign, and Female*.

17. Ruben Rumbaut, quoted in James Freeman, *Hearts of Sorrow: Vietnamese American Lives* (Stanford, 1989), 18–20.

18. *San Jose Mercury News, West* magazine, December 4, 1994.

19. Freeman, *Hearts of Sorrow*, 17 (the success stories), 8 (the effect on downtown).

20. *San Jose Mercury News*, March 19, 2000.

21. Ibid., March 4, 2000.

22. "Bridging Borders," 122.

23. AnnaLee Saxenian, *Silicon Valley's New Immigrant Entrepreneurs* (San Francisco, 1999), 26. The breakdown among the firms is 562 in hardware manufacturing, 716 in software and business services, and 723 in computer wholesaling. On June 2, 2000, I attended a conference sponsored by the Asia Pacific Research Center at Stanford University that brought together high-tech business leaders from a number of Asian countries, including China, and that highlighted this pattern.

24. As quoted in Edward Jang-Woo Park, "Asian Americans in Silicon Valley: Race and Ethnicity in the Postindustrial Economy" (Ph.D. diss., University of California, Berkeley, 1993), 118.

25. Ibid., 107.

26. *San Jose Mercury News*, March 9, 2000, column by Mike Cassidy. See also the discussion of Indians in Silicon Valley in Michael Lewis, *The New, New Thing: A Silicon Valley Story* (New York, 2000).

27. My information about Solectron comes from Tim John Sturgeon, "Turnkey Production Networks, Industry Organization, Economic Development, and the Globalization of Electronics Contract Manufacturing" (Ph.D. diss., University of California, Berkeley, 1999). See also *San Jose Mercury News*, June 28, 1999.

28. *San Jose Mercury News*, June 27, 1999.

Suggested Readings

Freeman, James. *Hearts of Sorrow: Vietnamese American Lives*. Stanford: Stanford University Press, 1989.

Hondagneu-Sotelo, Pierette. *Gendered Transitions: Mexican Experience of Immigration*. Berkeley: University of California Press, 1994.

Hossfeld, Karen J. "Why Aren't High-Tech Workers Organized? Lessons in Gender, Race, and Nationality from Silicon Valley." In Daniel Cornford, ed., *Working People of California*. Berkeley: University of California Press, 1995.

Lewis, Michael. *The New, New Thing: A Silicon Valley Story*. New York: W. W. Norton, 2000.

Saxenian, AnnaLee. *Silicon Valley's New Immigrant Entrepreneurs*. San Francisco: Public Policy Institute of California, 1999.

Ueda, Reed. *Postwar Immigrant America: A Social History*. New York: Bedford Books of St. Martin's Press, 1994.

Suggestions for
Further Reading and Research

Almaguer, Tomás. *Racial Fault Lines: The Historical Origins of White Supremacy in California*. Berkeley: University of California Press, 1994.

Bouvier, Virginia M. *Women and the Conquest of California, 1542–1840: Codes of Silence*. Tucson: University of Arizona Press, 2001.

Chan, Sucheng. *This Bittersweet Soil: The Chinese in California Ag. uculture, 1860–1910*. Berkeley: University of California Press, 1986.

Deverell, William, and Tom Sitton, eds. *California Progressivism Revisited*. Berkeley: University of California Press, 1994.

Gutierrez, Ramón, and Richard Orsi, eds., *Contested Eden: California before the Gold Rush*. Berkeley: University of California Press, 1998.

Hass, Lisbeth. *Conquests and Historical Identities in California, 1769–1936*. Berkeley: University of California Press, 1995.

Johnson, Susan Lee. *Roaring Camp: The Social World of the California Gold Rush*. New York: W. W. Norton, 2000.

Lotchin, Roger W. *Fortress California, 1910–1961: From Warfare to Welfare*. New York: Oxford University Press, 1992.

McWilliams, Carey. *California: The Great Exception*. Berkeley: University of California Press, 1999; originally published, 1949.

Pitt, Leonard. *The Decline of the Californios: A Social History of the Spanish-Speaking Californians, 1846–1890*. Berkeley: University of California Press, 1966.

Rohrbough, Malcolm. *Days of Gold: The California Gold Rush and the American Nation*. Berkeley: University of California Press, 1997.

Saxton, Alexander. *The Indispensable Enemy: A Study of the Anti-Chinese Movement in California*. Berkeley: University of California Press, 1967.

Schrag, Peter. *Paradise Lost: California's Experience, America's Future*. Berkeley: University of California Press, 1998.

Starr, Kevin. *Americans and the California Dream, 1850–1915*. New York: Oxford University Press, 1973.

Web Sites

http:\\www.learncalifornia.org
http:\\www.socalhistory.org
http:\\www.calhist.org

Index

Emmons, Delos, 167
Employee benefits, 237
Employment: for African American
women, 150–51; blue-collar, 236, 237;
film industry growth and, 122, 126–27;
for Silicon Valley immigrants, 231–37.
See also Domestic service; Farmworkers;
Workplace
Endo decision, 171
End Poverty in California (EPIC), 135
English language, and immigrants, 74–75,
204, 226, 227
Entertainment, 126–27. *See also* Film
industry
Epidemics, 11–12, 24
Equality, social. *See* Social equality
Equity League, 111
Esselen Indians, 7
Ethnic groups: gold rush and, 47, 50, 54–
56, 57–59, 60; population of (2000),
205; in Southern California, 189; in
suburbs, 182
Ethnic studies, 202, 203, 205, 212
European contact, 6, 9–12
Exclusion laws. *See* Chinese Exclusion Act
Executive Order 9066, 161, 166–67

Fair Housing Act (1963), 193
Family life, 183–85, 230
Famous Players, 121
Fandangos, 57, 59
Farm Labor Law (1976), 213
Farms: corporate, 140, 210, 214–15, 220,
232–33; family, 140, 144; fruit and
vegetable, 140, 232–33. *See also*
Agriculture; Farmworkers
Farm Security Administration, 142
Farmworkers: "bindlestiffs," 140; Chávez
and, 209–10, 215–20; camps for, 138–
40, 141–42, 143; Chicano Nation and,
210–12; ethnic composition of, 141;
forced repatriation of, 135; grape
boycott and, 212, 214, 216; immigrants as, 140–41, 144, 209–10, 221;
labor contractors and, 210, 215; labor
unions, 135, 138, 140, 141–45, 193,
209; Mexican Americans as, 221–22;
Mexican American students and, 211–
12; Mexican immigrants as, 141, 144,
147, 221–22; New Deal programs for,
142; Okies as, 136, 138–45; strikes by,
144–45, 219–20; supporters of, 216–

17; United Farm Workers and, 216–17,
219–20; wages, 209, 210, 222. *See also*
Agribusiness; Agriculture
Federal Bureau of Investigation (FBI),
161, 164
Federal Housing Administration, 180–81
Fifteenth Amendment, 105
Filipinos: as farmworkers, 141; forced
repatriation of, 68, 135; population of,
235; in Silicon Valley, 228–29, 234,
235
Film industry, 119–33; Americanization
and, 126; censors, 126; frontier myth
and, 122, 123–25, 127–28, 129–32;
Great Depression and, 131; immigrants
and, 122, 126; life-style and, 119–20;
Progressive Era reform and, 123–27;
socioeconomic status and, 122–23,
127, 131. *See also* DeMille, Cecil B.
Finney, Charles Grandison, 102
Fisher, William, 73
Flower Festival Society, 107
Fonda, Henry, 143
Food sources, for Native Americans, 4–5, 6
Foote, Henry S., 71–72
Ford, Leland, 165
Foreign Miners Tax, 47, 59, 65
Forty-niners, 47–64; Anglo, 47, 48, 51,
53, 54–56; behavior of, 48, 58–59;
Chinese, 47, 50, 54–55, 56–57, 59;
Mexican, 50, 54–55, 59; Native
Americans and, 55, 58, 59, 60;
socioeconomic status of, 47–48, 49–50,
51, 56–57, 61; stereotypes of, 55. *See
also* Gold rush
Franciscans: missions of, 9, 18–27; Native
Americans and, 2, 21–25
Fraternal organizations, 53
Freedman's Bureau, 103
Free Kindergarten Association, 109
Free Speech Movement, 193
Freeways, 182, 188–89
Frémont, Jessie, 111
Friday Morning Club (FMC), 99, 100,
105, 107, 110–11, 112
Frobel, Friedrich, 108, 109
Frontier myth, 122, 123–25, 127–28,
129–32
Fruit industry, 140, 232–33

Gabrielino Indians, 7, 33
Gallup poll, on places to live, 179

Made in the USA
San Bernardino, CA
15 January 2014